W9-ACA-556

WITHDRAWN

Gramley Library
Salem College
Winston-Salem, NC 27108

READING BERLIN **1900**

READING
BERLIN
1900

Peter Fritzsche

HARVARD UNIVERSITY PRESS 1996

Cambridge, Massachusetts London, England

Gramley Library
Salem College
Winston-Salem, NC 27108

Copyright © 1996 by the President and Fellows
of Harvard College
All rights reserved
Printed in the United States of America

Library of Congress Cataloging-in-Publication Data

Fritzsche, Peter.
    Reading Berlin 1900 / Peter Fritzsche.
        p.   cm.
    Includes index.
    ISBN 0-674-74881-6
    1. Berlin (Germany) in the press.   2. German
newspapers—Germany—Berlin—History.   I. Title.
PN5219.B59F75   1996
073′.155—dc20   95-37608
                                                                    CIP

ACKNOWLEDGMENTS

I first had the idea for this book in the summer of 1989, while working in Hamburg. That small ideas grew into longer chapters is largely thanks to the confidence so many friends and colleagues had in my sometimes quirky assumptions. Very early support was provided by the Research Board of the University of Illinois, and an Alexander von Humboldt Research Fellowship, augmented by generous leave from the Department of History at Illinois, allowed me to spend the year 1992-93 in Berlin. I am most grateful for the help and advice of Reinhard Rürup, with whom I spent many wonderful hours. This book would not have been possible without the help of Rainer Laabs at the Ullstein archive in the Springer Verlag; I profited greatly from Jonathan Huener's research assistance. Thomas Childers, Modris Eksteins, Gerald Feldman, and Shulamit Volkov were also most helpful along the way.

Numerous discussions with colleagues sharpened my thinking in fruitful ways, and so my thanks go to Stephen Brockman, Courtney Federle, Sybille Fritzsche, Peter Garrett, Dilip Goankar, Sabine Hake, Martin Jay, Peter Jelavich, Thomas C. Leonard, Thomas Lindenberger, George Mosse, Karl Prümm, Leslie Reagan, Erhard Schütz, and Peter Steinbach; to members of the German Colloquium, the Social History Group, the Cultural Studies Group, and the Institute for Transcultural Studies; and especially to my ongoing interlocutor, Harry Liebersohn. One hot day in July, Jerry at Hyde Park Computers saved Chapter 2: thanks a lot! I am also very grateful for the still and wintry day on which Aïda Donald of Harvard University Press read and commented on the manuscript. And thanks to Anita Safran, who was a great editor.

Karen Hewitt put in plenty of overtime on the playground on Rüdesheimer Platz to give me time to write the first drafts. She also read those drafts, and made the whole venture worthwhile. At the same time, the verve of Lauren and the birth of Eric gave me wonderful live examples of the urban turbulence that I was only writing about. One sad victim of that turbulence was Lucie Berlin, of Berlin, murdered in 1904 at the age of nine; in the face of flux and ephemerality, I wish to commemorate her name here.

CONTENTS

ILLUSTRATIONS

READING BERLIN **1900**

INTRODUCTION

This book is about the "word city," the accumulation of small bits and rich streams of text that saturated the twentieth-century city, guided and misguided its inhabitants, and, in large measure, fashioned the nature of metropolitan experience. In an age of urban mass literacy, the city as place and the city as text defined each other in mutually constitutive ways. The crush of people and welter of things in the modern city revised ways of reading and writing, and these representational acts, in turn, constructed a second-hand metropolis which gave a narrative to the concrete one and choreographed its encounters. By way of the most mundane but also the most indispensable and widely circulated metropolitan texts—that is, the countless pages of daily newsprint—and by way of the example of imperial Berlin, at the turn of the nineteenth century among Europe's fastest-growing and most populous cities, I intend to explore the terms of mediation between city and text. My two-way argument is that reading and writing in the city invited as well as contained public movements through the city. To demonstrate this, I will keep in place the broad strokes of narrational order and bring in the sharp counterstrokes of interpretative disorder, both of which emerge out of the relations between readers and texts and contexts.

I have chosen to focus on the period in the early twentieth century (1900–1914) when Berlin was still in the stages of rapid growth and newspapers first established themselves as metropolitan institutions, fashioning new, more assertive journalistic practices. Both the metropolis and the metropolitan newspaper were relatively novel forms before World War I, and it is in this formative period of mutual definition that a study of how reading and writing worked on the city is most useful. The word city that I examine here encompasses imperial Berlin's major mass-circulation newspapers and includes advertisements, broadsides, and a variety of other curbside texts. The *Berliner Morgenpost*, which, after 1902, was not only far and away Berlin's largest newspaper but really *the* Berlin daily, and *BZ am Mittag*, the popular tabloid or "boulevard newspaper" founded in 1904, were both published by Ullstein and form the basis of this study. Although Ullstein set the tone, other publishers competed successfully, and I have accordingly also examined Scherl's *Berliner Lokal-Anzeiger*, the city's first properly local newspaper, and the *Berliner Tageblatt*, published by Mosse, perhaps Germany's best-written paper. Despite this intensive survey of the press, my intention is not to study newspapers or journalism as such but rather to focus on the construction of the narrated city and analyze its impact on the built city. The great advantage of newspapers for such a purpose is their sharp focus on the metropolis combined with their wide readership and ubiquitous presence. A study of the popular press, which is the foundation of the word city, keeps in view all three elements of the project—new aspects of the city, new readers, and new readings.

Over the course of the last century or two, metropolitan readers came to think about the city as a vast, enticing spectacle, as movement, as motley and mysterious and, in effect, democratic. Yet the appealing image of the big city in flux elides over established relations of power and often misrepresents the basic sameness of outwardly colorful differences. Texts in the city were at once orderly and disruptive, they reframed and juxtaposed and reiterated and left unsaid, they led as well as misled, and worked for and against concretions of power. Because it wished to be all things to all people, the word city remained an unstable, pliable form, which allowed readers to make sense of the changing inventory of the city and to respond to its speculative, playful voices, but which also guided readers simply by measuring and standardizing the urban inventory.[1] Even as metropolitan narratives encompassed considerable diversity, they organized detail and difference and thus invariably regulated ways of seeing and not seeing. Accordingly, like the city in history, the city of words has always been characterized by refreshingly cosmopolite and dangerously coercive aspects.

No city can be clearly seen yet most cities delight the eye with their marketplace variety, labyrinthine streets, and surprising changeability. Again and again in the history of modern thought, cities have been a challenge to clarity of vision: the details, in themselves decipherable, do not come together to make a full picture. In the first place, the city has always been characterized as a Babel of contesting voices and intentions. This social and political diversity has a crucial epistemological aspect, in that the incompleteness of civic rule is accompanied by the instability of narrative authority. In the metropolis there are as many stories as viewpoints. At the same time, however, the metropolis doubles as the capital, which enforces regimentation and discipline in the name of imperial mastery and economic efficiency.[2] Nonetheless, the metropolis and the capital coexist in the same urban place. Cities remain fascinating to this day precisely because they put into question delusions of order and fantasies of disorder alike and because they indicate the extent to which aesthetic preferences for either are ideological fallacies. The city frustrates both the dictator and the ragpicker.

What heightens the fascination is the link between the city as geographical place and the city as narrated form. From the beginning, written records and urban existence have gone hand-in-hand. This correspondence created an imaginary symbolic order that was as important as the city itself. The primary functions of the ancient city as "a storehouse, a conservator and accumulator" required the maintenance of permanent records. Over time, the purely notational tablets found at Ur developed in abstraction, allowing the preservation, selection, and commemoration of ideas and traditions. As Lewis Mumford observes, "the rulers of the city lived a multiple life: once in action, again in monuments and inscriptions." Indeed, "living by the record and for the record became one of the great stigmata of urban existence." This was so not just because monuments recorded life in an overdramatic or even deliberately false way, as Mumford suggests, but because reading and writing were crucial to using the city as a "container" of goods and services and also of memories, laws, and customs.[3] Once the built city was overlaid with the word city, the functions of the metropolis became more specialized and the power of rulers and priests appeared more formidable.

As the word city acquired more layers, however, the uses to

which words could be put multiplied, enhancing their disorderly potential. Written history recorded edicts broken and laws overturned and thus exposed the contingency of tradition. At the same time, the spread of literacy in the modern era gave permanent form to the memories and hopes of new arrivals into the city. Soon enough the Babel of voices corresponded to a flood of broadsides, stories, and newspapers. And finally, the extraordinary triumph of consumer culture at the end of the nineteenth century insured that the word city would make use of the notational skills of its inhabitants while it appealed by means of advertisements and images to their desires and prejudices. Around 1900, the messy debris of print culture seemed to overwhelm the well-ordered archive of economic and political power. From morning until night people walked through the city encountering schedules, advertisements, regulations, handbills, instructions, clocks, labels, newspapers, and myriad other printed forms, so that any shared jargon, standard version, or dominant genre quickly lost authority. Provincial dialects clashed with bureaucratic formulations, music-hall jingles with the language of commerce. The word city still mediated the built city, but it no longer guided readers in the same uniform way as had the earliest monuments in Sumer. To borrow the vocabulary of the linguist Mikhail Bakhtin, the modern word city, like the modern novel, proved to be astonishingly heteroglot in the indeterminate forms and various readings it assumed.[4]

And yet, by necessity, the word city was not simply a collage, and it remained inscribed with all sorts of authorial directives. Even the most popular metropolitan texts reveal narrative strategies that controlled heteroglossic readings in important ways. All narrative forms impose some kind of coherence on the events they describe; representation fashions the "experience of the real."[5] Literary structuralists have taken the realist novel, for example, which Bakhtin considered among the most free and creative genres, and shown how authority was enacted by plot sequences, favored viewpoints, and protocols of introspection. Insofar as literary forms such as novels or newspapers organized or suppressed evidence and made claims to comprehensiveness, they established compelling disciplines.[6] The power of these texts to inscribe world views should not be ignored. Although the degree to which readers' ideas are formed by what they read remains contested by literary scholars—a question which will be considered in more depth in the chapters to follow—the potential of texts to prefigure or, for that matter, to subvert perceptions is not in question. This ambivalence is a troublesome but rewarding part of my argument. Precisely because it manifests itself in such unstable, narrated forms, the word city has the effect of dramatizing the tension between metropolis and capital.

Cities have been built on land wrestled from nature; their manufactured forms and designs still retain the unfinished, mutable aspect of something made and remade on a changing landscape. No city escapes this duality. But surely the most awe-inspiring aspect of the great cities in the industrial epoch was their restless, fugitive quality. During the same nineteenth-century decades when the city came to be a permanent part of national and individual ambitions, the constitution of the city grew more impermanent: the metropolis kept slipping out of the frame of the capital. More than anything else, the machinery and the social relations of industrial development reworked the looks of cities to the point of unfamiliarity. They did so not simply by tearing down medieval walls or by adding immense factories and settling thousands of new laborers, although these were undeniably dramatic events, but by sustaining this busy activity over time. Neither industrial progress nor commercial activity were geared to preserve the physical character or the social makeup of urban space. As a result, the nineteenth-century city was less of a new creation and more of an incalculable, ongoing process. Victorian London, Second Empire Paris, and Wilhelmine Berlin were no longer best described by sturdy four-cornered nouns referring to old squares and new buildings but by a more tentative vocabulary that denoted movement, surprise, and discontinuity. The industrial city was distinctive as much for the everyday experience of unfamiliarity and flux as for the infiltration of smokestacks and proletarians.

No century was more strongly marked by, or had become more aware of, the experience of transience than the one hundred years up to 1914. And no major city in Europe underwent quite so dramatic a transformation as Berlin. The provincial capital of the Prussian kingdom reinvented itself as a major metropolis over the course of only a few decades. Between 1848 and 1905, the population of Berlin leaped from 400,000 to 2 million; huge suburbs ringing the city added another 1.5 million. By 1920 Greater Berlin had become the world's third largest city. Not surprisingly, the dizzying pace of development in the span of one lifetime fixed the city's identity. Without permanent form or common history, Berlin was widely praised or else dismissively condemned as a "nowhere city," a place that was "always becoming and never is."[7] Of course, Vienna, Paris, and London, too, were substantially rebuilt and had millions of new residents in the nineteenth century; they shared with Berlin the experience of instability. But these cities never lost sight of their Roman origins or their medieval prosperity, and not even master builders such as Baron Haussmann wrecked all of their baroque facades and preindustrial proportions. What sets Berlin apart is not so much the intensity of industrial development as the city's almost exclusive identification with it. Any story of Berlin therefore adds an extra measure of turbulence to an account of the modern city. The constant motion of the industrial city left a lasting mark on city texts, and these, in turn, heightened the fugitive nature of the metropolis. At the most basic level, the urban sprawl that altered regional maps around 1900 could not be used without instructions and labels. With the daily influx of hundreds of newcomers, the breakdown of older neighborhoods and turnover of residents in newer ones, and the widening physical separation of home and workplace, a great crowd traversed the city more frequently and for longer distances than ever before. These strangers found in newspapers indispensable guides to unfamiliar urban territory. Indeed, newspapers found a mass readership only with the emergence of big cities. At the same time, municipal authorities literally posted the modern settlement with signs, regulations, and prohibitions. Merchants and agents added their promotional advertisements and handbills. More and more bits and pieces of text littered the streets. The sheer number and assortment of words lent to turn-of-the-century metropolitan exchanges an unmistakably fortuitous quality.

The fluctuating inventory of the modern city had the effect of generating more numerous though more provisional texts. The daily newspaper is only the most obvious example of such constantly revised versions of the metropolis. The stepped-up pace of reportage made good business sense, as the financiers and speculators who personified mature capitalism required up-to-date market reports and eagerly purchased the latest telegrams from abroad. But daily (re)editions also catered to the ebb and flow of different groups—workers and women and shoppers and spectators—through public places. As a result, fleeting reportage seemed best to fit the unprecedented fullness of city life. At the end of the nineteenth century, feuilleton sketches, short stories, line drawings, motion pictures, and "real life" eyewitness accounts became increasingly popular, since these formats caught so well the occasional and surprising aspects of the metropolis. Intellectuals, too, made a point of rejecting the more authoritative and encyclopedic accounts of the city as gross falsifications of the flux of urban circumstances. The great industrial city, more than any other geographical place, justified turn-of-the-century experimentation with new artistic principles that sought, by techniques of shock, juxtapostion, and displacement, to demonstrate the basic incongruity of modern experience.

Because the industrial city took on such spectacular, eye-catching forms, its ephemeral quality can be easily exaggerated. At each turn, the various mediations of the word city increased the sense of precariousness in the built city. Artistic avant-gardes zealously promoted the mutations of the metropolis in the name of countercultural resistance and perceptual instability. At the same time, the images of contrast and contradiction they generated found an appreciative metropolitan public of sightseers and connoisseurs. The avant-garde also mesmerized cultural conservatives eager to use lurid city views to reaffirm traditional values. Both the aesthetics of modernism and the culture of consumption distorted the city by embellishing its most fantastic characteristics. To this day, observers fail to comprehend the metropolis because they see it from particular vantages selected to produce extraordinary effects.[8] But drawing the limits and puncturing the insights of modernism will take critics only so far. Coffeehouse poets, peep-show exhibitors, vaudeville artists, and police-beat reporters sensationalized the city and also recast it in their image. The terms of mediation cannot be separated from the metropolitan experience; the falsification of the city, its people, and its history has become a permanent part of the city. Tourism is perhaps the best way to consider how the act of consuming an imagined city can transform the physical nature and economic base of the built city.[9] No conception of the modern metropolis would be complete without holiday tourists, press empires, and huge billboards. The word city, at least since the turn of the century, is not just a fabrication that overlaid, sensationalized, and falsified the actual city; to a large extent it came to be part of it, through the industries of sensationalism. As the boundaries between the real and the imagined become blurred, the potential to fabricate the city has in fact made the city more fugitive.

In the seven chapters that follow I propose to explore how the industrial city reworked and proliferated versions of the word city, how the word city, in turn, re-viewed and fashioned the city, and how the resulting margin of distortion eventually became part of the experience of the city itself. Truly an elaborate fabrication, the word city should be regarded as a social text that simultaneously reflected, distorted, and reconstituted the city. While the terms of mediation define the organization of the book, each chapter has a secondary purpose as well: to tell about Berlin while highlighting how the media shaped what is seen and how. The first chapter provides a theoretical overview and looks more closely at the links between the industrial city and modernist forms, of which the metropolitan newspaper was one of the most important and vital. Chapter 2 examines the history of reading in the city and the growth of the metropolitan press. The remaining chapters identify different ways of making sense of the metropolis and suggest how reading about the city fashioned the encounters with the city. That the city can be taken apart and its various parts and people identified and contrasted under a sharply focused physiognomical lens is the subject of Chapter 3. A careful reading also reveals the fluctuating inventory of the city. The colorful contrasts and fine variations encouraged viewers to see the city as a vast spectacle. In this manner, the city could be encountered simply by browsing, a disengaged and largely passive apprehension that is the subject of Chapter 4. At the same time, the constantly changing metropolitan collage that the browser enjoyed threatened always to dissolve into incoherence. The question of whether the readable city made syntactical sense at all is discussed in Chapter 5. Narrative strategies that served to provide the seemingly chaotic city with a set of governing images, and the part the press played in choreographing the metropolis, are treated in Chapter 6. Finally, in the concluding chapter, I compare the newspaper to other texts and discuss more generally metropolitan readership and modernism at the beginning of the twentieth century.

Gramley Library
Salem College
Winston-Salem, NC 27108

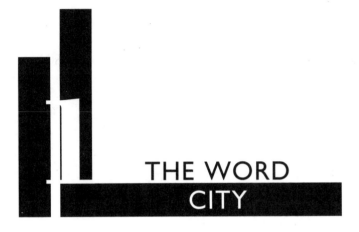

THE WORD CITY

Twenty-three-year old Jakob van Hoddis first read his most famous poem, "Weltende"—"End of the World"—in an obscure Berlin cabaret. A few weeks later a revised version was published in the January 1911 issue of the literary magazine *Der Demokrat*. Nothing van Hoddis wrote later had the impact of these eight lines:[1]

> The bourgeois' hat flies off his pointy head,
> The air shrieks with a thousand screams.
> Shinglers plunge off roofs and break in two,
> And the tide is rising all along the coast (we read).
> The storm is here, a wild ocean has jumped
> On land, the swollen dams have burst.
> Most everyone has a cold.
> Locomotives everywhere drop off bridges.

Things no longer hang together in van Hoddis's rendering of the sensible world. The juxtapositions and causal nonsequiturs indicate a disheveled universe torn by surprise and shock. Just a few years after the great Messina earthquake of 1908, only months after Halley's Comet had swept by the planet in spring 1910, van Hoddis probed the supernatural behind the natural. Written a few years before the outbreak of World War I, "Weltende" also anticipated the coming catastrophe, at least according to generations of literary critics for whom Jacob van Hoddis was a sensitive "outsider" able to discern turbulence beneath outwardly tranquil appearances.[2]

Indeed, van Hoddis's companions took his images as revealed truths to be set against the deceits of the established order. Johannes Becher, later "culture tsar" of the German Democratic Republic, remembered "Weltende": "These eight lines seemed to transform us into entirely different people, to raise us out of a world of bourgeois convention . . . These eight lines seduced us again and again. We sang them, we hummed them, we murmured them, we whistled them . . . we shouted them at each other across the street as if they were battle-cries." Armed with "Weltende," Becher found the "indifferent, horrible world" of the imperial epoch "no longer quite so solid."[3] Forty years after the poem was written, Becher mobilized van Hoddis against the bourgeois order and thereby enlisted him in the socialist politics of the "other Germany."

Yet this insurrectionary text itself had a defining context. Berlin in 1911—nearly four million inhabitants in a brand new industrial conglomeration—contained its own version of disorder in which the fugitive appearances, unexpected encounters, and rapid fluctuations of the city challenged nineteenth-century certainties again and again. To account for this unstable perceptual field, writers and artists experimented with new representational techniques. The "snapshot" style of *kleine Prosa*, the antinarratives of the modern novel, the disruptions and displacements of Expressionist poetry have all been related to a distinctly metropolitan way of seeing at the turn of the century, which can be summed up as modernism.[4]

So perhaps it was not van Hoddis shouting at the city, but the city shouting back at van Hoddis. We know that Berlin was a powerful presence in the life of the poet. The painter Ludwig Meidner used to take nighttime walks with van Hoddis (born Hans Davidsohn, Jewish son of a Berlin physician). They walked until dawn along the edges of the city—Berlin Nord, Berlin Ost—where, amidst construction sites, newly erected tenements, and ramshackle carnivals and dancehalls, the crackling sense of things becoming metropolitan was most apparent.[5]

Van Hoddis/sensitive poet/Davidsohn/metropolitan could be made to stand for two approaches to modernism. One draws attention to the experimentalism of an avant garde in rebellion, the other indicates the disorienting impact of the metropolis in the fullness of its historical and industrial contexts. But "Weltende" brings in an interesting complicating factor, which insinuates itself between the insurrectionary experimentalist and the disorderly city. Recall the line "And the tide is rising all along the coast (we read)." The parenthetical "we read" signals just how much the press mediated and amplified the improvised and dangerously precarious nature of big-city surroundings. The newspaper report of the events itself constituted part of the eventfulness of the city.

The aside "we read" deepens our understanding of modernism, a movement that owes its insights not simply to far-seeing genius or new-fangled industry and technology but also to the idea that perception is constructed and circumstantial. Van Hoddis suggested that in some measure metropolitans and readers lived in a looking-glass universe composed of signs and images that were connected only incompletely to actual events and happenings. Both the unaccountable growth of the metropolis in the nineteenth century and the busy streams of people, goods, and information that flowed more and more quickly through its precincts created an increasingly mediated public sphere. The modern city became inseparable from the commercial records, advertising broadsides, and newspaper stories that embellished it. An encompassing symbolic order informed the city and left behind countless versions and editions. The degree to which the urban inventory was legible or illegible, eventful or well-ordered, was at least as much function of the city's thorough narrativization as it was of industrialization and commercialization. Even the conviction that appearances are always deceptive and not stable is simply one story that modernism likes to tell about itself, something van Hoddis acknowledges when he approaches a disheveled universe first and foremost as a reader. Van Hoddis is not saying that the topsy-turvy world is mere appearances, is not real, but rather, that appearances make up the world and leave it astonishingly contingent, indeterminate, and charged with possibility. This sense of precariousness, which extends to include the concept itself, is the predicate of modernism.

The great text of the big city around the turn of the century had a wide range of authors. Any number of genres—the novel, drama, vaudeville, photography, advertisements—represented the metropolis. But none was as indispensable or as focused on the metropolis as the mass-circulation newspaper. It was the most versatile guide to the huge and ever-changing inventory of the industrial city. By the end of the nineteenth century, most city people read newspapers and, often enough, only newspapers. Indeed, Robert Ezra Park, founder of the Chicago School of Sociology, referred to the newspaper's "universe of discourse."[6] Yet popular newspapers did more than introduce the metropolis; they calibrated readers to its tremulous, machine-tempered rhythms. They fashioned ways of looking in addition to fashioning looks, and they trained readers how to move through streets and crowds in addition to guiding them among sensational sights. Somewhat later in the twentieth century film and television would organize reality in more compelling images, though they never took as their primary subject the city. That is why the turn-of-the-century metropolitan newspaper is the most suitable entryway into the nature of urban experience.

CITY TEXTS

Merely a glance at old photographs depicting the busy metropolitan intersections of Berlin around 1900—Potsdamer Platz, Belle-Alliance-Platz, Alexanderplatz, Friedrichstrasse, Spittelmarkt, Tauentzienstrasse, Jannowitzbrücke—reveals the presence of newspaper readers, newspaper vendors, and newspaper kiosks. No newly built square or thoroughfare (Schlesisches Tor, Zehlendorf-West, Rüdesheimer Platz) lacked an eight-sided green kiosk, a truly basic urban amenity. "Every hour in Berlin," wrote Hans Brennert, playwright and reporter, "flings millions of newspaper pages onto streets, into houses, into offices, banking suites, factories, taverns, and theaters." Newspapers had "completely changed the face of the street."[7] Even schoolchildren tucked newspapers into their drawings of the city: "Every morning I see the milkmaid and the newspaperman on Perleberger Strasse," explained one young artist.[8] Indeed, Berlin had the greatest newspaper density of any city in Europe. By the 1920s, the city's three great publishers were all putting out special noontime, evening, or late-night papers—Ullstein's *BZ am Mittag*, Mosse's *8-Uhr Abendblatt*, Scherl's *Nacht-Ausgabe*—in addition to various editions of their big flagship dailies, the *Berliner Morgenpost*, the *Berliner Tageblatt*, and the *Berliner Lokal-Anzeiger*. Daily newspapers tailored for suburbanites *(Die Grüne Post)*, highbrow Westend readers *(Vossische Zeitung)*, or businessmen *(Berliner Börsen-Courier)* flourished as well. A total of 93 newspapers appeared each week on the city streets. Only the onset of the Great Depression in 1929 set limits to this astonishing marketplace diversity.[9]

No city could have supported so many newspapers had city people not browsed their way through the diverse selections of the press. If Berliners subscribed to a morning paper, in most cases the *Morgenpost*, delivered to their homes by newspapermen, they also purchased paper after paper at streetcorner kiosks and perused any one of the latest editions lunching in cafés, waiting for buses, and riding streetcars. When Berlin's great twentieth-century chronicler, Walter Kiaulehn, recalled the irrepressible feel of summer, he remembered bus passengers on "the Eleven" riding down Unter den Linden, their feet perched on the edge of seat frames, happily eating from a bag of cherries, turning the pages of tabloids.[10] "Almost everybody reads" the *Morgenpost*, the *Lokal-Anzeiger*, or the *Berliner Tageblatt* in the 416 streetcars that rolled across Potsdamer Platz each daytime hour, noted Anselm Heine in 1908.[11] *Zwölf Uhr Mittagszeitung, BZ am Mittag, Berliner Illustrirte*—one of these brushed the cheek of Franz Biberkopf riding into town from Tegel Prison on streetcar Number 41 in the opening scene of Alfred Döblin's *Berlin Alexanderplatz*.[12] And newspaper headlines played catch with the thoughts of commuters in Lion Feuchtwanger's short-story sketch, subway car "Number 419."[13] Number 11, Number 41, Number 419—municipal buses and streetcars and subways were crowded with avid newspapers readers; an impression confirmed in scholarly surveys. According to one

Viennese study, every other streetcar rider read big-city dailies going to and from work. In one car scandalous headlines or editorial commentary or final sports results absorbed twenty-three of thirty-four commuters.[14]

The extraordinary correspondence between metropolitans and readers suggests the city simply could not be used without the guidance of newspapers. Newspapers not only reported on a mechanized city that had grown so large so quickly that it had become impossible for a single individual to survey; they also revealed a city whose diverse parts even less prosperous inhabitants had come to use more deliberately. That most Berliners around 1900 took streetcars as a matter of routine and read a newspaper every day represented a startling change in metropolitan habits, which had been far less cosmopolitan and regular just one generation earlier. Long gone were the days when city people worked and lived in the same neighborhood and could construct adequate city maps on a foundation of personal experience. Twentieth-century Berliners took streetcars to go to work and to shop and, on weekends, to travel to outlying metropolitan sites. If in 1890 Berliners took nine still rather unusual streetcar journeys per month, the number grew to sixteen in 1900 and became a very regular twenty-five in 1913. When young children, the very old, and homeworkers are factored out, it is clear that the streetcar had become a thoroughly quotidian conveyance for most city people.[15] Hence it is not surprising that the delights of the city—the Wertheim department store on Leipziger Platz, Lunapark at the end of Kurfürstendamm, the beach resort on the Wannsee, the parade grounds at Tempelhof—attracted a socially diverse public of proletarians, employees, and merchants and of men, women, and children: it was no longer simply well-to-do flâneurs who were "at home" around and about in urban places. By the end of the nineteenth century Berlin, like Paris

"Just Out! *Berliner Illustrirte Zeitung*." In
this ad everyone is reading *BIZ*.

or London or St. Petersburg, had truly become a settlement
where strangers were likely to meet, which is Richard Sennett's very fine definition of a city.[16] As Berliners participated
more widely in the cosmos of the city, they read more avidly
about its occasions and events. City people encountered the

strange, enticing, prodigious city first and foremost as readers.

For newcomers, the city was retrievable most easily in the newspaper. It was the popular or penny press that first tried to make the new world of the industrial city sensible to readers, recasting location (the newspaper in the metropolis) into function (the newspaper for the metropolis). The *New York Sun* pioneered this sort of urban reportage in the 1830s, and publishers in Paris and London followed suit. It was not until half a century later, in 1883, just when thousands of immigrants had begun streaming into Berlin, that the *Berliner Lokal-Anzeiger* and, after 1898, the *Berliner Morgenpost* introduced the practices of the "new journalism" to Germany. Thereafter both papers served as informative guides to the confusing protocols and hectic rhythms of the metropolis. New arrivals depended on newspapers to find work and housing, to sell goods and services, and to identify urban types and negotiate local institutions. Increasingly elaborate local reportage provided readers with sketches of homelife in tenement buildings, public life along fashionable streets, and work discipline inside factories and department stores. Over time newcomers —readers—filled in the blank spaces of their mental maps of Berlin. Not to read the newspaper was to risk losing orientation.

The complicated city that made the newspaper such an indispensable guide to immigrants also provided diverting entertainment to residents. Vicarious expeditions into proletarian neighborhoods, introductions to an improbable cast of curbside characters, and descriptions of visits to asylums, prisons, and hospitals gave the city an exotic quality that fascinated readers. But Berlin was sensational on many counts: its particular geography (medieval alleyways, proletarian precincts, parvenu suburbs), picturesque sociology (chimney sweeps, prostitutes, speculators), and also the instability of the city's inventory, the restless motion of its transformation. Reassembling crowds in ever-changing urban tableaux, reconfiguring buildings and landmarks with every passing year, grafting on new factories, tenements, and streetcar lines, the city lacked a distinctive, permanent physiognomy. Its extreme variability resulted in a persisting sense of bewilderment. By the end of the nineteenth century the story of Berlin had become the story of constant change. Observers as diverse as Mark Twain, Walther Rathenau, and Karl Scheffler all found the city's lack of innate character to be its distinguishing trait. It follows, then, that the efforts of the popular press to guide readers through a strange land complemented perfectly its rapacious appetite for sensational news.

The picture of Berlin that metropolitan newspapers constructed had little in common with previous views of the residential city. Excursions into department stores and neighborhood streets or tenement courtyards revealed a fabulous metropolitan garden that could be traversed time and again yet never look the same. A fixed topographical idea of Berlin as the seat of commercial and royal power established along Unter den Linden or, more typically in the sootier age of industrialization, as a menacing moloch *(Feuerland)*, gradually dissipated. In place of the unitary image there was a slideshow of closely observed sketches on the rich variety of trades and inclinations and social ties that made up the big city. The startling variations included the ceaseless fluctuation in the fortunes of individuals and the ongoing renovation of neighborhoods. Again and again, journalistic detail confounded any pat summation of the growing city. Whether they came as surveyors of urban wilderness or merely as collectors of metropolitan exotica, reporters kept Berlin's transitory aspects sharply in focus. Describing the strangers who mingled on the streets or following the rapid development along the city's periphery, they gave urban portraiture a new geography: Friedrichstrasse and Potsdamer Platz, streetcars and tenements, blue-collar Rixdorf and the well-groomed Grunewald. In the hands of the metropolitan press, the city encompassed the outer precincts of Berlin N. as well as the elegant districts of Berlin W., Friedrichstrasse as well as Unter den Linden; metropolitan sociology had been amended to include workers, street vendors, and small tradespeople; and the city's forbidding nature challenged by introductions to an array of robust individuals and improbable habitats.

The sensational content of popular newspapers was matched by the sprightly form in which they were written. Assorted news—national, local, sports—clashed uneasily on the front page and upset conventional hierarchies of what was considered important. The rapid succession of juxtaposed articles recreated the big-city crowd of strangers.[17] Individual columns were laid out in a perhaps more attractive but frankly tendentious manner. Edited stories replaced political chronicles, and loud and contradictory opinions broke down the authoritative voice of newsmakers. The fashionable late-nineteenth-century literary form of small sketches (kleine Prosa) was particularly suited to chronicling the contrasts of the city.[18] Gripping headlines and active verbs mimicked metropolitan rhythms as well. Editorial philosophy, layout design, and feuilleton sketches collaborated to emphasize how provisional city matters had become.

Front-page formats intensified the urban experience that front-page stories sought to report on. Headlines and slogans, for example, at once reproduced the quick tempo of metropolitan speech and supplied readers with additions to their vernacular. The papers' focus on dramatic, astonishing events made of the city a convulsive, never-ending spectacle, heightened by the succession of morning, afternoon, evening, and extra editions sold in growing numbers on the street. Newspapers were themselves exemplary of the nervous rhythms of the big city.[19] No account of Wilhelmine or Weimar Berlin has been complete without a description of the gigantic linotype machines that set big-city editions, the fast-pedaling cyclists who distributed the bundled papers, the colorful vendors who sold them on busy streets, or the hurrying commuters who scanned headlines in streetcars and subways. To take just one well-known example, Walter Ruttmann's 1927 film, *Berlin: Symphony of the Big City*, went to some lengths to depict the business of the newspaper as an indispensable part of the sensational story of the city. It featured close-up shots of rotation presses, front pages, and street sales and even ripped apart headlines to leave oversized words on the screen: "crisis," "murder," "stock market," "marriage." Indeed, mass-circulation newspapers actually played a major role in organizing twentieth-century spectacles, which assembled the reading public on the street to witness car races, aviation rallies, and other city-wide events.

The newspaper was inseparable from the modern city and served as a perfect metonym for the city itself. Already in the 1860s Charles Dickens compared the disjointed assemblage of articles on the front page to the haphazard space of the metropolis: "As we change from the broad leader to the squalid police report," he observed, "we pass a corner and we are in a changed world."[20] The rapid alternations that Dickens described enhanced a spectacular view of the city, a "dreadful, delightful" place that could be easily consumed.[21] The reading and writing of the city as spectacle has prompted judgments ranging from uncompromising condemnation in the face of trivialization and reduction of the metropolitan experience, to appreciation of the ceaseless replenishment of city matters.

The lively debate over mass media and metropolitan culture will inform this book throughout; it is neatly introduced by the different approaches of two novelists, Paul Gurk (1880–1953), an undeservedly neglected Berlin writer, and his near contemporary and occasional mentor, Alfred Döblin (1878–1957). At the end of Gurk's Weimar-era novel *Berlin*, the itinerant bookseller Eckenpenn boards a streetcar which hurtles along the street like a screeching "monster." Eckenpenn sits down, pays his fare, and is at once blindsided by a newspaper that another commuter unfurls in front of his face. This inconsiderate act accounts for Eckenpenn's demise. In a time when Berliners hurry along in streetcars and steal glances at newspapers there is simply no place left for books or booksellers. In a few masterstrokes, Gurk puts the industrial schedules of the metropolis in tandem with the debased regimes of reading and writing. What is more, the insistent rhythms of the city have disfigured its physiognomy as much as they have distracted its readers. Eckenpenn no longer recognizes his hometown. By the 1920s, the stretch of the old city between the Tiergarten and the Spree River where the bookseller had wheeled his cart has been torn up by speeding automobiles, undermined by roaring subways, and overshadowed by glass buildings.[22] To be sure, Eckenpenn still encounters a city of readers, but they now mainly consume newspapers during minute-long intervals, driven by a relentless tempo that has obliterated contemplation and robbed experience of its savor. As the story ends, it becomes clear that the bookseller cannot adjust to "the new time," an incompatibility which lends dramatic tension to the novel.

Gurk himself languished in a backyard tenement in the working-class neighborhood of Wedding. He was not able to make a living as a writer or find an accommodation with the urban forms that surrounded him. It is revealing that at his death in 1953 over 600 watercolors were found in his rooms, most depicting the coarse ochre-tinted countryside around Berlin and many augmented by careful meteorological notations, as if Gurk were trying to fix the optimal conditions for the revival of preindustrial virtues.[23]

For Gurk, the city is a form of knowledge, although the twentieth-century incarnation in which newspapers supersede books is distinctly inferior. His feelings were seconded by contemporaries, who deplored the effects of mass literacy, particularly the "overconsumption" of newspapers and other "trivial literature," and the challenge these posed to the authority of classicism.[24] Without adopting such a heavy-handed tone, a number of modern critics more or less stand in Gurk's corner and regard newspapers and other metropolitan media as notable agents of homogenization and spiritual impoverishment. Cultural conservatives, Frankfurt School theorists, and Gramscian neo-Marxists apply similar broad strokes to their analyses: since the turn of the century, the culture industry has not only steadily abolished the intimate experience of reading books but has gradually extinguished diversity as it has pulled various social groups into its vortex. Intramural debates about timing or the survival of archaic folk traditions and the possibility of formulating alternative women's spaces have generally honored the assumption that the mass media have the ability to reduce both men and women to passive spectators, consumers of compelling images of a homogenized population in the pursuit of like-minded goals.[25]

In his analysis of discourse and counterdiscourse in nineteenth-century France, Richard Terdiman identifies commercial newspapers as vital agents in the production of the "seamless serenity" and apparent inevitability of a hegemonic culture. Despite the juxtaposition of items on the front page according to the abstract requirements of layout, there is little about the newspaper, in Terdiman's judgment, that can teach readers to perceive contradictions. "In its routinized, quotidian recurrence, in its quintessential prosaicism, in its unrepentant commercialism," the press flattens out and elides over differences and leaves power relations unquestioned. According to Terdiman, the capitalist investment in newspaper texts, which no longer addressed political partisans but city readers at large and which consequently commodified news as disposable consumer items, shaped a dominant discourse that reconstructed and naturalized the nineteenth-century world. Newspapers "seemed to go without saying," representing the universe as a wonderfully complicated, colorful creation, a world view that went unquestioned and unchallenged. Although Terdiman allows for counterdiscursive interventions of the occasional sardonic feuilletonist or caricaturist, these forays only highlight the hegemonic workings of the genre as a whole.[26]

There is much that is persuasive about Terdiman's analysis, and his observations about the way the newspaper calibrated readers to the operations of commodity culture are filled with insight. Yet there is an overly serene, even static quality to his own portrait. Very little about the newspaper genre or the city life it depicts disrupts the monologic meanings Terdiman reconstructs. "Counterdiscourse" is restricted to intellectuals—Daumier, Flaubert, Baudelaire—who struggle to maintain distinctions in the face of general contentment and experiment with subversive forms—caricatures, exotic journeys, prose poems—in opposition to the larger, encompassing social text.

For Berliner Alfred Döblin, in contrast, the social text itself has lost coherence. The newspapers, handbills, advertisements, and anecdotes he accumulates are anything but serene or seamless. In Döblin's big-city epic, *Berlin Alexanderplatz*, almost constant movement from all directions keeps the city in turmoil. From the very beginning of the story, when a page of newsprint grazes (but does not blindside) Franz Biberkopf on streetcar Number 41, texts interrupt and interject and jostle, and they continue to do so throughout the novel, disrupting and mocking narrative coherence. What characterizes the city are fast-moving streams of information. The excessive number, simultaneous appearance, and rapid alternation of texts preclude stability. Under the turbulent conditions of twentieth-century Berlin, Döblin's account of Franz Biberkopf negates the possibility of narration in the modern city.[27] There are, of course, famous scenes in the novel where the movement of city people around Alexanderplatz is synchronized in precisely the stiff, passive manner suggested by critics of mass culture, but Döblin adds to these so many other studies in disorderly motion that the lingering impression his interspersed city texts leave is a disquieting sense of surprise and intrusion.

Döblin imparts to *Alexanderplatz* a restless and mutable quality that keeps texts from functioning in uniform or authoritative ways. As a result, Berlin gradually loses its single-mindedness. The unforgiving industrial city which destroys its inhabitants was a staple image in the second half of the nineteenth century. Now the monolith has broken up into countless pieces—odd adventures and unexpected experiences which do not add up to a coherent whole. In this fragmented social universe, to which no single interpretative template applies, people make their way and encounter the city in disparate, idiosyncratic, and solitary ways. "Tenants, landlords, Jews, anti-Semites, poor people, proletarians, class warriors, hustlers, dispossessed intellectuals, little girls, prostitutes, teachers, parents, trade unions"; Döblin described the Berlin that inspired his writing with a roll-call of characters whose versions and editions of the city were even more proliferate: "two thousand organizations, ten thousand newspapers, twenty thousand reports, five truths."[28] Perpetually decomposed and wonderfully precipitous, the modern metropolis passes, in the words of literary scholar Philip Fisher, from "killing machine to playground."[29]

The exuberant view of the playful, insurgent city in which the center does not hold should not be romanticized. Terdiman's analysis is valuable precisely because it draws attention to the "always same" behind the appearance of the "always different." In this view, the representation of flux covers up the hegemonic logic of social reality and thus poses an ideology of abundance amidst conditions of scarcity. Yet Terdiman risks flattening out differences in the analysis of social texts because he ignores the city, the defining context, which in its haphazard and dizzying explosion at the end of the nineteenth century produced more disorder and encouraged more undisciplined readings than he allows. Even as social imperatives rewrote the city and imposed on it some measure of narrative order and legibility, the fugitive city continued to replenish its energies and to loosen these bonds.

THE MODERN CITY

The nineteenth century remade cities into new and strange places that challenged conventional literary representations. Within just a few generations, industrial machinery drastically renovated the physical layout of the early-modern city. What had been the seat of administrative, commercial, and religious power with a familiar *Altstadt* (old town) topography of royal palaces, town halls, and church spires increasingly gave way to the geography of manufacturing that Friedrich Engels described so well for Manchester in the 1840s. Factory districts, commercial avenues, railway yards, and tenement blocks overlaid and overwhelmed the older city. Both in physical extent and in the number of inhabitants, the industrial city was much larger than its preindustrial counterpart. By the middle of the nineteenth century thousands of newcomers were moving in from the impoverished countryside; the hastily built suburban sectors to house them, along with railways and boulevards to move them about, had given urban settings a completely new face. A generation of writers, from Eugène Sue to Charles Dickens and Emile Zola, attempted to account for this remade city, guiding readers through busy streets and imposing institutions and introducing them to a range of improbable characters both rich and poor.

But the industrial city in the nineteenth century was different from the commercial and administrative towns of the eighteenth century not only because of its factories and factory workers. The crucial difference lay in the ceaseless mutability of the modern city. It is this process of relentless change rather than particular economic functions that I want to keep in focus when I refer to the industrial city, and I prefer the term "industrial" to others that might emphasize more precisely the business of exchange and commerce because it identifies the nineteenth-century combinations of technology, capital, and speculation that presupposed the city's disorienting fluctuations.

The pull of social and economic relations into the capitalist market, the expansion of a uniform and universal monetary exchange that transformed even the most refined landmarks into perishable commodities, the never-ending introduction of new wares and fashions, and the steady arrival of newcomers all collaborated to transform the modern city over and over again. A surfeit of impressions and diversions insured that the city would be experienced over time as merely provisional. That urban experience of extreme impermanence, which has its origin in the last century and which we have come to associate with modernity, profoundly unsettled everyday life.[30]

What was true for the industrial city in general was epito-
mized by Berlin. Unlike Paris, London, or Vienna, Berlin had
been a rather insubstantial royal residence until the rise of
manufacturing in the 1830s and the concentration of banking
and other commercial services in the new capital after the
unification of Germany in 1871. In the thirty years before
World War I, the population of Greater Berlin doubled from
two to nearly four million. Entirely new zones, grafted at
sharp angles onto the old Prussian center, indicated the city's
rapid growth: the largely proletarian precincts of Berlin N.
(north) and Berlin O. (east) and the more affluent west end,
Berlin W. Whether they lived up north or out west, most Berliners in 1900 had been born elsewhere, usually in small towns
or rural villages in Brandenburg, Silesia, and East Prussia.
Their very presence in the city represented a sharp discontinuity with their remembered rural pasts. The city remained
strange even to long-time metropolitans. The noise of commerce and bustle of traffic; the heaps of goods in markets and
warehouses; the diverse backgrounds and professions of
neighbors; and, most of all, the restless transformation of the
city's physical layout continually augmented the shock and
astonishment that newcomers felt upon arrival.

Contemporaries marveled at the city's dynamic energy, but
felt increasingly disoriented in its midst. Arthur Eloesser, a
journalist born shortly before unification on the northern
edge of Berlin, regretted losing the city of his youth "in the
ceaseless influx of new inhabitants who lived from day to day,
without memory, without tradition, without a sense of duty to
the past."[31] This confession contained a critical insight into
the modernist condition: to live from "day to day" was to live
without memory or a sense of continuity. A similar lament
came from Karl Scheffler, author of the most famous survey

of the city, *Berlin. Ein Stadtschicksal* (1910). He concluded
that the tragedy of Berlin was its fate "always to become and
never to be."[32] His essay remains astonishingly perceptive and
has established the essential plot to the city. For the three
generations of observers who have followed Scheffler and witnessed the devastation of two world wars, the thirty-year division of the city, and in 1990 reunification, Berlin has remained the paradigmatic modern city because its character
has been so forcefully determined by the experience of transience.[33]

The modern city etched deep traces in the consciousness of
metropolitans. Both Eloesser and Scheffler identified a new
type, the city person who lived without a stable sense of identity or memory. In the barrage of new sensations, city life
amounted to a series of improvisations that foreclosed on an
integral personality. Walter Benjamin made a similar distinction between the rooted experience *(Erfahrung)* of the villager
or the artisan and the discontinuous eventfulness *(Erlebnis)* of
the metropolitan or the factory worker. A more sociological
perspective argued that the fluctuations and contradictions of
the big city required a dramatic process of psychological ad-
justment—"inner urbanization"—which was distinguished by
heightened sensual dexterity but also by emotional indifference.[34]

Georg Simmel, celebrated sociologist in turn-of-the-century
Berlin and perhaps the most illuminating investigator of city
life, related the loss of inner security, which had estranged
Eloesser so keenly, to "the shocks and turmoils which we con-
front in the immediate proximity and contact with people and
things." "The clamorous splendor of the scientific technological age," as Simmel called it, had become part of the inner
world of the individual, who was by turns stunned and awed

by the continuous rearrangement of city things. Feelings of tension, longing, helplessness were the result:

> The lack of something at the center of the soul impels us to search for momentary satisfaction in ever-new stimulations, sensations and external activities. Thus it is that we become entangled in the instability and helplessness that manifests itself as the tumult of the metropolis, as the mania for travelling, as the wild pursuit of competition and as the typically modern disloyalty with regard to taste, style, opinions and personal relationships.

Inconstancy characterized the inner world of the metropolitan as much as it did the outer world of the metropolis.[35]

Simmel's vocabulary is generally lachrymose—"disloyalty," "wild pursuit," "helplessness" indict the city on behalf of an imagined past that offered more coherence and integrity. Traveling madly, competing wildly, tasting promiscuously, Simmel's city people lived completely on the surface. In response to a barrage of "rapidly changing and closely compressed" shocks, they adopted a blasé and self-complacent attitude (*Blasiertheit*); "perhaps no psychic phenomenon," Simmel added, "has been so unconditionally reserved to the metropolis."[36]

Simmel recognized that this ability to live unmoved amidst the "clamorous splendor" encouraged a studied lack of conviction. In the face of public outrages passersby remained indifferent spectators, and the public square a mere amusing laissez-faire playground. Metropolitan virtuosos risked losing themselves in the "labyrinth of means," unmindful about the "ultimate goal."[37] They could read a schedule, catch a train, but they had forgotten where they were going. Yet Simmel was also powerfully attracted to this urbane sensibility. He made what amounted to a distinction between the careless and the carefree, between lack of character and lack of prejudice, identifying *Blasiertheit* with a heightened self-reliance and intellectuality. By cloaking individuals in anonymity rather than eliminating them completely, life in the city made possible the cultivation of the personality.[38] An "overtone of hidden aversion . . . grants to the individual a kind . . . of personal freedom which has no analogy whatsoever under other conditions," Simmel observed, although this freedom did not delete loneliness or alleviate nervous discomfort.[39] Simmel was thus torn between "fate and utopia."[40] He acknowledged both the moral emptiness and intellectual virtuosity of metropolitans.

Simmel's seminal contribution was not simply to identify the fluctuating and fragmented nature of metropolitan life but to follow its effects on the body and the senses. City matters formed city minds.[41] Along with roads and railways the city also projected angles of perception, and it is these that the modernist tradition in the arts attempted to represent. From the turbulence of quickly passing impressions, the detached observer came to determine the impermanence of the social world and its relations. And this determination of impermanence has characterized the idea of modernism. Not only was the present increasingly experienced as brand new, completely different from even the recent past, but it was itself doomed to be merely transitory. Fashions, fads, and all ideas of the moment were thus typically modern creatures, bursting onto the scene with great energy before falling into disuse, persisting for a while as ruins, then disappearing again. It followed that any attempt to capture the essence of the age had to focus on these occasionals, which Baudelaire described as "le transitoire, le fugitif, le contingent." To track the merely transitory was to represent the enduring nature of the age.[42]

Baudelaire's modernist heralded a crisis in the authority of representation. Insofar as artists accepted the contingent and fleeting nature of phenomena, indulged in the merely fashionable, and even claimed no longer to recognize the indelibility of rank and distinction, they threatened conventional hierarchies of knowledge. The provisional quality of their city views imperiled an encompassing and ordered world view in which objects were known and relations fixed. The industrial city's ceaseless flux had a vertiginous effect on observers; henceforth, any account of modern times would have to focus on the mutability of society and, at the same time, to acknowledge the provisional nature of description and representation. As a result, the fragmentary nature of the modern city came to be identified with new ways of seeing. Perspectives that had once been dismissed as marginal, subjective, or hallucinatory gained new credibility. This promiscuous visuality ultimately challenged the whole process of sight and even the idea of certainty and clarity. Throughout the nineteenth century, artists and writers turned to the city as a new organum to explore the mediations and circumstances of consciousness.[43]

The development of the modern novel, which has often been identified as a classic metropolitan genre, indicates the ways in which the city revised the operations of literary representation. Since the novel did not flourish in Germany until the end of the nineteenth century, in part because of the absence of great cities, I will now and then draw on French and British examples. But the point here is not to establish an authoritative genealogy of metropolitan reading in Germany; it is simply to suggest the heteroglossic impact city contexts had on narrative forms.

Already at the beginning of the nineteenth century, in the "wonderful new time" after the French Revolution,[44] as coal and coalers set the first steam engines in motion, novelists, poets, and other literati sought out cities because they believed that only the inconstancy that was peculiar to the metropolis could lead to a new comprehension of the world. According to E. T. A. Hoffmann, no amount of reflection or education could yield more wisdom. He espied the "signs of an epoch . . . in which the questionable once again opens the gates to the fundamentals of all things." As Marianne Thalmann explains, German Romantics such as Novalis, Kleist, Schlegel, and Hölderlin joined Hoffmann in Biedermeier Berlin. No longer satisfied with "walking forth and back across the room, rummaging through papers and books, as if that was where the answer to everything could be found," they were convinced that knowledge required skepticism and experimentation, not serenity and contemplation.[45]

For Hoffmann especially, as he felt his death approaching (he died in June 1822), the city provided "a true depiction of the constant flux of life." From one moment to the next, the busy activity of streets and markets gave way to desolate silence: "the voices, raised pell-mell in the wild confusion, have fallen silent, and each deserted spot expresses all too clearly an awful: 'it once was!'"[46] How different was this restlessness from Goethe's carefully maintained garden of literary production in the small town of Weimar, which enclosed reflective walks along the river, a well-insulated atelier, and one or two confidants.[47] In contrast to Goethe, who visited Berlin only once, younger Romantics sought the city out as a site of stimulation, doubt, inquiry. And they accordingly furnished their imaginary cities in the "twilight of truth." "Bridges, alleys, windows, steps, masks, dawn, and dusk" were physical suggestions for the emotional uncertainties that Romantics sought to realize in their art. In their enchanted tales, streets doubled as "secretive paths to the interior." "The endpoint of each perspective opens onto a new one," and the city traveler "constantly awaits the unexpected." "In this criss-crossing of streets, at each of the corners and curves, people become transformed into the antenna for a thousand experiences."[48]

It was the novel rather than Hoffmann's tales or Kleist's dramas that provided the industrial city with its first distinctive mirror. According to Volker Klotz in his acclaimed study *The Narrated City*, the novel achieved a suppleness that drama lacked. It retold city matters more ably because scenes and characters could depict the breadth and social diversity of the metropolis more freely. The various walks of city life, exploded "the playtime of a drama or the playroom of a stage." Moreover, the center-stage focus on a few individual characters and carefully conceived dialogues kept dramatists from adequately representing the collective nature of city life.[49] Novelists, in contrast, worked with a huge stock of characters whose movements and impressions built a veritable word city. More than that: the novelist could quickly change scenes, lead readers into asides, and introduce a range of social mechanisms such as letters, conversations, rumors, and newspapers to convey or exchange information, all of which erected an increasingly complex labyrinth in the mind's eye.

Even when the novel did not take the city as its subject, it assumed the formal properties of urban life. Readers had to become much like detectives to make sense out of a welter of literary images and portraits. "The rhythm of mystery and solution," in which the reader followed the lines of narrative in a state of suspense, translated the disconnected experience of the city. Philip Fisher leans on Simmel to make the important argument:

> The city . . . intellectualized men [and women] by demanding more and more consciousness, more alertness and inference, more balance and tolerance for the unexpected, more processing of the immediate environment. The novel trained and fed this psychology of detection with its intellectual keenness, its suspicion, its playfulness and speculation in the face of what it sees, but created simultaneously an emotional passivity that amounts to a reserve in the face of what can't be anticipated or understood until the moment

when it is unexpectedly revealed. In achieving this training the novel in Dickens, James, Conrad, and Joyce carried to a spiritualized level the rhythm of obscurity and illumination.

However, the narrative of the novel comes to an end, whereas that of the city does not. A contradiction thereby ensues between the form and the subject of representation. Fisher describes the conclusion to which the detective work of reader and writer leads as a "web" that eventually "replaces a set of knots." At the end of Dickens's *Bleak House*, for example, the key characters, who occupy the most diverse social stations, reveal their improbable interconnections. The "puzzled anxiety" of the reader in the face of the labyrinthine city is relieved before the last page is turned.[50] Emile Zola, too, for all his effort to present the fast pace, the roilsome flux, and subjective states of the city, closes his thick novels with unwieldy narrational devices that collapse the many dimensions and dispel the nagging uncertainties he has laboriously constructed.[51] The metropolitan rhythm the novel has accomplished over its course is thus offset by the closure, the visibility of the web at the end of the narrative, as if the labyrinth of the city were built with exits after all.

The experimental novels of the twentieth century, by contrast, gained their stylistic originality by attempting to accommodate the city's disharmony. Discontinuity, dissociation, and unpredictability steadily overruled the orderings of plot and narrative. Already in Dickens's last novel, *Our Mutual Friend* (1865), the city is "an agglomeration of crazed parts . . . whose relationship to each other has been jumbled" rather than simply hidden from view.[52] "The feverish babble of constant digressions," which was so consonant with the experience of walking down the big-city boulevard, became louder still in Andrei Bely's celebrated surrealist novel, *Petersburg* (1913–1916).[53] Set in the revolutionary year 1905, *Petersburg* ostensibly tracks the attempt of comrades to throw a bomb and accomplish a political end. "Everything seems to head toward a final end," comments Klotz: "the steady hand of the central symbol of the time bomb; the busy routines of characters with their sundry tasks and responsibilities; the limited duration of the action, which quickens the pace" of the novel. But, in fact, "not only do all intentions fall flat"—the assassins fail, the plot is derailed, the bomb does not go off—but, what is more, Bely's protagonists are constantly being diverted, scattered, turned around, and kept waiting. By cutting from one scene to the next, changing perspectives, repeatedly revising previous statements, and censoriously inserting himself in the dialogue, Bely attempts to reproduce the discontinuities of the city in an almost tactile way to the reader. Petersburg prevails not as a place but as a force that arbitrarily gathers up and disperses its inhabitants. It devours the dramatic storyline about the bomb, an iterative process that is, in the end, the plot.[54]

The most ambitious effort to overcome the limitations of the novel to comprehend the unstable experience of the metropolis was Alfred Döblin's *Berlin Alexanderplatz* (1928). Döblin's originality lay in bending the novel to the city, eschewing a narrative line in favor of techniques of montage, layering, and serialization. The irritation that Döblin produced in his readers who were accustomed to a plot, however slowly revealed, also reproduced the irritation and incoherence of the city.[55] Döblin's readers, like Berliners at large, were flooded by streams of words and impressions, which tumbled over one another in rapid sequence and resisted arrangement into hierarchically ordered beginnings and endings. Any storyline, Döblin felt, would extinguish the transient and contradictory nature of city life. In constructing *Berlin Alexanderplatz*, Döblin presupposed that "the many folds that make up the cloth of life and the interconnections between events would be cut and torn by the red thread of narration."[56]

Döblin also dismisses his hero, Franz Biberkopf, leaving him muttering and bewildered on streetcorners. "'What was that?' 'What am I gonna do?' 'What's to become of me?': such are the discouraged questions of a person who, like Biberkopf, has been tossed out by the city," writes Helmut Jähner. Any step into the world, like Biberkopf's ride into the city on streetcar Number 41, was a step into an ungraspable order to which the individual was subordinated. Although Biberkopf was not completely powerless, he had to contend with powerful characters, namely the underlying rhythm of the city and the press of the crowd.[57] The composition of *Berlin Alexanderplatz* allows Döblin to shuttle back and forth between two levels: the chaos of the city and the wider crisis of meaning for which the city stands. Döblin uses the city to question the ability of the individual to see and oversee reliably and to move about purposively. Biberkopf is not only left helpless on the street, but his utterances and thoughts are contaminated by advertising slogans, household words, biblical quotations, and newspaper items. Both the city and the subject in the city are composed of fragmentary bits and pieces that resist summation. To achieve this effect, Döblin manipulated the form and language of the novel, moving well beyond the conventional alternation of first-person dialogue and third-person narration. Whereas Bely's characters still speak and think in clear, educated voices, a second-hand voice which Bely himself assumes in narration, Döblin tries to recreate an unmediated inventory of dialects, voices, and colloquialisms. In addition, he splices different kinds of texts into the pages of the novel: headlines, advertisements, schedules, notices jostle alongside and often run into the speech of the protagonists.

Browsing over many items, accumulating along the way a

motley array of stories, predictions, asides, and statistical data, *Berlin Alexanderplatz* reads much like the tabloids it repeatedly cites. In many ways, the newspaper provided Döblin with a miniaturized version of his entire project. Its unity is purely formal; there is no narrative line to order the disconnected elements. As Fisher points out, "column by column, weighted without account of importance, the heroic and the trivial repose side by side."[58] A rapid series of events burst onto the front page and just as quickly fade and disappear. Berlin newspapers profiled precisely those events that were fleeting and provisional and with each edition produced a brand new version of the metropolis, thereby adding to the "spectacle of incessant actuality."

What made the format of the newspaper so attractive to writers was its ability to reproduce the discontinuous and haphazard arrangements that seemed to be the most marvelous aspect of the modern city. But the experiments of Döblin, and those of John Dos Passos and James Joyce, who also manipulated the novel to read like a newspaper, indicated limits in the ability of the novel to depict the city. That literary form's claim to comprehensiveness, its narrative continuity, and its reliance on a stock of retrievable characters tended to enclose and harmonize the urban setting. Improvisational writing, in contrast, caught more fully the modern city's restless nature.

Not long after his arrival in Berlin from provincial Swiss Bern in 1906, the essayist Robert Walser reflected on the metropolis and the metropolitan arts. "I prefer the street to the theater," he wrote to Christian Morgenstern, "and the most crudely printed newspaper article to a well-crafted novel."[59] Newspapers threw open their front-page windows to life on the boulevards in ways that books did not; the brief style and rapid succession of articles more nearly fit urban rhythms. The hectic tempo that the modern city had decreed also completely infiltrated Joseph Adler's description of reading. "And when do I read?" the critic asked in 1913: "On the streetcar, on the platform of the omnibus, in an entryway during a rain shower, in the half-hour before falling asleep." Moreover, he added, the reading material had to complement this busy, unmistakably metropolitan routine better than "long-winded plots, a horse-and-buggy style, and deep psychological analysis."[60]

Walser and Adler both suggested that the style and content of the newspaper were more equal to the tumultuous activity of the city than the leisurely narrative of conventional dramas or novels. In other words, they pointed to the curious fact that the big city supplied its own form to represent the riotous and colorful scenes it put on stage day after day. The representative arts bent to accord with their novel subject. Modern "art not merely mirrors a world in motion," ascertained Georg Simmel, "its very mirror has itself become more labile."[61]

At the turn of the century, artists and writers picked up newspapers again and again to convey the provisional and fragmented nature of metropolitan vision. Variety shows, for example, typically featured what was known as "la revue de l'année," a run through the past year's events cobbled out of newspaper headlines, fashion tips, and *faits divers*. In the evenings before World War I, audiences stormed Berlin's Metropol-Theater to take in the show "Neuestes, Allerneuestes!!" (1903) or "Ein tolles Jahr" (1904). And on the Friedrichstrasse, the Wintergarten was famous for its number "Der Biograph," an innovative cinematographic review of "das Aktuellste vom Aktuellen" which closed the show. The format of the revues, in which political satire followed society gossip or hyperbolic advertising slogans, mimicked the juxtaposition of trivial and serious items in big-city newspapers. Indeed, one Parisian revue, showing at the Théâtre de l'Athénée, was called "Le Journal joué," the performed news-paper.[62] This "aesthetic of the newspaper" lent cabaret per-formances a popular realism. They recycled scraps of printed words—posters, public notices, municipal prohibitions, ad-vertisements, schedules, labels, newspapers—that could be collected on any streetcorner and were thus accessible to everyone. A century later, however, the shows have become impenetrable. No doubt they required an audience that was thoroughly literate in the words of the moment. The revue made audiences fluent in the transitory, which was itself com-prehensible only so long as the cabaret's inventory of jokes and allusions remained current.

In their prewar work, Pablo Picasso and Georges Braque repeatedly experimented with newspapers. Between Novem-ber 1912 and January 1913, for example, Picasso created three dozen newspaper collages. By rearranging headlines, advertisements, and other urban debris, Picasso focused at-tention on the improvisational nature of city words. As Jeffrey Weiss points out in his excellent study of these collages, "the anti-illusionistic shallow or flat pictorial space that results from the predominance of pasted paper signals a new role for the picture plane as a field of transience." Composed of news-print, stuck together with glue, Picasso's pieces themselves have faded along with the urgency of the words and messages they contain. They thereby carry a "fleeting contemporan-eity" into our own time.[63] Rearranging newspapers into kiosks of his own making and watching the collages fade over time, Picasso drew attention to the words that formed the universe of city people and to the contingency of meaning that results from their ever-changing constructions.

Some artists gathered up newspapers to tuck into their novels or glue onto their canvases; others dropped their pro-jects altogether to write for the papers. Metropolitan writers such as Theodor Fontane, Alfred Döblin, Lion Feuchtwanger, Martin Kessel, and Arnold Zweig all penned dozens of feuilleton articles between writing their novels. The period between 1890 and 1930 ranks as the golden age of the feuilleton, or feature article. There was an obvious advantage in keeping one's name constantly before the reading public, and big-city newspapers paid well-known authors princely sums. But the format of the daily press was also well-suited to representing the city. Snapshots, vignettes, and other sketches captured the endless variety of city inventory.[64] *Kleine Prosa,* which became increasingly popular at the end of the nineteenth century, adhered to Baudelaire's insistence that a "rapid . . . speed of execution" was necessary amidst "the daily metamorphosis of external things."[65] Metropolitan newspapers offered writers a happy medium to experiment with writing styles that were equal to the provisional and fluctuating states of the city.

Although cultural historians have usually strictly separated the feuilleton from the rest of the newspaper, celebrating its intellectual virtuosity and critical thinking, even going so far as to accord it the status of a "counternewspaper" *(Gegenzeitung)* spun off an otherwise purely commercial enterprise,[66] both the feuilleton and the rest of the newspaper shared an indulgence in disorderly detail. Theodor Fontane made just this point in a celebration of the playful, provisional voice of the English press:

> The leading article in *The Times* represents the complete victory of the feuilletonist style over the last remains of the style of the chancellery and other deformed sons and daughters of Latin classicism. Long periods are disdained; the sentences follow one another quickly like shots from a revolver . . . Knowledge and details must not take up too much space. The well-written *Times* article is an arabesque, wrapped carefully around the question, an ornament, a witty illustration; it is coquettish and wants to

please, captivate and conquer, but it does not at all intend to convince, once and for all.

Fontane lauded the impressionistic, playful style of the feuilleton for refusing to submit to stable and clear hierarchies. As Russell Berman observes, "the newspaper's renunciation of the comprehensive overview" is part and parcel of "the crisis of meaning: to the advocates of bourgeois culture, the world, seeming to grow more and more absurd, refused to submit to the rational ordering" that had informed the worldview of earlier generations of intellectuals.[67] Not conforming to the predominant regimes of knowledge, full of ironic possibility, the feuilleton attracted writers at the end of the nineteenth century much as the labyrinthine city had attracted Romantics at the beginning of it.

The feuilleton, like the other serious, trivial, and merely curious stories on the newspaper page, served up an excess of details. For the most part, the feuilleton writer observed, rather than explained. Just a short sketch, two or three thousand words at most, without any pretensions to analysis and conclusion, the feuilleton was an ideal form for recounting the pointillist splendor of the industrial city. By focusing on singular or astonishing details or coincidental events the writer had noticed because they disrupted expectations, the feuilleton demonstrated that things were not always in place or properly understood. Producing a spectacle of surprise, feuilletonists pleaded the case for the confusion of meaning. They surpassed novelists in their ability to present the city as an accumulation of co-incidents, in which grand designs and compositions were elusive or merely provisional and in which meanings were ever contested and undermined.[68]

The industrial city was neither fully defined by the improvisational forms of representation, nor was such a definition the whole aim of these forms. While the speed and velocity of modern life and the hurried turnover of fashions and commodities had profound effects on everyday life, and Simmel's speculative sociological insights attempt to verify these empirically, the city was also fabricated by nineteenth-century artists eager to promote the idea of the fugitive in opposition to the classicism of the artistic establishment. The very modern notions of diversity, blurred boundaries, and self-styled identities are as much the predicates as they are the results of late-nineteenth-century city viewing. The famous Impressionist "blur" constituted a bold claim that modern life had become indeterminate. Yet, as T. J. Clark and Christopher Prendergast have argued, it was also a refusal to acknowledge the class divisions and political conflicts that would have clarified both the sensible and sinister workings of the city.[69] To stand on Potsdamer Platz in the middle of Berlin and to revel in the surprises and shocks of noontime traffic, in the unlikely combinations of pedestrians and commuters, and the ever-changing inventory of buildings and entertainments was to miss some crucial aspects of city life such as conditions of employment, housing, and upbringing. Enough newspaper stories continued to expose "how the other half lives," indicating just how much of the city simply fell outside the modernist frame of reference.

And yet the fugitive city in the metropolitan feuilleton cannot be simply dismissed as a modernist fantasy. Overly blurred or unjustifiably illegible, the image of the unknowable city leads as well as misleads. Twentieth-century ideas about sight and perception owe much of their force and insight to the Impressionist "blur." Manet and his followers collaborated in a scopic regime which, even if it rests on an ideologically tendentious view of nineteenth-century Paris, as Clark claims, has had profound political and cultural implications for the twentieth century, providing, for example, many of the tools to dismantle authoritarian habits of mind and to revive the fancifulness of individual choices.

At the same time as the city was so described, the idea of the city as sensational and spectacular had reconstituted the city itself. This was so not just because popular texts such as newspapers told about city affairs, giving them a common, sensational profile, but also because their mode of reporting intensified the contradictory and fragmented experiences of city people. To the newspapermen who worked for Ullstein (or for Scherl or Mosse), Berlin was in constant motion. The city literally splintered underneath the long strides of A. H. Kober as he made his way to the Ullsteinhaus on Kochstrasse:[70]

> I've got an hour. That's enough time. . . . The streetcar, running in both directions, half-minute intervals, masses of people. On the right, spectators leaving the circus; on the left, strollers, students, girls, tired workers returning home . . . houses, restaurants, dives, beer halls, cafés, clubs, show windows . . . darkened entryways to offices, sweatshops, apartments, rooms, pawnshops, loan sharks, pensions (elegant rooms, to let even by the hour), doctors, lawyers, tutors, the wine bar with the red lanterns and the female personnel . . . Friedrichstrasse! . . . Past the exit to the new subway station: Mohrenstrasse, at the corner of Charlottenstrasse . . . then down to the corner of Jerusalemer: Mosse . . . Next corner, Zimmerstrasse: Scherl . . . royalist to the bones. And finally to the third cross street: Ullstein!

It was not only Kober's second-hand word city that moved faster and faster, but the city itself. Readers felt events leap, jump, and crash. And papers such as Ullstein's *BZ am Mittag* quickly became among Berlin's most familiar and noisy features. For over forty years, until the end of World War II, uniformed street hawkers shouted the rhythmic "Bezett! Bezett am Mittag!" down Berlin's boulevards at noon. Siegfried

Kracauer described how their cries "tumble over each other without end, squeeze themselves into the tiniest openings, and blend together in a thousand ways." Even after the vendors had sold their goods and gone home, Kracauer thought he still heard their calls.[71] Texts were active on city streets. They blindsided Eckenpenn, grazed Franz Biberkopf, tumbled over Siegfried Kracauer, and interrupted, defied, and jostled other metropolitans. Again and again, the word city insinuated itself into the city. Reading about Berlin cannot be separated from being in Berlin.

A NOTE ON READING THE CITY

The act of reading is a complicated and personal experience that cannot be deduced effortlessly from the text itself. Texts do not speak for themselves in one voice, and they are not understood in the same way by all readers. Our own common-sense experience tells us that newspapers have always been used in various ways—readers glance at, peruse, or pour over text; some readers read headlines first, others the sports pages, and others still examine advertisements and classifieds; readers may use newspapers for entertainment or to gain vital information that will lead to a job or apartment; children, men, women, workers, and commuters read and fold and tear out and dispose of newspaper pages in different ways; newspapers tell stories, and they also wrap fish and make paper hats. Insofar as reading is an individual act of "poaching," in the words of Michel de Certeau, it might be hazardous to suggest that any sort of text worked on readers and, through readers, on metropolitan experience in common, knowable ways.[72]

The creative labor of reading should stay very much in view, and one of the arguments of this book is that metropolitan newspapers represent a relatively weak literary form which encouraged multiple readings and provided the foundation for the construction of multiple cities. Nonetheless, reading is a socially informed act. In the case of metropolitan newspapers, turn-of-the-century readers approached the text in order to render their surroundings more comprehensible. After all, the newspaper is an indispensable guide to the city, not a literary form like a novel or a poem. At the turn of the last century, readers read newspapers to make sense of the city and they were therefore predisposed to legitimate the form and accept the substance of reportage. At the same time, the newspaper, like any other genre, had distinctive attributes which guided readers. Headlines, columns, subheads, succinct narration, and other typographical elements created protocols of reading.

This study cannot resolve the basic debate between literary scholars who emphasize the role of the text in governing interpretation and those who argue that interpretation is provided by the reader from outside the text. Both approaches are valid and one will be more useful than the other depending on the question being asked. In this book, I am more interested in the creation of metropolitan rather than other identities. Therefore, while I accept the creative autonomy of the reader, the accent will fall on the ways in which reading is inscribed by texts and by the social assumptions under which readers approach texts. For this reason, I have also accepted the identity of the genre of the mass-circulation newspaper without explaining how each paper or each story came to be. Although the *Lokal-Anzeiger* and the *Morgenpost* had different staffs and publishers—Scherl and Ullstein were bitter political enemies—I have chosen to focus on the common attributes of newspapers and their circulation in the city. Of course, a comprehensive study of the press would include a business history and an examination of reporters and editorial philosophy; this exploration of the word city cannot substitute for such an analysis.

This said, a central argument of mine is that the metropolitan newspaper gave its readers choices for moving about the city without compelling a particular itinerary. While the city was presented as the locus of spectacle, the word city could be rummaged in diverse ways. Middle-class women, white-collar commuters, and proletarians all made their own way. The distinctions I make between reading and browsing, between discovering and consuming, and between the city as an unknowable, fugitive formation and the city as a choreographed spectacle indicate the absence of a single, determining encounter with the metropolis. But the idea that the city was a fabulous place where its multiple actors could take journeys, collect impermanent images, and construct a sense of themselves does give metropolitan diversity a common, inclusive note. In the end, I go on to suggest that the years before World War I witnessed the formation of an identifiable metropolitan culture in which city people increasingly used and viewed the city in like-minded ways. Even so, this shared culture did not snuff out other countervailing identities based on class, ethnicity, or gender, and it certainly did not homogenize Berliners. It established protocols to allow strangers to roam the city, to bathe in its sights, and to interact with one another in familiar ways. It also anticipated the broader culture of consumption later in the twentieth century. As it happened, though, the civic unity that cohered around 1900 was itself impermanent. By the 1920s the word city was threatened by deep political polarization and its versions became unreadable and uninteresting to people city-wide. Metropolitan culture was also transformed by the increasingly national operations of new media such as radio and film.

Words and narrative forms worked on the city in broad and unmistakable strokes, while they also generated countless alternative versions and editions. At every point, the word city

pointed out instability and inadequacy as well as predict-
ability; it worked to startle and invite as well as to control
movement; it showed the contradictory as well as the coherent.
It was not possible to get around that two-way narration,
which was at once promiscuous and authoritative and which
continuously wrote and rewrote both the metropolis and the
capital.

2
READERS AND METROPOLITANS

The revolution in reading that historians identify at the end of the eighteenth century was characterized by increasingly private and introspective reading of imaginative literature and, at the same time, by extensive reading of useful, practical books. Yet in Germany this revolution remained quite limited in its social reach until well into the nineteenth century.[1] Even if educated readers had by and large put aside traditional religious texts, ceased to invoke passages from the Bible as guides to daily life, and acquired habits of choosing and perusing from among hundreds of titles now available in libraries, catalogues, and bookstores, still, according to Jean Paul, their number barely exceeded 300,000 in the 1820s. This was a dramatic increase from the bookseller Friedrich Nicolai's estimate of 20,000 in 1773, to be sure, but nonetheless a small minority among 27 million Germans.[2]

Again and again, nineteenth-century writers attested to the frustrating scarcity of books as they were growing up. The dramatist Friedrich Hebbel, for example, recalled the arrival of any book in his hometown of Wesselburen as a momentous occasion in the 1830s. And it took some bowing and scraping for young Hebbel to get the local pastor to lend him the town's only copy of Goethe's *Faust* for a few stolen hours one night. Other places must have been without books altogether, since at the time three in four Germans lived in localities smaller than the 1,000 inhabitants who made up Wesselburen.

Even in larger towns, workers and artisans rarely purchased books, and subscriptions to lending libraries were prohibitively expensive. Long working hours and difficult living conditions further curtailed the reading habits of the lower classes.[3] The few books that proletarian autodidacts did acquire were read and reread. Novelist Karl May, born in 1842 into a family of weavers, remembered his grandmother and great grandfather reading out loud and discussing together the contents of their modest shelf of books some twenty times.[4] Devotional items, cheaply bound adventure stories, and family journals were less expensive than leather-bound books, but these came with the wares of itinerant peddlers who visited irregularly and generally kept to the main roads.

The few sheets that made up the first newspapers did not readily find a mass readership either. If newspapers began to appear daily in the larger German cities in the first decades of the nineteenth century and could rely on a cadre of metropolitan readers, they were generally purchased only by the propertied and educated middle class. As late as the 1870s, Arthur Eloesser recalled, the shoemaker and tailor who lived in the streetfront apartments of a Prenzlauer Berg *Mietskaserne* (tenement) shared one subscription to save expenses; poorer families, housed in the *Hinterhäuser* (back buildings) around the dark interior courtyard, spared themselves the effort of reading altogether.[5] Although the numbers of newspapers for each citizen that Rolf Engelsing has calculated for Bremen indicate the rapid rise in reading throughout the second half of the nineteenth century, from 25 potential readers per newspaper in 1841 to 9 around 1850 and 5 in 1885, his figures show that only the onset of the twentieth century saw the formation of a truly national readership in which every other citizen bought a newspaper.[6]

It was the low-brow metropolitan newspaper, more than anything else, that enfranchised nearly all Germans in the republic of readers. By 1900, city people especially were making use of literacy skills acquired over the course of the nineteenth century and hitherto underused. In 1914, for example, an astonishing 4,200 newspapers and 6,500 journals were published in Germany. They found particularly large circulations in urban areas. In the imperial capital itself the *Berliner Lokal-Anzeiger* and the *Berliner Morgenpost* alike boasted daily sales of well over 200,000 copies after 1900; the fast-growing *Morgenpost* reached the 400,000 mark on the eve of World War I. By that time Greater Berlin, with some 3.5 million inhabitants, counted more than 1 million subscribers of, say, Ullstein's *Morgenpost*, Scherl's *Lokal-Anzeiger*, or Mosse's *Berliner Tageblatt*, the flagship dailies of the city's three big publishers. All around Alexanderplatz, Alfred Döblin reports, Berliners read papers—on streetcar Number 41, as we know, but also while waiting for an omnibus, browsing by a kiosk, sitting in a café, or eating pea soup at Aschinger's.[7] Newspaper peddlers also found buyers outside factory gates and in suburban districts. At the beginning of the twentieth century, newspapers had become everyday items in proletarian tenements. Newsprint accumulated amidst other household trash, and cutouts from the Sunday illustrateds were taped to decrepit plaster walls, telltale signs that reading had become commonplace among all classes.[8]

In the span of the single generation that encompassed Eloesser and Döblin, Germans had acquired the habit of picking up and reading daily newspapers and popular journals. At the same time, new preprinted bureaucratic forms, the instructions and labels that came with manufactured goods, and the many advertising placards along roads and railroad tracks contributed additional material to the print culture. In 1900, it was no longer necessary to inculcate reading habits or to locate reading materials as it had been in Hebbel's time. But if critics did not bemoan the scarcity of books, they worried about the excessive number and undifferentiated variety of texts: scandalous penny romances, brash advertisements, and sensationalist boulevard newspapers, all of which allegedly corrupted reading and unsteadied moral authority. In particular, critics pointed again and again to the deleterious influence of popular newspapers. These were especially dangerous because they had the same format as their more respectable counterparts and were so easily available to passersby. According to Rudolf von Gottschal, writing in 1908, "the newspaper" had become "as indispensable a prop as a glass of beer." Liters of beer, reams of newsprint—what was so disturbing about these early items of mass culture was their incidental, quotidian, and unconsidered aspect.[9]

Somewhat later, in the 1920s, surveyors found a veritable *Lesewut* (reading addiction) among countless metropolitans who required daily "fixes" of newspaper pages. "I couldn't even imagine breakfast without a newspaper," confessed one subscriber.[10] One German scholar discovered to his horror that the "overconsumption" of newspapers prevailed even "in respectable bourgeois families:"[11] "Only the head of the household still reads the customary subscription newspaper. His wife, who now has the right to vote, forms her opinions according to another paper and the grown children consider it a matter of honor to hold views different from their begetter. They all have their favorite newspapers which they buy from a street peddler." Of course, it was not necessarily freethinking "new women" or unruly children who bought newspapers at streetcorner kiosks; vendors testified that it was usually men about town who had a spare 10-pfennig piece to buy an additional afternoon or evening paper, a business courier, or the sports pages.

Kurt Tucholsky described all this perusing, cutting, and accumulating of newspapers as a "craving." This is how he set the scene for his 1927 *Sprechchor* (speaking choir), "The Newspaper Reader's Prayer": "Room. The newspaper reader in a robe. Piled on the table, scattered and balled up on chairs, are newspapers of all shapes and sizes." Alone in this room, the newspaper reader prays:[12]

Dear God . . . I have to read them all, all of them.

About the civil war between the North Chinese and the
   South Chinese;
about the gymnasts' festival with straddle jumps and
   balance beams;
about the flag conflict in Schaumburg-Lippe;
about Abegg, Lübeck, Ahlbeck, Becker;
about Schiller's executor;
about the Prince of Wales and Richard Strauss—
all that and more, each day at home!
And still I buy the stuff, as soon as I see it,
fixe Idee:
"Acht-Uhr-Abendblatt! Acht-Uhr! B.Z.! Die Nachtausgabe!"

I'll trot anyplace that has a newspaper—
it's a craving

for paper—always more paper—
I stop and read on the street:

The western Baltic very rough;
Pola Negri finally rescued;
Churchill overthrown; parliament furious;
the Pope and Mary Wigman engaged;
(suits him too!)—Storm in the Azores;
missing: Ludendorff's dachshund's tail;
boom in Greenland swimwear;
one hundred farces for Pallenberg;
Ain and Kabel to be filmed;
the smallest bellybutton ever;
Mussolini, black shirts, monograms
news, news, telegrams, telegrams,
telegrams

Like Walter Benjamin's flâneur, who restlessly seeks out the next street, turns the next corner, Tucholsky's reader buys one paper after another.

How do we account for the sudden popularity and relentless consumption of newspapers after 1900? There is an important political explanation. As the public gained a political voice over the course of the nineteenth century, the German press grew in volume and importance. The revolutions of 1848 marked a crucial juncture, after which newspapers became more critical of government and more progressive in tone. Not all newspapers endorsed Germany's middle-class revolutionaries, to be sure, but, as daily reworked versions of the world, newspapers legitimated new ideas. They were associated with the forward movement of the times.[13] Revolutionary activity and newspaper reading accordingly went hand in hand. Eyewitnesses reported that the first intense political debates in Berlin in spring 1848 took place in literary cafés and reading rooms. These indoor sites quickly became overcrowded and

meetings spilled into the streets, where orators and pamphlet-
eers found ever larger audiences. Thanks to newspapers, and
also to broadsides and satiric cartoons, the revolution acquired a circle of activists and the city more readers.[14]

Technology also made things easier for turn-of-the-century
readers. James Smith Allen's splendid history of reading in
France, for example, points out developments such as better
lighting at home, first with the introduction of gas lamps, then
with electrification, which reached 43 percent of Berlin households in 1927.[15] The nineteenth century's acquired habits of
drinking tea and coffee and smoking tobacco turned out to
have a great affinity with reading as well. And more people
wore reading glasses.

Outside the home, the growth of a bourgeois public sphere
and the accessibility of cafés, parks, and waiting rooms invited
reading.[16] At the same time, many potential readers in that age
of iron and steam found time to pick up books and browse
through newspapers during railway journeys; this, in turn,
prompted the popularity of the cheap fiction that the English
quickly labeled "railway reading."[17] And railroads transported unprecedented numbers of books and newspapers,
filling small-town mailboxes, stocking small-town kiosks, and
finally replacing itinerant vendors as the primary sources of
reading material. Village libraries, bookstores, and reading
clubs followed soon after.[18]

Nonetheless, newspapers in the railway age were still a commodity for the educated and middle-class subscribers. Engelsing's statistics for nineteenth-century Bremen show a
rapid increase in the number of readers, but they indicate as
well the continuance of a majority of nonreaders. What came
to constitute a genuine mass reading public was the huge mi-
gration from the countryside into the cities in the last third of
the nineteenth century and the concurrent development of the

General-Anzeiger (official advertiser) press, which catered to the needs of millions of new city people. It was local news and information, and plenty of advertisements, rather than sharp-witted commentary on high politics or polished feuilletons, that won newspapers a genuinely metropolitan readership. Moreover, by relying on advertisements to finance their papers, publishers were able to lower costs and attract additional subscribers.

At the end of the nineteenth century, the big-city daily had become the primary source of information and entertainment for metropolitans. It was cheap and easy to get either at street-corner kiosks or by weekly subscription, and it was at once workaday in orientation and comprehensive in scope. Rather than painting a portrait of parliamentary and diplomatic politics, it mirrored the familiar hardships, misfortunes, and amusements of tradespeople, workers, and their families, and did so in an economical but entertaining style. According to Rudolf Schenda, this formula had first been devised in the eighteenth and nineteenth centuries; it was successfully adopted by family magazines such as *Die Gartenlaube* and *Kladderadatsch*, which appeared in the 1850s and 1860s; and once elaborated by the metropolitan press, it did indeed make the newspaper as commonplace and indispensable and satisfying as a glass of beer.[19]

LOCAL NEWS

In a New Year's verse for the year 1700, the *Münchner Merkur* prized its comprehensive account of events far and near:[20]

> Wide and far, from land to sea,
> all things new and strange.
> What fame has earned and fortune brought,
> and money has turned and art rendered,

around the world, at home and far afield
our embassy will report each week.

This promise remained unredeemed until the end of the nineteenth century, however. There was little in the first German
newspapers that touched on home, and much more from "far
afield." International cabinet politics or national affairs completely overshadowed local news, which either was consigned
to a bare summary in the back pages or went unreported altogether. For almost three hundred years, concludes Jürgen
Wilke in a study of German newspapers from 1622 to 1906,
they did not serve as a medium of local communication. A
broad cast of "non-elite" characters on a municipal stage appeared only after the middle of the last century.[21] Even then,
local news received little attention from publishers, editors,
and reporters. One west German paper, which published over
150 articles detailing various incidents of murder, robbery,
and suicide in the last two weeks of December 1910, had contented itself with publishing only three similar notices just
thirty years earlier.[22] Often enough, it took a spectacular
murder, like that of nine-year-old Lucie Berlin in 1904, for established newspapers to take notice of the poor neighborhoods
in Berlin N., "the other Berlin," in any detail. "Finally, arrived," exclaimed a disoriented reporter from the *Berliner
Tageblatt* as he got off the streetcar and walked to a murder
site in unfamiliar Prenzlauer Berg.[23] The upper-class precincts of Berlin W. continued to attract the exclusive interest
of the influential paper during the Weimar era. "Do you sometimes drive through the Eastside or the Southside or the
Northside," Fred Hildenbrandt once asked the city editor,
who replied laconically: "No, why, what would I do there?"[24]

Pages of parliamentary protocols, long-winded political
articles, and seemingly uninterrupted coverage of royal court

life turned most German newspapers even in the early twentieth century into what one historian aptly describes as a "uniform lead desert."[25] Without practical information on shopping or stock prices, without advertisements for Saturday night theater or Monday morning job offerings, without reports on yesterday's sporting events or last night's family row down the street, without warnings against corrupt marriage brokers or perfidious real-estate speculators, the opinions and editorials of established newspapers were not terribly useful or interesting to most city people.

As soon as newspapers reported on the traffic and growth of the metropolis, however, they quickly found a huge readership. The shared turbulence of city life stoked an intense interest in topicality, to which popular literary forms from newspapers to novels had to respond.[26] Thousands of confused newcomers arrived in Berlin's train stations every year, the great majority from small villages, many of them Poles and Jews who spoke German poorly, and all hungering for information to orient themselves in the big city.[27] To report on what Gunther Barth has aptly described as "the greatest news story of the nineteenth century—modern city life"—the metropolitan press had to reinvent itself.[28] In short order, the practices of the "new journalism," pioneered first in the 1830s in New York and Paris, then ventured in London and later in Berlin, revolutionized the look and contents of newspapers.[29] They told newcomers about the myriad ways to survive and succeed, and also revealed the many paths to misfortune in sensational front-page stories about murder, suicide, and corruption. Urban life stories helped metropolitans to move about the labyrinthine city with greater certainty. By introducing readers to novel arenas and unlikely characters, newspapers also "overcame ignorance perpetuated by convention," "encouraged tolerance born of knowledge," and thus refined a common metropolitan sensibility.[30]

Newcomers appreciated straight talk about manners in the city: "whether to throw away cherry pits or orange peels, how to behave on the streetcar, the proper conduct of pedestrians."[31] The *Berliner Morgenpost* ran stories about how to find quality meat, butter, and eggs in the teeming indoor markets, and *BZ am Mittag* detailed the virtues of punctuality and offered other hints for success to enterprising white-collar employees.[32] Again and again, newspapers calibrated city people to city rhythms by offering guides and introductions to metropolitan economies of scale. City newspapers gained readers when they discussed the problems of maids and coachmen rather than the problems of finding domestic help or hailing a taxi, which was precisely the difference between the *Berliner Morgenpost* and the *Berliner Tageblatt*.[33] And when publishers turned their papers into plainly commercial enterprises by selling advertising space ranging from a full page to a single line, they garnered harsh criticism from the established press for blatantly catering to the material needs of readers rather than trying to educate them. In fact, though, they did benefit city people anxious to find work, rent or let a room, or enjoy nighttime amusements. Not until the newspaper reformulated itself as an encyclopedia of daily life and "grasped the reader from all sides"—a process which corresponded to the fantastic growth of the industrial city at the end of the nineteenth century—could it become a quotidian item in the people's inventory.[34]

USING THE CITY

As Berliners made greater use of the city and crossed its various zones and neighborhoods on a daily basis, newspapers became more useful. In the year 1913, for example, each Berliner took 306 trips on streetcars, riding three times more often than the city dweller had done in 1890 (in New York, by way of comparison, the 1913 figure was 419).[35] In the last years

Potsdamer Strasse, c. 1913. Double-decker omnibuses
and streetcars dominate the boulevards. A kiosk and an
advertising pillar are on the left, and advertisements for
the *Berliner Morgenpost* and the *Berliner Lokal-Anzeiger*
form a proscenium to the street scene.

before World War I, no fewer than 750,000 and occasionally
as many as 1.2 million commuters used the city's streetcars
every day; thousands more rode motorized buses, underground subways, and the suburban *Stadtbahn* (elevated) so
that a daily average of nearly 2 million Berliners were mechan-
ically moved about the city.[36] At the busiest time of the day,
around half past seven in the morning, streetcars passed the
main suburban intersections every twenty seconds.[37]

"Four standard speeds existed for the man of the crowd,"
recalled Walter Kiaulehn about Berlin at the end of the Em-

pire: "pedestrians at five kilometers per hour, streetcars at fourteen, omnibuses at sixteen, and subways at twenty-five."[38] In new gear, Berliners—women as much as men—entered the city center more frequently and circulated around it much faster than the city grew. Over the course of sixteen hours on 1 October 1900, for example, 146,146 people walked across Potsdamer Platz compared to the 87,266 counted just nine years earlier; by 1908, the number of daily pedestrians on the square had reached some 174,000.[39]

Many of the new arrivals on Potsdamer Platz and Berlin's other metropolitan intersections were stiffly dressed employees who commuted to centrally located banks, offices, and department stores. As a walk around the Gendarmenmarkt and Hausvogteiplatz or past Behrenstrasse indicated, Berlin had become a major commercial hub in the last quarter of the nineteenth century. The city's double function as imperial and Prussian capital added thousands of bureaucrats as well. The growing numbers of employees to be transported undoubtedly lengthened the Berliner's average commute, which had reached four kilometers in 1913.

At the same time, more and more women crowded the city center. Thousands of female typists and clerks joined the army of white-collar workers. By 1907 the service industry accounted for 11 percent of employed persons in Berlin and Charlottenburg (20 percent if civil servants are included), up from 8.5 (13) percent in 1895; of these, 27 (35.7) percent were women, a startling contrast to 19.6 (18) percent just twelve years earlier.[40] With just these steadily advancing troops in mind, the *Morgenpost* ran a lengthy series on possible professions for prospective female employees: in January 1899 it was "How Do I Become a Nurse?" Other articles in the twenty-odd-part series reviewed opportunities for working women in the garment district, the restaurant trade, and private households. The *Morgenpost* undoubtedly attracted female readers by paying attention to their concerns in the various spheres of the new city.[41]

After work ended each evening at eight, the "girls" as much as the "boys" in business crowded public places, meeting beneath the *Normaluhr* (standard clock) on Potsdamer Platz or the Spittelmarkt and going on to visit city restaurants and suburban dancehalls. And from across the Atlantic and the Channel came a new daytime repertoire of "lunches," "five o'-clock teas," and "cocktail hours" as department stores, restaurants, and hotels vied for the business of affluent ladies and gentlemen. In particular, Berlin's great department stores, which were all established around the turn of the century, became regular stops on the metropolitan itineraries of middle-class and even working-class shoppers—Jandorf was known as the proletarians' emporium, Wertheim on Leipziger Platz and especially Kaufhaus des Westens on Tauentzienstrasse in the Westend attracted a well-heeled crowd, while Tietz on Alexanderplatz was firmly middle-brow. Housewives were even advised by the *Morgenpost* to take a weekly streetcar to Alexanderplatz to visit the food central markets, which offered more variety and lower prices.[42]

In this blossoming consumer culture, conventional gender roles became blurred. By the onset of World War I it was increasingly rare for unchaperoned women to be denied service in public places. As a busy place of retail commerce and exchange, the city had become a visual field of pleasure in which women as well as men could safely move about "just looking."[43] Dozens of small items of local news and especially the eye-catching full-page promotional ads that the big stores purchased every day charted and invited the casual movements of shoppers and browsers, with the result that older maps of the dominant views of the city, drawn by privileged

Edmund Edel's publicity poster for the *Morgenpost* (1901)
connects women, shopping, and the media.

male flâneurs, had become obsolete. Art-nouveau posters for the *Morgenpost* made the links between the sale of goods, the readership of newspapers, and the movement of women in public explicit. If ads dressed women for men, the layers of enticing clothing demonstrating, in the words of one trade magazine, that "*die Frau* is as beautiful as she makes herself out to be," they also addressed women in a more cosmopolitan spirit, celebrating the pleasure of consumption and overturning the discipline of parsimony.[44]

Hotels full of tourists—the one-million occupancy was reached in 1906—confirmed the extent to which Berlin had become a place to visit. Like other Western cities at the end of the nineteenth century, Berlin had become aware of itself as a tourist attraction. The newly minted *Weltstadt* (cosmopolis) displayed its sights on thousands of picture postcards, relaxed morality codes and censorship in deference to international visitors, and its papers commented readily on the provincial ways and odd habits of so many "out-of-towners."[45] Crowded with workers, typists, shoppers, spectators, and visitors of all kinds, the urban terrain had become even more congested and contested after the turn of the century. It was nearly impossible to make use of this capital of entertainment and commerce without the aid of a local newspaper such as the *Lokal-Anzeiger*, the *Morgenpost*, or *BZ am Mittag*, each one featuring pages of advertisements, announcements, and local stories that reported on the value of metropolitan excursions.

It was not just on workdays but also (and especially) on Sundays and holidays that Berliners traveled through their city. Despite deep pockets of poverty, more and more workers could afford weekend entertainments and metropolitan diversions.[46] (A morning newspaper or a streetcar trip anywhere in Greater Berlin cost 10 pfennigs; entrance into the *Freibad* (public beach) on the Wannsee between 10 and 30 pfennigs.)

As a result, streetcar traffic was always busiest on holidays. On Sunday, 17 June 1906, for example, a record 1,188,773 passengers, about one in three Berliners—and the great majority certainly workers and their families—had boarded trams. Subsequent Sundays—13 October 1907, 4 October 1908—established new records.[47] A total of 3 million streetcar tickets were sold over the long Easter weekend in 1907 and an astonishing 6 million over *Pfingsten* (Whitsuntide) in 1911.[48] A substantial majority of Berlin's 3.5 million inhabitants proved adept at using the entire city. From the city's proletarian districts in the North and East or from more affluent neighborhoods in the West, families dressed in their Sunday best poured into the city center, wandered about the Hohenzollern palace, strolled down Unter den Linden, and picnicked and listened to brass bands in the Tiergarten. Farther west, at the very end of the Kurfürstendamm, the amusement park Lunapark opened in May 1910. According to one newspaper, the ubiquitous slogan of that summer was "every Berliner at least once to Lunapark." At the end of two months, by the middle of July, over one-million sightseers had visited the fair grounds.[49] The twentieth-century city rapidly unfolded as a spectacular showplace for a variety of metropolitan browsers.

Most weekend streetcar and *Stadtbahn* riders journeyed well beyond the Tiergarten or Lunapark into the parklands, forests, and lake regions surrounding Berlin. "Hinaus ins Grüne"—on sunny Sundays, Berliners headed out of town into the Grunewald, to Tegel, Rummelsberg, or the Müggelsee. Easter streetcar traffic to the lakeshore at Tegel, for example, had more than doubled from 47,300 passengers in 1901 to 112,400 in 1906.[50] In each case it was newspapers, especially the *Lokal-Anzeiger*, with its weekly article "Hinaus ins Freie" on where to go and how to get there, or "Ausflüge mit der *Morgenpost*" and Ullstein's holiday poems and sketches celebrating Berliners at play, which encouraged city people to explore the metropolitan perimeter.

No suburban destination was quite as beloved by Berliners as the beach and cabanas at the *Freibad* on the Wannsee, which opened in summer 1907. Early opponents of the mass incursion of the working class to the beach tried but failed to raise entrance fees.[51] Thereafter, faraway Wannsee became an enchanted outpost of hometown Berlin, celebrated by the *Morgenpost* and immortalized by the city's beloved artist, Heinrich Zille. The prewar guidebook *Berlin für Kenner* sketched the scene: "bakers, shoemakers, milliners in bathing suits. Golden models and salesgirls in stockings—just like ladies. A mixture of earthy roughness and saucy insolence, of nonchalance, impertinence, and petty-bourgeois comfort."[52] As many as 200,000 Berliners enjoyed "Wannseeligkeit" (a double pun on "Seligkeit"—bliss—and "Wahn"—illusion) on summer Sundays. The *Morgenpost's* vernacular verses convey the convivial atmosphere:[53]

> Kaum die Wagenklassen fassen
> All die Mengen und die Massen;
> Kinder, Junggesellen, Bräute
> Und die vielen Eheleute
> Teilweis' mit, teils ohne Eh'ring,
> Eingepökelt wie die Hering'

"Eingepökelt wie die Hering'" (packed in like sardines)—the experience of a city weekend was not complete without the press of the crowd. In fair weather, all Berlin seemed to be out and about, on streetcars, in outdoor cafés, in the Grunewald, "to eat and drink," invited the *Morgenpost*:[54]

> Come along
> for a song
> bass with dill

what you will
ham on a bun
a bottle of rum;
Oh, there are the crowds,
but it's a waste
to rush in haste
for tables or just one seat.
You see, they've always got you beat.

Well into autumn, Berliners were still exploring the outdoors. "That was quite a day of turbulence around and about Berlin," commented the *Morgenpost* in October 1907: "On Sunday, the city must have been deserted, judging by the enormous crowds streaming onto public transportation to get outdoors!" When merrymakers returned home by train and tram in the evening, the pushing and shoving became "life-threatening."[55] At the end of a festive Sunday, the *Lokal-Anzeiger* noted wistfully, streetcars were littered with wilted bouquets that thousands of day trippers had left behind.[56]

By the eve of World War I, a modicum of discretionary income and an extensive network of public transportation had turned Berlin and its environs into a vast playground. As Zille made clear, nothing was more "volkstümlich" in Wilhelmine Berlin than a trip "ins Grüne."[57] Beloved Berlin chansons— "Rixdorfer," "Der Tempelhofer," and "Rimmel, Rammel, Rummelsburg"—commemorated long weekends spent on the outskirts of the city.[58] After the turn of the century, concludes one historian, city people moved about in increasingly dense crowds, "whether in the workaday traffic or during weekend expeditions, whether shopping or at sports events, whether at aeronautical rallies or military parades."[59] At the same time, as metropolitan sights grew more attractive and more crowded, observers noticed a concomitant decline in purely neighborhood amusements such as the one-carousel carnivals (*Rummel*) hastily erected on empty construction sites.[60] Even working-class Berliners snacked in the chain restaurant, Aschinger's, treated themselves to an evening in the cavernous hall of the Rheingold near Potsdamer Platz, and danced under the electric lights at Lunapark, participating in the novel rhythms of an emerging metropolitan culture.[61]

This city-wide stage was closely covered by mass-circulation newspapers. They reviewed Berlin's various recreations and reported on the ways and means of using them. But no metropolitan institution received quite as much attention as the "Grosse Berliner," the city streetcar company. The *Lokal-Anzeiger* and *Morgenpost* were full of small items about new routes, extra cars, overcrowding, and collisions, and they published the unending stream of complaints and suggestions sent in by disgruntled commuters. As city people spent more time on public transportation, newspapers devoted more articles to questions of public behavior—"When should you pull the emergency brake?" or "Should you get up or stay seated?"[62] Streetcars became part of the familiar interior of the city; articles reported on the life of streetcar conductors, told of the types to be found on the night bus, and examined the different ways passengers had of holding their tickets.[63] In addition, a new genre of feuilleton articles detailed flirtations and awkward encounters among commuting strangers.[64]

The growing familiarity with streetcars indicated just how accustomed Berliners had become to moving about the city as commuters, strangers, and spectators. As city people circulated more widely and more frequently, the city acquired an increasingly cosmopolitan quality. With its streetcars and streetcar destinations, Berlin had become, in the words of Richard Sennett, a "gathering of strangers," a place where "strangers [were] likely to meet."[65] The busy commerce and

"So Where Are We Going Today? To the Busch Circus,
Bahnhof Börse." Heinrich Zille's sketch shows a working-
class family using the newspaper to plan
an outing by train.

recreation centers of the metropolis gradually overwhelmed
the official parade-ground bearing of the capital. Moreover,
the delights of the metropolis attracted a large and socially diverse audience of proletarians and employees, men and
women: it was no longer just well-to-do flâneurs who were "at
home" in the city.[66] And as strangers and cosmopolitans, Berliners relied increasingly on the press for orientation. Local
newspapers were not organized around work; it was only after
the city became an emporium and a spectacle, in addition to
being a workplace, that Berlin's two biggest newspapers—
Ullstein's *Morgenpost* and Scherl's *Lokal-Anzeiger*—attained
their pervasive influence and came to be treasured alongside
the "Grosse Berliner" streetcar company, the Wertheim de-

partment store, and Aschinger's beer palaces, as quintessential Berlin institutions. With the onset of consumer culture at the end of the nineteenth century, Berliners came to see their surroundings through the perspective of the city newspaper.

BERLIN'S CITY PRESS

August Scherl published the first newspaper intended to serve Berlin rather than merely to appear there. The venture succeeded by making the most of a few basic ideas gleaned from thriving dailies in New York City and Paris. Scherl was convinced that money could be made by packaging a newspaper to meet the needs of the thousands of small tradespeople, employees, and workers who had moved to the new capital in the years after German unification in 1871. To make money on volume the product had to be cheap, and Scherl announced his good intentions by delivering the first number of his *Berliner Lokal-Anzeiger* on 4 November 1883 free of charge to all households listed in the Berlin address book. To entice readers, Scherl offered subscriptions at low monthly rates and stimulated their interest with the first chapter of *Pistole und Feuer* (Pistol and Fire), a steamy novel that was serialized over the next weeks. Anything that would offend or dismay his subscribers, however, was deleted from the paper. Scherl's editors carefully avoided taking partisan political stands or catering to particular social groups. Uninterested in persuading voters or refining cultural tastes, the *Lokal-Anzeiger* dropped the front-page *Leitartikel* (lead commentary) that was typical of most German papers and provided nothing but information and interesting tidbits written up in a concise and clear manner. While Scherl did not neglect news from abroad, he always reported on hometown happenings: "how the roof mender came to fall from the scaffolding in the next block, what occurred when the main water pipe burst in the neighboring village," as Hermann Ullstein put it, and, of course, stories about the growing number of Berlin's murders and suicides.[67] Scherl was the first German publisher who approached readers as depoliticized consumers, and he encouraged them to browse over news items much as they browsed over advertised goods. Scherl's Berlin was a city oriented toward consumption. It was nonpartisan, inclusive, and often complacent.

Scherl's formula quickly gained him a stable readership, and the paper soon attracted the steady business of advertisers. Department stores, specialty shops, and variety theaters all found the *Lokal-Anzeiger* a convenient means to reach thousands of potential customers, and readers took advantage of low-priced want ads to sell goods and services. Offering what Scherl described as "solide Hausmannskost," or "plain fare," the *Lokal-Anzeiger* quickly emerged as Berlin's largest newspaper with a circulation of 123,500 in 1889. Most copies were distributed by an early-morning army of *Zeitungsfrauen* (newspaper ladies), but thousands were also sold at the kiosks which appeared in the newly opened stations of Berlin's *Stadtbahn* and at other busy crossroads.[68] Both the substance of the paper and its disposable nature as a street-sale item addressed metropolitans first and foremost as consumers.

Commercialism was not the only thing that distinguished the Scherl's new journalism from the old. The idea that newspapermen peddled sensation merely to sell advertising space is too pat. Cities promised lucrative new markets, to be sure, but cities also generated the sensational novelties that newspapers served up to their readers.[69] Scherl's attention to information rather than commentary, along with his wide focus, gained him a genuinely metropolitan readership and kept the *Lokal-Anzeiger* from falling into the schoolmasterish tones of Berlin's more respectable papers. But the paper was missing some distinctive color. In the words of Peter de Mendelssohn, chronicler of the Berlin press, it had "no opinion, no character, no face," indeed, "no goal other than to bring in as much advertising and sell as many papers as possible."[70] With the ascension of Wilhelm II to the Hohenzollern throne in 1888, the *Lokal-Anzeiger* devoted more and more space to light entertainment. Scherl adopted a safely conservative tone, celebrating the young monarch and later following the amusements of the young crown prince—at the races, in St. Moritz—and otherwise, as Heinrich Mann satirizes so pointedly in *Man of Straw*, reporting on the sunny life of the imperial court. The paper thereby lost its sharp focus on city people.

The early success and subsequent limitations of the *Lokal-Anzeiger* invited competition. It was Leopold Ullstein who made the best improvements on Scherl's formula when he launched the *Berliner Morgenpost*, a paper that came closest to becoming a "Volkszeitung"—people's paper. On 9 September 1898, the first day of publication, the paper introduced itself: "Above all, the *Morgenpost* strives to be a genuinely Berlin paper and as such hopes to be at home in every household in the city. . . . the *Morgenpost* wants to depict Berlin, Berlin as its feels and thinks, as it works and dreams, as it suffers and loves, Berlin, the way it really is." Daily columns chronicled "Berliner Neuigkeiten" and "Berlin Allerlei" as well as suburban life "Rund um Berlin." More specialized features reported on Berlin's theaters and music halls and covered "accidents and crimes" and court dockets.

Sprinkled throughout the newspaper was Berlin's clipped dialect, which turned "g's" into "j's," "auf" into "oof," and "das" into "det." The *Morgenpost* even invented chatty Berliners: "Rentier Mudickes Stammtischreden" ("Regular Talk from Old Man Mudicke") was a weekly column. Direct in manner and disrespectful to authority, Mudicke became a Berlin favorite. He was joined by a portrait gallery of city characters, many of them sketched by Heinrich Zille from amidst a Berlin "milljöh" of backstreets, tenement court-yards, and tumbledown bars. Artists such as Zille, characters like Mudicke, cheeky copywriting, extensive and inexpensive classifieds (3 pfennigs a word), and a low-cost subscription plan that fit the weekly wage schedule of workers (first 10, then 15 pfennigs) made the *Morgenpost* Berlin's outstanding hometown paper.[71]

For all its local flavor, the *Morgenpost* did not neglect na-tional and international news, and its business pages earned the praise of professional economists.[72] Moreover, Ullstein's editors refused to accept Scherl's premise that a mass-circu-lation newspaper had to eschew political positions. Publisher Ullstein and his eldest son, Hans, both served as left-wing Pro-gressives in Berlin's town council and used the *Morgenpost* to campaign for civic improvement. According to a front-page editorial written by editor-in-chief Arthur Brehmer on the first day of publication, "whoever does not take a position in the difficult political debates of our times is an imbecile, an idler, or a coward." The political direction of the *Morgenpost* was clear enough—ameliorative social reform combined with political liberty in the name of a young, openminded leader-ship—but what really mattered was public service itself, "from whatever side."[73] Although the *Morgenpost* did not es-pouse socialism, it championed the "little people" against Prussian authority, reported on Social Democratic events sympathetically, and was surely preferred by most workers to the sober Socialist daily, *Vorwärts*. Given its brash tone and unabashedly democratic orientation, the *Morgenpost* was per-fectly suited to Berlin and quickly outstripped the *Lokal-Anzeiger*. Ullstein, himself a member of a prominent Jewish family, employed many Jews on his staff; this may have enhanced the newspaper's appealing "self-made," cosmopolitan, and reform-minded image.

If the *Morgenpost* told metropolitan stories in a column irreverently titled "Berlin Allerlei," Scherl paid far greater attention to the imperial court and to the official calendar of the capital in a buttoned-up local column, "Aus der Reichshauptstadt." The *Lokal-Anzeiger* also published pages and pages of fine print chronicling the commissions or promotions of Prussian officers and announcing the honors and decorations the kaiser had awarded his subjects. The sky would have to fall before Scherl's reporters wrote about the annual fall parade as Ullstein's did: "In short, this parade was much like any other."[74] And on Easter Sunday or Christmas Day, the *Lokal-Anzeiger* never failed to print a front-page sermon either by Hof- und Domprediger Kritzinger, Militär-Oberpfarrer Goens, or Potsdam's Hofprediger und Garnisonpfarrer Kessler. The *Morgenpost*, on the other hand, published a more congenial, family-oriented holiday edition full of short stories, pictures, poems, and other clippings from the people's archive.[75] Even the layout of the *Lokal-Anzeiger* looked dreary when compared to the *Morgenpost*'s art-nouveau subheads and half-page illustrations—neither paper introduced photographs until the 1920s. Long paragraphs reinforced the officious and circumlocutory tone of the *Lokal-Anzeiger*. Nothing expressed its dour and humorless face better than its reaction to the October 1906 "Köpenickiade." While all Berlin laughed, Scherl with punctilious consistency referred to Wilhelm Voigt, the costumed adventurer and gentleman robber, as "thief" and "scoundrel." Not even in suburban Köpenick could the paper let the dignity of the *Reichshauptstadt* slip.[76]

Although the *Lokal-Anzeiger* had been founded in the 1880s as a newspaper for Berlin's "small people," as the German ex-

pression has it, after the turn of the century it spoke out unmistakably against Social Democracy, the city's majority
party, and took the side of the police in labor disputes (during
the "Moabiter Unruhen" in 1910, for example). Most readers
of the *Lokal-Anzeiger* were shopkeepers, merchants, civil servants, or rentiers. In one marketing survey, less than one percent of all subscribers listed themselves as workers—an unre-
liable statistic but accurate self-appreciation.[77] The view from
the *Morgenpost* was rather different. Most of its readers certainly cooked for themselves and many bought the book *Ich
kann Kochen* (I Can Cook), which the paper published and
prominently advertised at Christmastime.[78] The *Morgenpost*
and, later, *BZ am Mittag* covered Social Democratic events
and honored working-class leaders such as Paul Singer and
August Bebel in front-page articles.[79] If historians are looking
for Germany's most progressive and popular newspaper, they
will find it in the *Berliner Morgenpost*.

The *Morgenpost* was an overnight success. Within eight
months after the appearance of the first issue, a notice on the
front-page boasted of 100,000 subscribers, a substantial challenge to the well-established *Lokal-Anzeiger*. With daily articles about Berlin crimes, Berlin cabarets, and Berlin parks,
the paper had an irresistible metropolitan appeal. And each
edition advertised its alluring topicality. In June 1899, for example: "Once again the *Berliner Morgenpost* is offering its
readers something new." And on this occasion the editors even
promised "something completely new." They proposed to send
editor-in-chief Arthur Brehmer on his honeymoon to Paris by
automobile. Readers subsequently followed the adventure in
daily installments which Brehmer wired back to Berlin. The
series would have nothing in common with the prosaic "eye of
the chronicler" or the sober analysis of the political reporter.
Its virtue, the *Morgenpost* emphasized, would be the "free,

wide-ranging perspective of the novelist." Nothing would better reveal the paper's "fin-de-siècle character" than the strong-armed verbs and hectic scenery of "a novel that is not a novel."[80] By all accounts, this front-page spectacle drew "colossal crowds" to Kochstrasse—starting point of Brehmer's expedition—and won the paper additional tens of thousands of Berlin readers.[81] Brehmer's honeymoon trip set a pattern which continued with round-the-world automobile races, zeppelin flyovers, and aviation rallies, all grand spectacles which Ullstein either choreographed or sponsored. Again and again, the *Morgenpost* inserted itself into the story as much as it reported on it, using a winning combination that had broad appeal and a thoroughly "berlinisch" character.

At the end of the hyped-up summer of 1899, after just one year of publication, a facsimile notarization on the front page indicated that the *Morgenpost* had "jut" 154,349 subscribers (to which the localism "jut"—"just about"—surely added more).[82] By the end of the year the paper's masthead declared that over 190,000 Berliners subscribed to the *Morgenpost*,[83] and soon after that it surpassed the *Lokal-Anzeiger* to become Berlin's biggest newspaper. In 1913 the *Morgenpost* claimed 390,000 subscribers.[84] No other Berlin (or German) newspaper approached this level of popularity. The *Lokal-Anzeiger* lagged behind with fewer than 250,000 subscribers, and so did Mosse's flagship daily, the *Berliner Tageblatt*. Although it had doubled its readership in six years to 220,000 in 1912, it remained far smaller than Ullstein's.[85] The *Welt am Montag* had 98,000 subscribers (1904), the *Berliner Volks-Zeitung*, 83,000 (1912), and *Vorwärts* about 50,000.[86] Berliners evidently took to heart the words with which "Rentier Mudicke" ended his *Morgenpost* column: "Fritze, noch ne Ufflage!" (Another edition, pal!). As Greater Berlin had a population of some 3.5 million inhabitants on the eve of World

War I, and most of these lived in families with several children, it seems safe to estimate that the *Morgenpost* was read in every third, perhaps even every second household. In any case, well over half of all Berliners regularly read either the *Morgenpost* or the *Lokal-Anzeiger*.

If the *Morgenpost* spoke for "Rentier Mudicke" in Berlin N., its midday companion, *BZ am Mittag*, which first appeared in October 1904, aimed at streetcar commuters, fashionable shopgirls in the garment district, motorcycle enthusiasts, and the city's nighttime demi-monde. "It was only a small door that led from the *Morgenpost* to the editorial offices of *BZ am Mittag*," remembered Egon Jameson, "but behind it lay another world," with "completely different ambitions, goals, and methods."[87] *BZ* did not greet its readers at home but grabbed them on the street amidst the daytime traffic. It gave them snapshots of the morning's proceedings in the courts, police stations, and stockmarkets, in addition to the latest telegrams from abroad; it made no pretense of covering all the day's events fully or serving the needs of its readers completely. Yet at heart *BZ am Mittag* remained a local paper. It reviewed the performing arts from cabaret and film to serious theater, maintained Berlin's largest staff of sports reporters, and led readers through the department stores, amusement parks, and soup kitchens of the city. *BZ* was a genuine boulevard newspaper not only because it was sold exclusively on the streets, but because it presented the streets as the distinctive stage of the metropolis.

It was *BZ*'s attention to sports that made the newspaper particularly popular among all social classes (before World War I, daily circulation reached 125,000). Workers did not usually have five pfennigs to spare for the noontime paper, but when they did, they bought it on Mondays, when *BZ* published its big sports section. Sports and recreation had become integral elements of big-city life. By the end of the nineteenth century, Germans joined athletic clubs and gymnastic societies in droves. According to one estimate, four percent of Germans belonged to a sports organization in 1914, a figure that was almost certainly higher in cities. Under the auspices of the Social Democratic Party, workers established an especially rich filigree of sports clubs.[88] Neighborhood athletic fields and bicycle stadiums filled with spectators every Sunday from early spring to late autumn. Special trains were pressed into service to bring sightseers to events in the outlying Grunewald and Weissensee. *BZ am Mittag* covered the horseraces on Easter Monday at Karlshorst:[89] "Just how many thousand spectators it is impossible to estimate. There and back, special trains had to be pressed into service; people even crowded onto the coal car behind the locomotive, and, in addition to the densely packed ticketholders, hundreds of onlookers stood beyond the fence and along the railway tracks up to the north ridge." Sports was no longer the amateur amusement of the upper classes but a mass phenomenon, drawing people out of "the dreariness of offices, factories, and apartment barracks."[90]

Sunday was the busiest day at the sports desk. "My God, it's Sunday again," recounted a harried local reporter, this time in the 1920s:[91]

I don't even know what to see and where I should begin . . . hockey is over now . . . a rugby game is scheduled to begin shortly on a sportsfield across town . . . I can just get there by car . . . Quick, back to the sports desk. I speed my car through the streets, run up the steps, rush into my office . . . Questions back and forth, what happened here, what took place there. Quickly I dictate reports to the typist and run with the rest to the composing room . . . paragraph by paragraph, line by line, horseraces, motorcycle rallies, sailing, boxing, soccer, handball—around the country, from abroad—names, scores—and the minute hand moves inexorably forward until finally: presstime, nothing more in the first edition. Layout. That was a hot day . . . and next Sunday won't be any different.

With six (later twelve) reporters working under a sports editor, *BZ am Mittag* was the best qualified to cover the Sunday recreation of Berliners. Publishing its first sports supplement on 15 April 1905, it reported on horseraces as did most of the other papers, but also covered boxing, motorcycle and bicycle racing, the early flying rallies at Johannisthal and Tempelhof, and the increasingly popular proletarian sport of soccer, and it did so in a lively style that wove compelling stories around the bare results that had once been tucked away in the pages of classified advertising.[92] Even when the hurrah-shouting, smoke-filled, champagne-drowned excitement of Berlin's six-day bicycle races, which claimed the front pages for one week every winter beginning in 1909, had passed, nearly half of every paper was devoted to sports, and spectacular events such as all-around-Germany aviation rallies merited an "Extra-Sport-Beilage." Sports was "volkstümlich," a thing of city people, and Ullstein won thousands of readers by giving extensive coverage to these events. The *Lokal-Anzeiger*, by contrast, had only a small sports section largely oriented to the international yacht and horse set.

Scherl and Ullstein won mass readership for their papers by coming up with the right mix. The *Lokal-Anzeiger* and later the *Morgenpost* became indispensable guides to the city. Newcomers inevitably bought and almost every working family subscribed to one or the other paper, which quickly earned their own streetcorner sobriquets—*Skandal-Anzeiger* and *Mottenpost*; coming after them, *BZ am Mittag* took its place among Berlin's largest dailies simply by being most people's second newspaper of choice.

Berliners poring over want ads, 1910.

Of course, it is impossible to gauge how vital or helpful the
perspective of the paper was to city people. Each person used
the paper differently. Perhaps the most attentive readers were
newcomers and the unemployed who poured over the job list-
ings, handed out for free as a separate section at specified locations. "Finally the newspaper boy appears. The silent crowd
begins to move. Hundreds of hands stretch out, reaching to get
a hold of the long-awaited paper and the possibility of employment. Hasty glances quickly move through the paper."[93] Tragedies and crimes in the city undoubtedly grabbed readers.
Here are two young girls in a Prenzlauer Berg tenement courtyard, whom the *Berliner Tageblatt* found "in front of a junk
shop crouching on small stools . . . slowly reading every word
out loud."[94] Other readers turned to the sport pages first,
glanced at the theater reviews, browsed through the big de-

partment-store ads, or dutifully read the lead articles. Newspapers were not always read carefully. They were picked up
and tossed aside to be retrieved again in waiting rooms, streetcars, and cafés. Franz Biberkopf "stepped into a little café,
took a Kümmel, thumbed the pages of the *Vorwärts* and the
Lokal-Anzeiger. Not much more in 'em than in the *Mottenpost*."[95] And yet all the browsing and glancing through the
pages left a distinct imprint.

On 13 November 1919, the *Morgenpost* produced a city-
wide event that was meant to revive a sense of metropolitan responsibility which had supposedly disappeared since the war.
According to Berlin police officials, citizens had grown disin-
clined to report criminal activity or to help authorities identify suspects at large. As a step toward retraining people to be
reliable witnesses and aid the police, the *Morgenpost* offered
2,000 Marks to the sharp-eyed individual who called out
"Augen auf!" (Eyes Open!) upon spotting its street-roaming
reporter Egon Jameson, whose face peered from hundreds of
Litfasssäulen (advertising pillars).[96]

For twelve hours the "wanted man" walked up and down
Berlin's streets unrecognized, collecting evidence to prove
where he had been:

> 10:00—Potsdamer Bridge. Proof: a copy of a burglary report
> prepared on a form provided by the Ullstein office there.
>
> 10:15—Potsdamer Platz. Proof: Telegram sent from the post
> office at Potsdamer Gate.
>
> 10:30—In Wertheim's department store on Leipziger Platz.
> Proof: Photo at an automatic photo machine.
>
> 10:45—Mauerstrasse. Proof: Pneumatic letter from the Post
> Office W. 66.

Although Jameson remained unidentified, he recalled feeling
the questioning glances of passersby. To avoid detection he
was forced to move on quickly: he jumped off streetcars, fled

into department stores, turned corners.[97] Hundreds of Berliners apparently joined to play the game, each one eager to find Jameson and to collect the reward.

Because the contest generated enormous interest, the *Morgenpost* decided to repeat "Augen auf!" a week later, this time providing readers with a rough plan of where and when Jameson might be seen. The odds were thus improved, and within three hours Jameson was caught by thirteen-year-old Willi Czerwinski on Berlin's Grimmstrasse.

Once again, Jameson reported having been watched carefully by scores of Berliners, though for three hours not one had been able to identify him. He concluded that the great majority of metropolitans lacked a keen sense of observation. In his opinion, the city favored anonymity because city people remained indifferent, a point Simmel had made already in 1903.[98] Yet Jameson also provided plenty of evidence to suggest that Berliners were indeed taking notice. The watchfulness he detected was encompassing, although not necessarily reliable. All morning long Jameson overheard excited discussions about the game—"No way that guy is a newspaperman," maintained one gruff commuter. Again and again, Jameson averted his eyes when someone appeared on the verge of recognizing him, and once found himself jokingly accosted by a stranger—"maybe it's you?"[99] Thanks to the press, the "Eye of the Metropolis" functioned rather well. Indeed, Jameson, like many suspects whom the press had portrayed in its pages, was eventually caught. Even if we consider that hundreds of Berliners saw and did not actually identify Jameson and hundreds more cried "Augen auf!" but caught the wrong man (as the *Morgenpost* reported), the stunt exposed a city of strangers whose gossip and glances and asides had largely been choreographed by the *Morgenpost*.[100]

It is interesting that the 1919 contest was a case of life imitating art—a reprise of Max Mack's 1913 feature-length film comedy, *Wo ist Coletti?* in which a popular police detective, Jean Coletti, criticized by *BZ am Mittag* for not using the press to help catch criminals, wages 100,000 marks that he can lose himself in Berlin for forty-eight hours without being caught. Coletti, master reader of hidden signs, sees little value in circulating pictures of wanted criminals in tabloids whose readership he considers too careless. To even up the odds, Coletti distributes wanted posters with his photograph overwritten with the reward sum, as did Jameson six years later. In the end, after numerous adventures, Coletti wins his forty-eight-hour wager.[101]

Although our hero remains at large, it is not because the film contends that city people are not observant. A look-alike barber whom the detective recruits as his stand-in is hounded in a wild chase involving a double-decker omnibus and a zeppelin. That the fake Coletti is not the "real" Coletti makes the relationship between the simulated and the real more precarious, but does not diminish the vigilance and single-mindedness of Mack's Berliners, who are seen devouring daily newspapers and avidly participating in the contest. True, the detective Coletti won the bet and therefore trumped the press, but director Mack paid careful attention to the presence of newspapers in the city: *BZ am Mittag* and the Ullsteinhaus were featured institutions in the film. Mack even got Ullstein to permit the filming of the pressrun of *BZ*, and it created quite a sensation when the fake bundled newspapers with the headline "100,000 Marks Reward" were delivered and distributed on the streets. As Mack filmed on location, the scripted action on film was repeatedly enlivened by the excitement of street crowds who joined the fifty paid extras in the frenzy of a chase they did not understand was merely staged.[102]

Wo ist Coletti? constantly blurred the boundaries between the story, and the story within the story. Coletti himself introduced a stand-in, and in the most famous scenes of the film he slips into a movie theater where he watches a newsreel depicting the chase in which the double eventually enters a movie theater, a remarkable sequence in which Coletti's shadow finally catches up with him. At the same time, the production of the film relied on the participation of passersby who did not always know that the excitement they felt around them was not real. Moreover, the film depended on a world mediated by newspapers, whose depictions of wanted criminals not only provided Coletti with the rationale for the wager but gave Max Mack the idea for the film. Even posters for the movie showed passersby reading boulevard papers, looking up, and scanning the streets.[103] Again and again, Mack indicated how the city was read before it was seen or encountered. Both in the use and depiction of the press, Mack's film and Jameson's subsequent stunt alike regarded the newspaper as a vital metropolitan script. Indeed, there is no better illustration of the narrativization of the metropolis than the *Morgenpost*'s choreography on a city-wide scale of the comical plot of a minor film. *Wo ist Coletti?* and "Augen auf!" revealed Berlin to be a city of readers and spectators who made sense of their urban surroundings by consuming images manufactured by the press. It is this city of readers, in which literary genres composed so much of urban experience, that the chapters that follow propose to explore.

3
PHYSIOGNOMY
OF THE CITY

The well-appointed salon faced north and therefore received little sunlight, so the widow mostly sat in a modest, sunny sitting room overlooking a side street. Ninety years old, she rarely left her apartment, yet was astonishingly alert and curious. For hours at a time she sat at the window and watched and assembled pictures of city life. Directly beneath her perch an empty lot served as a peephole that opened up unexpected perspectives. The widow focused first on the *Hinterhof* (back courtyard), where neighborhood children played or danced whenever the organ grinder came around. Some seemed easily frightened, most were pale and anemic, not like the pink-cheeked maids from the *Vorderhaus* (front building) who came out in the morning to beat the carpets of well-to-do employers. Birds nested in the trees bordering the courtyard: sparrows scolded constantly and every evening in summer a

blackbird came and sang. Like a calendar, the arbor registered the change of seasons, the alternation of rich and poor
months. Several back windows opened along the sides of the
courtyard, and the widow observed the busy activity in
kitchens and bedrooms. Housemaids got up terribly early:
they heated the kitchen stove, prepared breakfast, and aired
the bedding, which allowed nosy neighbors to inspect the
quality of the interior appointments. Sadly, some of the
building's windows remained bare all year long, except for an
occasional flower pot still wrapped in colorful birthday paper.
Higher up, though, the windows of the poorer tenants were
usually decorated with fuchsia and geraniums. And through
one of them the widow occasionally cast a compassionate
glance at an elderly woman trying to disguise her age beneath
layers of heavy makeup.

A variegated landscape typical of city outskirts lay beyond
the courtyard: on one side of a wooden fence, meadows, a nur-
sery, and a soap factory, and on the other the street, along
which ladies and gentlemen made their way and working-class
women hurried to market. Streetcars and omnibuses—the
widow counted thirty-seven cars in a single quarter-hour—
enlivened the metropolitan scene. At the end of the street, visible across the empty lot, three stores and a bus stop made for
a busy corner at which housewives shopped in the morning
and young people lingered in the evening to gossip or peruse
notices about upcoming theater openings and lost dachshunds
posted on an advertising pillar. Day after day, in this short
story published in 1905 in the *Berliner Tageblatt*, the widow
sat at her back window, watching the small business of city
people on the outskirts of the metropolis.[1]

This charmingly innocuous portrait of an old lady provides
a series of valuable hints about the way contemporaries looked
at and reconstructed modern cities. At first glance, "Der Fen-

sterplatz" adheres to a long tradition of reading meaning into surface phenomena. With their vast inventory of wares and customs and people, cities fascinated viewers who, in turn, tried to take stock by classifying sights and occasions and creating a usable lexicon of familiar and identifiable types. Louis-Sébastien Mercier's *Tableau de Paris* and London's "coney-catching books" indicate how established the practice of representing the urban physiognomy was already in the eighteenth century.[2] Mercantile hubs were portrayed as rich but completely legible habitats, as accessible to the practiced observer as flora was to the botanist or fauna to the zoologist. To be sure, metropolitan literacy did not always come easily; we know the widow collected her telltale traces carefully in various seasonal and daytime settings. Nonetheless, patterns eventually became clear. The widow rendered an intelligible and meaningful configuration. A study of faces and clothing disclosed the social structure of the apartment house, with its contrasts of rich and poor. The detail of window dressing revealed the melancholy loneliness of city dwellers, though flower boxes also told of everyday joys. Streetcorner traffic had its own order according to the time of day. Though deprived of the flâneur's mobility, the widow at the window fashioned a table of contrasts by which to make sense of the city.

The widow's perch recalls Edgar Allan Poe's bow-window in his tale "The Man of the Crowd." Sitting in a London coffeehouse, the narrator put aside his newspaper and peered through "the smokey panes into the street," turning his attention from one to the other as if reading the city were as easy as reading the paper. He observed "continuous tides . . . rushing past the door." At first only "abstract and generalized," the "sea of human heads" gradually took on detail and character. Poe eventually made out "innumerable varieties of figure, dress, air, gait, visage, and expression of countenance," which led him to identify "two remarkable divisions" in the "tribe of clerks," a "race of swell pick-pockets," as well as "darker and deeper themes" among peddlers, beggars, and diverse "women of the town." Although "night deepened" and the rays of the gas lamps "threw over every thing a fitful and garish lustre," the faces in the crowd revealed ever more distinctive features. "With my brow to the glass," "I could frequently read, even in that brief interval of a glance, the history of long years" for a single individual.[3]

The ability to read the city provided keys to moving about the city and thus corresponded to the ability to master the city. Although Poe himself challenged the value of evaluation at first sight, since the last "man in the crowd" in fact stayed elusive, urban tableaux and physiognomical sketches remained popular and largely unquestioned renditions. Indeed, the literary gestures of the physiognomist anticipated the more heavy-handed actions of nineteenth-century reformers, who attempted to survey and renovate entire urban settlements. Never before, realized Maxime du Camp about Paris in the 1870s and 1880s, had the city been "so minutely described, monitored, surveyed, classified, [and] generally 'cleaned up' taxonomically as well as practically." In Paris and elsewhere police officials, public-health experts, city inspectors, and other municipal authorities carefully traversed and reported on metropolitan surroundings, an exhaustive accounting which was the necessary foundation for the ameliorative reforms they proposed. Even the detailed descriptions, numerous characters, and intricately devised plots composed by nineteenth-century novelists represented labored attempts to faithfully map the great city.[4] But the most prevalent form of reading and cataloguing the metropolis took place under the aegis of the big-city newspaper, which took thousands and then millions of readers along on roving expeditions on street-

car lines, into quaint neighborhoods, or through the nighttime
city, and on visits to municipal institutions of all kinds, and introduced them to a variety of social facts. Indeed, reporters
were often the best-placed group and metropolitan newspapers the most accessible medium to represent the nineteenth-
century city.[5]

There was something presumptuous about these practices
of legibility. The widow in "Der Fensterplatz," Poe's man at
the bow-window, or the reporter on the street observed the
city with the detached, authoritative eye of the naturalist—
Walter Benjamin once referred to the flâneur "botanizing on
the asphalt."[6] Allegories drawn from the garden informed the
widow's vision of society. A reference to the alternation of rich
and poor months in the arbor, for example, served to explain
the contrast between rich and poor in the courtyard. With its
attention to geraniums and fuchsia amidst poverty, the picture
was all relaxing pastels, although details such as bare windows
or the old woman's makeup added more somber tones. Every
element had a place in Poe's description of the evening crowd
as well. The sea of faces outside the coffeehouse was divided
into tribes, races, themes. This structural model of society,
drawn from illustrious nineteenth-century sciences such as
anthropology, botany, and zoology, distinguished differences,
prepared typologies, assigned functions to the various parts,
and thereby supposed the discovery of underlying laws of cohesion.

To read the city as an ecological formation tended to break
up widely held images of the industrial metropolis as an undifferentiated vastness of stone and its people as a poverty-
stricken mass. Even Expressionist poets after the turn of the
century honed predominantly nocturnal and oceanic metaphors which stressed the uniform and aimless nature of
Berlin.[7] But if typological views painted the city in brighter,

more variegated colors, they presumed an overarching coherence and functionality that rendered social life explicable, but static.[8] The panoramas and dioramas that were so popular throughout the nineteenth century attempted to recapture the entire city as a working mechanism. The observer controlled the potentially chaotic aspects of urban crowds by locating their disorienting inventory in an encompassing machinery. Even the most improbable city types were depicted as basically harmless, variations on a theme of "perfect bonhomie."[9] Although the search for functional relations left the city looking more hygienically acceptable, it did so by obscuring questions of political domination and economic exploitation. The physiognomist's eye could be a rather cold eye, which at once naturalized and miniaturized the urban setting by eliding over its disorderly, treacherous, or blatantly political aspects.[10]

No physiognomy was without its pretension to the transparency, accuracy, and universality that draped scientific typologies. But readings of the rapidly changing industrial metropolis at the end of the nineteenth century tended to admit more disorder and flux than earlier tableaux of the mercantile city. The improbable onlooker in "Der Fensterplatz," for example, underscored the force with which less authoritative ways of seeing accompanied the turbulence of the modern city allowed. If early nineteenth-century recountings of the city had often been legitimated by the authority of age—Dickens, for example, invoked on elderly witnesses who had "observed human nature a long time" to justify his viewpoints in *Sketches by Boz*—longevity had no such advantage in Berlin 1905.[11] The widow is presented as a notable exception rather than a well-regarded authority. With its unexpected social combinations and rich mélange of styles, the modern metropolis had come to demand more alertness, more inference, more tolerance for the unexpected.[12] In this case, the fantastic growth of Berlin, a process still incomplete (as the story's reference to a wooden fence, which invariably encloses a new construction site, indicated), had overtaken the suburban repose of a ninety-year old widow and retrained even her sense of detection.

"Der Fensterplatz" thus serves as an elegant illustration of Georg Simmel's premise that urbanization intellectualized metropolitans. The sedentary must take account of the contingency and rapid alternation of metropolitan encounters. City matters were no longer established or fixed and they could not be held together in the frame of a lifetime's experience. Even in its sentimental form, "Der Fensterplatz" acknowledged a revised orientation toward the city in which the panoramic visibility that seemed possible along the main avenues had given way to the wayward details and ceaseless disruptions of interior courtyards. In other words, this *Fensterplatz* shows the city's inventory to an unusual degree because the window opens behind the scenes and takes in small scraps of life. The widow has taken the first steps in the modern journey that approaches the metropolis haphazardly, accidentally.

Likewise, feuilletonistic tours of turn-of-the-century Berlin described a city in which constant motion surprises, interrupts, and ultimately overrules the physiognomist's reliable classifications. Of course, journalists still prepared detailed typologies and tables of contrasts. Almost everything encountered could be typed: newspaper vendors, park benches, and Sunday afternoons. But the categories were often prepared so provisionally and given such circumstantial properties that they hardly provided a key applicable to other than immediate circumstances. Far from leading viewers to see general characteristics, a necessary operation if the city was to become familiar and safe, urban tours became more and more one-of-a-kind, taking note of precise details, singular occasions, and chance encounters. They did not construct an authoritative map to the city; they fashioned its impressionistic surface. In the early twentieth-century texts under review here the typologies did not nail down city matters but merely alerted readers to detail and fluctuation. As a result, the city became equally unknowable and equally astonishing to all its readers, whom newspapers addressed as travelers in a fantastic garden of possibility. This metropolitan place did not recognize privileged dwellers like the leisurely flâneur whom Walter Benjamin describes in the Paris of the Second Empire. On the contrary, the fugitive city invited even occasional readers to individually assemble and reassemble the urban debris and to fashion their own city versions.

Differences of "figure, dress, air, gait, visage, and expression," recounted and rearranged in newspaper sketches, revealed countless varieties of coffeehouses, marketplace shoppers, and streetcar commuters. This attention to, and even celebration of, diversity and difference tended to undermine a coherent vision of the city. On-site reports, behind-the-scene investigations, and portraits of specific places and passing events put the accent on the singular and did so at the expense of more generic patterns. What physiognomies lost in universality they thus gained in detail: *Skizzen, Momentbilder*, and other snapshots of city places and city people over the course of a single day collected little more than moments and incidents.

Described in terms of finely observed layers of difference, the industrial city resembled a complex, shifting mosaic that could not be easily or immediately explicated. Since the functional categories that urban naturalists deployed existed only in a larger system of differences, the practiced observer shuttled constantly between lumping things together and separating them; between explaining patterns and inquiring about contrasts. One operation persistently challenged the other and newly observed differences disassembled previously constructed templates. Thus the practice of urban physiognomy that threatened to typecast city people also trained observers to examine and reexamine metropolitan marginalia and to question any form-fitting cohesion that might be imposed on the city.

The fugitive appearance of the city was heightened by the highly selective angles of perception that metropolitan observers favored. The widow's vantage point, a back window overlooking inner courtyards and side streets, suggested that the city was no longer an unproblematical object set securely in clear lines of vision. It had to be approached with less certainty, from around the back. The view from behind also corresponded to a widely held notion that the girdle of industrial neighborhoods and suburban outskirts revealed the essential nature of new cities. Expeditions undertaken by Berlin's tabloids regularly left behind the baroque center of the Prussian capital. The traveler went down bustling avenues beyond the *Stadtbahn* ring and prowled newly built precincts of the *Vorstadt* (city periphery) in order to take stock of things becoming metropolitan. It was in these turbulent zones of transition that the most exciting and colorful reportage was to be found.[13] In the city as represented by Berlin's popular newspapers, Unter den Linden, the classical boulevard of embassies, palaces, and ministries that led from the Stadtschloss to the Tiergarten, gave right-of-way to Friedrichstrasse, the busy commercial thoroughfare that connected the proletarian neighborhoods, factory yards, and railway stations beyond the city gates at either end.

The picture of Berlin that emerged produced an entirely new map of public places, social battlegrounds, and individual fortunes. Thus commercial Friedrichstrasse came into view

while the officious Unter den Linden faded from view. Simi-
larly, the witnesses local newspapers called upon to tell about
the city now included loud working-class voices. Around the
turn of the century, the press for the first time broadcast the
opinions, conjectures, and aspirations of the "man on the
street," the peddler, the fresh-faced migrant, the drinker, the
clerk, the sportsman.[14] In unadulterated "first-hand" language, his (less frequently, her) testimony indicated that
urban space had become as contested as it was congested.
These representations do not repeat the "same difference"
that Richard Sieburth identifies in French physiologies of the
1840s, in which a "panorama of human diversity" rested on
the "systematic exclusion of the nonbourgeois."[15] Excessive
detail also rendered the city into the object of fantasy. Details
about particular incidents and particular lives created any
number of textured "humanitarian narratives" which allowed
the reader's imagination to penetrate the life of others. As a
result, the narrativized city appeared inclusive and self-revelatory to a broad range of readers, rich and poor, men and
also women.[16] The absence of unity and harmony in the face
of so much disparate, countervailing detail also tended to give
the city a tentative face. City stories rendered the city inconclusive, in flux.

COLLECTING DEBRIS

The colorful catalogues prepared by the physiognomist tended
to reduce the diversity they portrayed by representing it in a
system of signs that classified and organized urban inventory.
In this way, cities could be translated into an abstract second-
hand system of classification. But typologies only maintained
their authority as long as the categories they imposed were
widely adopted and corresponded to a recognizable set of particulars. As long as surveyors, census-takers, medical re-

formers, and other urban encyclopedists recognized the same occupational, social, and ethnic divisions, they continued to fix city matters in a way that appeared complete and legible.

This process of representation was modified in the big-city newspaper. Turn-of-the-century feuilletonists categorized to such a degree that each category signified little more than the particular it purported to describe. Moreover, each new installment of the newspaper came out with additional city views and city excursions and thus undermined the authority of earlier editions. Newspapers reworked the city on a daily basis, and thereby emphasized the novel and transitory nature of its contents. In this respect, the unsystematic nature of reportage portrayed the late nineteenth-century city far more precariously than had classical physiognomies.

Also city chroniclers argued that the modern metropolis could best be conveyed by means of the feuilleton's versatile and immediate description. That is to say, urban places resisted directories, maps, indexes, catalogues, surveys, and other authoritative references. Although the industrial city had been fabricated and designed piece by piece, it had quickly taken on fantastic proportions. Its corners were dark enough to attract explorers; its streets obscure enough to require the illumination of documentary exposés. Local guides offered to lead newcomers through a virtual labyrinth of city ways.[17] As the imagery suggests, the urban setting was regarded as largely unknown territory. This was not because technical handicaps or inadequate knowledge or even social disdain had left parts of the city unexplored, like the blank spaces on a European's nineteenth-century map of Africa, but rather because the industrial city was such a brand new conglomeration. Its mystery lay in its perpetual newness and in the fleeting and abrupt nature of its movements. According to Hans Ostwald, who in the years 1904–1908 oversaw the publication of fifty pamphlets documenting Berlin, Hamburg, and Vienna, metropolitan life was "most modern"; its fullness had become apparent only in the "last decades." The bewildering speed with which cities had developed precluded their representation in a single work of art. And, however comprehensive, academic studies were too dry and detached; they failed to respect the singular, to report at first hand, or to tell life-stories. By challenging the ability of Realist modes to represent the fantastic big-city compound of passing sensations, Ostwald posed the central question of literary modernism.

A plausible account of metropolitan diversity, Ostwald argued, required new literary forms which forsook complete inventory for "short, crisp" reportage. Quickly assembled documentation—and the newspaper feuilletons on which it was based (and where the evidence was often first presented)—was exactly suited to report on the fluctuating contents of the city.[18] The great advantage of the feuilleton was its ability to capture the fluctuations of the modern city in its precise and highly stylized fragments. One student of the subject compared the genre to entries in a diary, a telling image since diaries do not purport to address a set of specific questions or to survey a life with the priorities of a biographer but simply put down in an unsystematic way immediate and often digressive impressions.[19] It was imperative to approach the city without definite purpose. The feuilletonist should simply, as media scholar Wilmont Haacke later summarized, "go out on the street, encounter life, capture it on the spot, and interrogate it for the newspaper."[20]

The newspaper's interrogations of Berlin revealed a protean city that was always surprising and never the same. Feuilletonists attempted to reproduce how it felt to meander through the city without purpose or direction, slipping into a stream of sensations. Along the way, they collected the debris of the city—

occasionals, incidentals, chance encounters, outstanding characters—and wrote these up in an unsystematic way as *Momentbilder* or *Skizzen*. The feuilleton was the flâneur's protocol.

The most typical journey was simply to pass the day in a
single place—the Tiergarten was a favorite location—and observe the panoply of contrasts unfold. "At the crack of dawn,"
the park belonged to an elegant public of riders: "gentlemen,
cavalry officers, and ladies with their blond hair topped by a
sporty hat." A while later, early-morning walkers appeared.
They were followed by businessmen getting a breath of fresh
air on their way to work. Batches of schoolchildren and finally
an "army of nannies" and their charges filled the park with
late-morning games and shouts. A noontime quiet returned
when old men sat on favorite benches and talked about the lost
city of their youth. Teenagers met their dates in the afternoon,
relieved at dusk by pairs of lovers who wandered in the twilight. The Tiergarten was clearly the preserve of the prosperous middle classes, but it followed a schedule of activities
that revealed its various aspects. A generation later, Walter
Ruttmann (in his film *Berlin: Symphony of the Big City*) and
Walter Benjamin (in "A Berlin Chronicle") would produce
nearly identical physiognomies.[21]

The *Morgenpost* even provided a map to the sociology of the
Tiergarten. Between Wilhelm II's monstrous broadway of Hohenzollern statuary, nicknamed *Puppenallee* (dolls' alley) by
impertinent Berliners, and the popular beer tents behind
Krolloper, milled a mixed public composed of the "demi-
monde" and drifters. More "mondaine" company could be
found around the goldfish ponds all the way to Rousseau Insel,
which, in turn, was the domain of nursemaids and nannies.
Completely different types strolled along the shore of the
Neuer See: "solitary people who commune with nature,
painters making their studies . . . lovers." North of Charlot-

At the skating rink. Sketches and feuilletons in the
Morgenpost make up these "city characters."

tenburger Chaussee, "matrons with their kniting, aunts with their nieces, mothers with their neighbors" indicated a "solid bourgeois element."[22] Excursions into the Grunewald, to a suburban ice-skating ring, a homeless shelter, the Prussian courthouse at Moabit, or simply a neighborhood savings bank fashioned similar typologies to character, timetables to routines, and maps to social niches, references that allowed readers not only to oversee the diverse makeup of the city but to verify the social meaning of metropolitan detail—"matrons with their knitting," for example, indicated *gutbürgerlich.*

The social contrasts that the maps and schedules to the Tiergarten attempted to bring to light could be encountered more dramatically by rambling through the entire city searching for variations on a theme. Eberhard Buchner, for example, made a study of popular theater, describing "Volksvarieté," "Familienvarieté," "Vorstadtvarieté," "Räuberhöhle," and "internationale Varieté." For his part, Hans Ostwald journeyed to a half-dozen different *Tanzlokalen* tucked into interior courtyards, clustered around the garish "golden corner" at Oranienburger Tor, or scattered "ganz weit draussen" along the city's outer precincts.[23]

These rather conventional tours brought to light an extensive cast of original characters. Yet they also imposed upon this motley collection reliable schedules and accurate maps. The search for variation and color provided the impetus for more digressive journeys that revealed again and again unpredictable aspects to the city. In order to reproduce more nearly the leisurely, unmindful movement of the flâneur, whose great talent, as Franz Hessel recognized, was the ability to get lost, physiognomical operations became increasingly banal. "Momentbilder" in the *Berliner Morgenpost,* the *Lokal-Anzeiger,* or the *Berliner Tageblatt* took up the most ordinary themes— Sunday afternoons, typists at their desks, or commuters on the streetcar—to introduce "everyday" people, that is, particular individuals rather than social types as had been the case on excursions to the Tiergarten. The whole point was to find a theme that would portray, as a sketch of Berlin's coachmen promised, an "exceptionally interesting human picture," or gather, as in "Types in the Typing Bureau," "a colorful collection of more or less original types . . . some burdened with manuscripts, others only with the insubstantial weight of passing fancies."[24] The more haphazard the tour, the more engaging the human-interest story.

That Paul Schüler of the *Berliner Tageblatt* did nothing more than take readers along "on the electrical" indicates how digressive the genre had become. Many of Schüler's streetcar encounters were simply diverting, describing, for example, the embarrassing "battle" between the top hat of "Herr Referendar" and the broad-rimmed hat of "Frau Landgerichtsdirektor," but some were more melodramatic, as an account of a flustered young lady who couldn't find her ticket suggests:

> Twenty stubs—each put to the acid test. The twenty-first was the one. Thank god, she thought to herself. Thank god, whispered the whole car. But the conductor took in all in stride. Apparently it was not the first time.
>
> "One of these days, you should clean out your purse and throw away the tickets you no longer need," he suggested.
>
> "But I need them," replied the young lady. "They are my receipts. Otherwise, my boss won't reimburse me for expenses."

Among the quirky habits and amusing dissonances of everyday life, the feuilletonist revealed snippets of overheard conversations, small scraps of autobiography, and grainy traces of minidramas that compelled the reader's imagination.[25] A ride on streetcar line Number 74 assembled a collection of a different sort. From affluent Schöneberg, over Potsdamer and Alexanderplatz, to proletarian Friedrichshain, the journey exposed the variagated physiognomy of the city: sleek automobiles, dusty trucks, quiet gardens, busy intersections, pounding factories.[26] A sketch of Tempelhofer Feld, the expansive parade ground where Berlin families spent fair-weather weekends, presented readers with minor one-act dramas interspersed with songs and political commentary in local dialect: "Willem hätte ja och mitjemusst. Und der Kleene veleicht och! Wejen Marokk'n!" (Willy would've been called up. The little one probably too. 'Cause of Morocco!).[27] Again and again, excursions to music halls ("Im Theater der kleinen Leute"), cafés, and hotels, encounters with streetside vendors, or simply a walk across the street ("Unsere Strassen"), reported on the rough voices and particular manners of Berliners.[28] Erasing the generic altogether, reducing Berlin to particulars, the urban physiognomist held up a mirror that reflected the city in fragments.

On excursions in and around Berlin reporters collected the debris of the city and displayed it as rough-hewn collage. Indeed, the organizing principle of dozens of newspaper stories was to recreate as nearly as possible chance encounters along busy commercial streets. One series in the *Morgenpost* in 1905 paid visits to various "number ones" in the city. What did readers find in this grab-bag? "Der lange Hermann," courier "Number 1" for the Berliner Express-Kompagnie since 1875; and Nicolaus Berg who drove Taxicab Number 1 in Behrenstrasse; and Car Number 1, a rather undistinguished streetcar in operation since 1897; and, finally, Ernst Gottfried Stauch, Policeman Number 1.[29] Even before Döblin, very *berlinisch* feuilletonists had begun working their way through the var-

ious and sundry that added up to the city and allowed readers
to browse among charity-kitchen menus—

> Bouillon
> Rice and apple
> Lung hash with potatoes
> Peas with sauerkraut
> Coffee and doughnuts

—extravagant advertisements ("Flea Circus, the most distinguished act in the Royal Capital"), parade-ground songs
("Gestern noch auf stolzen Rossen, Heute durch die Brust ges-
chossen")

—working people's budgets:

Rent	6.00 M
Baked goods	4.20
Lard and butter	2.40
Milk	1.10
Wurst for the man	1.50
Potatoes	0.50
Vegetables	1.00
Shoes	3.00
Gas	1.20
Insurance	1.80
Streetcar	1.80

—and even chalk traces of children's games ("Erich . . .
Kaiser; Hans . . . King; Emil . . . Nobleman").[30] Practiced in
this haphazard, unmindful way, physiognomy provided a
method to store the bits and pieces of the metropolis.[31]

The feuilletonist's "Skizzenbuch" recreated the city as a
junkman's collection of types, manners, and artifacts. Just a
short list of the themes pursued by the *Berliner Tageblatt* in

the years 1904 to 1911 indicates the minor key and sideways glance local reporters preferred:

"Berlin Rendezvous"

"Salons of Silence"

"What's Doing in the Garden Colonies"

"Taxi!"

"On the Litfasssäule"

"Children's Paradise"

"Autumn in the Botanical Garden"

"The Theater of the Working People"

"Our Streets"

"Old Berlin Idyl"

"Berlin Arcades"

"Homeless Shelter"

"At the Construction Site"

"Carnival"

"Conversations on the Stadtbahn"

"At the Pawnbroker"

"The Horn"

"Berlin Underground"

"Automatic Amusements"

"'Five o'clock'" in the Department Store

"Characters at the Ice Ring"

"White Sale"

"The Waiting Room of the West"

"Berlin at Night"

"Berlin Junkmen"

"On Strike!"

"On the Streetcar"

The textual shift from the generic to the particular, the center to the periphery, and the panorama to the snapshot found a congenial form in the short feuilleton sketches of metropolitan newspapers. The descriptive attention to detail—chalk marks on the sidewalk or gossip overheard at Tempelhof—was typical. Feuilletons trained readers to see and hear the jarring diversity of the city by striving for precision: by using just the right gradation of adjectival modification, borrowing from a technical vocabulary to sharpen the portrait, favoring singular and proper nouns, introducing particular streetcorners, giving names and addresses, and quoting paragraphs of Berlin dialect.

The city threatened to dissolve into a pointilist splendor as the feuilleton sought complete precision. A Sunday in the park

was captured in the most concrete terms possible:[32] "Father
. . . Dress coat, turned up trousers, open vest, paper napkin
bulging over the hunter's shirt . . . collar and green cravat un-
buttoned in the left hand, in the right hand the *Fresskorber*
[picnic basket] adorned with a pearl-stitched puppy and the
merry saying 'Happy Trails." The direct quotation from the
basket provided the last discrete detail. To be sure, writers
did not purge social types and collective nouns from their descriptions, and references to the sassy lady from Berlin W. or
the ruddy boy from Berlin O. remained commonplace, but the
retrieval of so many artifacts, quotations, and conversations
and the effort to create atmosphere by means of well-chosen
adjectives, specific nouns, and impressionistic verbs had the
effect of placing the reader directly on the scene.

The feuilleton reveled in the moment, and to enhance the
fleeting existence of time and place it deployed items from a
full stock of abbreviations, slang words, breezy asides, nouns
lifted out of an advertisers catalogue, and references to
today's fashions and yesterday's news ("Wejen Marokk'n!").
To set a scene in theatrical terms, as did the *Berliner Tageblatt* in a four-station tour of "sin city," exaggerated the
swirling motion that the feuilleton tried to reproduce:[33]

> Eleven thirty! In the Admiralspalast: it's Sunday on Friedrich-
> strasse. People from N., S., O., NW. and SW. and NO. live the life
> of the city . . . For the six-year-old it's chocolate from a vending
> machine, for the father it's a cigar with a fancy band, for the
> grown-up daughter the beginnings of a flirtation with that very el-
> egant gentleman who has already passed by three times. . . .

Ellipses, incomplete sentences, unanswered questions, inter-
rogatives, imperatives, and other short-order exclamations
augmented the report's inconclusive, purely impressionistic
effect.[34] In comparison to more prosaic newspaper articles,

feuilleton prose tends toward shorter and shorter fragments that pile up at a faster and faster pace. *BZ am Mittag* recounted a night at the six-day bicycle race in an almost telegraphic style: "Conceded: It's crazy, it's a waste, it's American—say what you will." In the next paragraph, the words seem to have gotten away altogether as they tumbled down the side of the page: "Thousands chased alongside, hunched over, eyes running, hands pressing, as if they could help, could push, could shove."[35]

This sort of writing, which turned into finely fashioned essays with unexpected twists and turns, became a highly regarded form of expression, replacing a more authoritative academic style. The welter and exactness of detail composed a playful rhetorical politics that put into doubt the validity of collective nouns and monumental generalizations.[36] By inviting richer observation, specificity did not so much invalidate typology as proliferate its practice; each type threatened to dissolve into a new mosaic since each sketch was no more than a picture of a single moment in the flow of impressions. With its focus on the singular, its point of vantage on the margins, and its projection of collected images in the daily, snappy little feuilleton pieces, a distinctive metropolitan eye caught the variation and inconstancy of the modern city most vividly.

POINTS OF EXCHANGE

The city represented as a point of commotion and exchange mimicked the restless motions of consumer capitalism. Commerce was at once an economic foundation and a sensory experience. Again and again, newspapers described the city as a place where chance encounters took place, new fashions and things arrived, and no thing could be relied on to remain in place for very long. In both the themes they developed and the style they honed, feuilletonists emphasized fashion, discontinuity, and diversity. Although the metropolitan press occasionally explored in an explicit way precincts invariably described as dark, unknown, or impoverished, and wrote up informative exposés on the ghetto, the tumbledown tenement, or the homeworker, for the most part the city as a whole was reviewed as a place of perpetual change.[37] Even sobering subjects such as asylums or food kitchens were approached by way of unlikely characters. The focus of interest was not on the harsh social pictures of industrial settlement but on the busy exchanges of the commercial metropolis, and reportage accordingly led readers to see the city's ephemeral aspects more vividly than its "other sides." The word city rewrote the ontology of the metropolis and generally ignored its sociology. To tell the story they wished to tell, Berlin's newspapers returned again and again to Friedrichstrasse and Potsdamer Platz, on which so much city traffic moved and intersected; to the nighttime metropolis in which types mixed and identities blurred; and to the *Vorstadt*, the margins of the city where rapid urban development was most apparent.

The best way to develop an eye for seeing variety was to enter a zone of transition in which the differences of social class and official bearing would be most visible. Specific locations such as the heavily transited Friedrichstrasse and Potsdamer Platz, or certain hours in the day, usually early evening or early morning, allowed observers to witness the interaction of various city types. To be sure, these vantage points were not chosen at random; they were selected to present a picture of the city in bright, jarring colors and rapidly passing moments. Berlin's chroniclers repeatedly strolled down Friedrichstrasse, lingered in the Kaiser-Passage, the showy arcade at the corner of Behrenstrasse, turned right at the busy intersection with Leipziger Strasse, and continued south, down to the traffic circle at Potsdamer Platz. This crooked corridor through the central city purportedly offered the most diverse alternation of characters and atmosphere. Walking just a few hundred steps along Friedrichstrasse provoked an explosion of the senses:

> Cacophonous blowing of horns in the traffic, melodies of organ grinders, cries of newspaper vendors, bells of Bolle's milkmen, voices of fruit and vegetable sellers, hoarse pleas of beggars, whispers of easy women, the low roar of streetcars and their screech against the old iron tracks, and millions of steps dragging, tripping, pounding. At the same time, a kaleidoscope of color . . . neon lights, bright electric lights of offices and factories . . . lanterns hanging from horse-drawn carts and automobiles, arclighting, light bulbs, carbide lamps.[38]

Berlin's busiest streets seemed to bring new and ferocious forms to life, and for this reason they attracted Germany's most famous Expressionist painters, Ernst Ludwig Kirchner, Ludwig Meidner, and later George Grosz and Otto Dix.[39]

Potsdamer Platz—"every second a new picture," marveled *BZ am Mittag* in 1905—"the world of elegance and the world of work, workers, traders, teachers, a sampling of the Berlin's entire population."[40] Only there did "everything that makes up a metropolis flow together, elegance and work, tragedy and harmlessness, commerce and entertainment."[41] Over the course of the day, this "colorful mix" took on various tones and colors. On Leipziger Strasse, for example, the afternoon crowd rushed to the hurried rhythm of business. "They stream past the show windows, excitedly, nervously, quickly," while alongside the overflowing sidewalks streetcars "crawl at a snail's pace," omnibuses "slide heavily laden along the slippery pavement, carriages navigate across the streetcar tracks, automobiles strain to make any progress at all." These moving parts constituted a huge "commercial machine." But the whirl and hum of wheels did not quite drown out the cries on the street: "Good-day, Sir—fifteen cents a rose—two for a quarter."[42] These rich evocations of Potsdamer Platz, delighting in its variety and contrasts, were exemplary of local feuilletons in the decade before World War I.[43]

Never at a standstill, the machine was still in motion in the evening—"Potsdamer Platz is swarming"—but in a new gear. "Lamps light up," and closing time releases hundreds of salesgirls, "with cheery faces, young bodies, and tiny salaries," out on the streets. An agreeable night out beckons, perhaps a meal at Aschinger's or dancing on the Kreuzberg: "Emil's waiting up at 'Potsdamer' . . . 'Mieze's guy' is taking her along to Schultheiss." A few hours later, toward midnight, after the stores had all closed and street vendors packed up their wares, pedestrians were still "calmly, quietly" strolling down Friedrichstrasse.

Journeys into nighttown deepened the texture of the city and sharpened its contrasts. The wide panorama and sure contours of the day faded as the sun went down and the lanterns brightened. Writing in the 1880s, Max Kretzer noticed a "second Berlin" come into view.[44]

> Houses no longer looked the same; people seemed to have changed appearances. . . . The thousand-headed mass, still recognizable as it moved through the streets against the dim light of dusk, has grown out of proportion beneath the deceptive light of lanterns. The crowd lacks a clear form, and distinct colors and movements suddenly give way to dark spots and deep shadows.

Thirty years later, when electrical lighting had replaced gas lamps, and department stores, municipal offices, and insurance companies let their employees go according to exact bureaucratic schedules, the first Berlin gave way to the second more rapidly: "In the quarter-hour after eight, the doors of thousands of shops and businesses close and the doors of thousands of cafes and restaurants open . . . the strong, healthy, and hard-working Berlin by day transforms itself into the corrupt, nervous, burning Berlin by night."[45]

The contrast was sharp at daybreak too, a moment of transition which typically concluded the newspaper's excursion into a city famous for its long-lived nights. "This, too, is Berlin," was the refrain of a famous prewar guidebook, *Berlin für Kenner*. At midnight, roilsome crowds spilled out to the pavement of Friedrichstrasse, barely making way for caravans of brightly lit buses and speeding automobiles. Streetcars ran until three in the morning, on the weekends some lines never stopped, and around Nollendorfplatz there were bars that stayed opened until dawn.[46] Even then, not all nighttime revelers went home. "Go home? What for?" *BZ* explained the next noon: "The paradox fascinates: others go to work, but [here] they lap at life one more time!" As deliverymen and streetcar and subway workers set the day in motion, certain bars kept their doors open and, drawing their heavy curtains, shut out the grey light of dawn. "We pour strong schnapps and hot chocolate down our throats" until eight, nine in the morning. An hour later, you can see a "very tired gentleman in the subway. His eyes sunk back in his head, he surveys the workaday world with complete indifference."[47]

Nighttime was such an intriguing literary terrain because it relocated, juxtaposed, and heightened the contrasts of the industrial city. As Gottfried Korff remarks, night was the "site of pleasure and entertainment," also the "site where passions vibrate and new forms of work discipline (night work) are tried out." It was the "site of apathy and relaxation," and the "site of heightened nervousness and sensual vigilance."[48] Moreover, the bars, cafés, and dancehalls that were the primary destinations of nightstalkers enclosed and recombined

Berliners in promiscuous social arrangements. "Only in night-life," noted Hans Ostwald, "do the classes merge a little bit." At Tante Brüsch in Jägerstrasse, for example, young women of the middle classes mixed with a rougher crowd of men, mis-leading, Ostwald imagined, their parents about the nature of their affairs.[49] Again and again, newspaper articles set the scene at dusk: from their overcrowded apartments in Acker-strasse or Pappelallee, dozens of working-class girls set out at night to sell roses and matches, moving about from restaurant to restaurant along Friedrichstrasse, where they encountered raucous parties of men on the town and learned about the various trades of the nighttime street. Students from the Friedrich-Wilhem University, doctors from the Charité Hos-pital, and stockbrokers from the Börse all took part in the tawdry "Tingel-Tangel" around Oranienburger Tor at the north end of Friedrichstrasse.

Sharply defined boundaries blurred in busy intersections such as Potsdamer Platz or at transitional moments such as dusk, and they were transgressed by the prostitutes, dancers, and shopgirls who featured so prominently in metropolitan stories. Crossing conventional class and gender demarcations, these women stood as symbols for the disorderly spectacle of the city. Tales of transgression circulated and recirculated in the press, popular because they confirmed both the antiurban prejudices of cultural conservatives and the avant-garde sen-sibilities of cultural modernists. No account of "die Passage" (the Kaiser-Passage), for example, failed to remark on the flir-tatious looks and whispered asides traded between men and women.[50] By all accounts, Berlin had considerable numbers of prostitutes; of course, it also had many thousands more skilled workers and white-collar clerks and schoolchildren. The reason the figure of the prostitute or the location of the dance-hall or the hour of dusk fascinated was that each embellished

Friedrichstrasse as a place charged with possibility, pleasure, and deception. It was mostly male pleasures that journalists mapped out on Friedrichstrasse—Ostwald at one point listed the going price of prostitutes block-by-block—yet female readers found the escapism of the night streets enticing as well.[51] Friedrichstrasse was a corridor of chance encounters and fleeting glances that offered a boisterous but safe location for the erotic imagination.

Friedrichstrasse and Leipziger Strasse to Potsdamer Platz occupied a central place in the imagination of imperial Berlin. It was from these sites that mass-circulation newspapers reported on the modern city, while they ignored almost completely Berlin's *Prachtstrasse* Unter den Linden, the classical parade route of the Kaiserreich, or Wilhelmstrasse, on which most government buildings were located. (The important exception was Scherl's *Berliner Lokal-Anzeiger*, which reported fully on the official jubilees, dedications, and appointments that took place Unter den Linden.) Friedrichstrasse connected the industrial *Feuerland* north of Oranienburger Tor with the suburbs that proliferated beyond Hallesches Tor, and it served Berlin's most important railway stations: Stettiner Bahnhof, Bahnhof Friedrichstrasse, and nearby Potsdamer Bahnhof and Anhalter Bahnhof. In a city that was increasingly characterized as a dense network of work and energy, Friedrichstrasse constituted a vital link: "The electric rails amble between rows of houses . . . subways zoom beneath the streets . . . wires pull themselves along giant masts." As a major north-south circuit in the *"Geschäftsmaschine,"* Friedrichstrasse assembled diverse types day and night: workers, office-girls, salesmen, bankers, flâneurs, criminals, prostitutes, children selling roses.[52] It was a "Plattform eines neuen Wesens," as Lothar Brieger put it, a parade route for the new Berlin, the Berlin that was born somewhere else, in Silesia or

East Prussia or Brandenburg; the Berlin that went to work in the morning with a spare *Fahrgroschen* for the streetcar; the Berlin that hurried to Aschinger's after work (the chain operated three restaurants on Friedrichstrasse alone), gathered at Bötzow's huge beer garden in the evenings, and spent Sunday afternoons underneath the *Zelten* (tents) on the edge of the Tiergarten; the Berlin that was mostly working-class, or else belonged to the "tribe of clerks," and voted overwhelmingly Social Democratic.[53] Unter den Linden was a mere tangent of these busy movements.

To understand turn-of-the-century Friedrichstrasse, today a desolate thoroughfare that cannot conjure up its sensational past for sightseers, it is worth considering the notoriety of Alexanderplatz in the Weimar era, when the precincts of Berlin were better known to an international literary group of readers and writers like Vladimir Nabokov and Thomas Wolfe. The center of urban renewal projects since 1906, the year the Scheunenviertel slum began to be knocked down and room made for the Volksbühne (people's theater), the district around Alexanderplatz provided startling contrasts between old and new. Just a few streets away from the ceaseless subway and high-rise construction, Alfred Döblin found Grenadierstrasse, which was not much different from a Polish shtetl. Berlin's poorest neighborhood, laid out helter-skelter in the late seventeenth century with four- and five-story brick apartment buildings that lacked indoor plumbing and still housed thousands of tenants in a warren of basement and entresol rooms, lay beyond the central square, now newly dressed up in white iron-girded concrete. Encircled to the north and east by the massive vaults and masonry bridgework of the Stadtbahnring, Alexanderplatz was full of nooks and crannies and improbable little deadends left over from another century, which made it the perfect site for petty criminals and also for

the headquarters of Berlin's police.[54] Alexanderplatz, like
Friedrichstrasse before it, was another perfect emblem for the
modern city.

VORSTADT

Friedrichstrasse, Potsdamer Platz, Berlin by night—these
were appealing destinations not simply because they offered
such a rich admixture of sensations but also because they permitted an extensive study of Berlin's "little people." The busy
traffic of curbside vendors, traveling salesmen, and shopgirls
around Potsdamer Platz or the nighttime trade of prostitutes
and merrymakers along Friedrichstrasse looked like the work
of a gigantic machine that set in motion and recirculated city
people. Buses and streetcars shuffled and reshuffled metropolitans as well. "Berlin by Omnibus," a show featuring tem-
peramental passengers, familiar cityscapes, and a colorful
"moving sidewalk," played to packed audiences at the Apollo-
Theater, its success a testimony to the urban public's fascination with haphazard social combinations.[55] The 1913 city
guide, *Berlin für Kenner*, recommended that visitors hazard a
real trip on the *Nordbahn* (third-class, of course) to see the diversity of working-class Berlin—"this, too, is Berlin."[56] The
passengers Anselm Heine observed on the streetcar that traveled to and from Berlin O. seemed to have stepped right out of
the city address book:

> Apprentices riding to their workshops: the porcelain gilder, the
> furniture maker, next to him a cutter at a dress factory, the tiny
> girl from the flower shop, maids and laundrywomen, commercial
> employees, accountants, doctors, lawyers, liftboys rushing to
> their hotels . . . the baker's assistant is sleeping, [so is] the car-
> riage washer, who has worked all night . . . glassblowers, cob-
> blers, copyeditors, reporters, agents of all sorts, bill-boys, mas-
> seurs, hairdressers, construction workers.

Heine marvelled at the exotic variety of trades, each one animated by so much "sweat and willpower and diligence and pa-
tience, which for a moment takes a hurried break:" "Each one
of them hopes for some sort of lucky break, for something to
happen, for a class to be cancelled, for a promotion, for a raise,
for overtime, for a great investment . . . *Vorwärts, vorwärts.*"

Vorwärts, vorwärts—the doubled word set the city's surg-
ing tempo, echoing in its streetcars, unsettling its commuters.[57]
This forward movement was most clearly visible on streetcars
that transported thousands into town from the newly surveyed
precincts of Berlin O. or Berlin N., Wedding, Prenzlauer
Berg, Luisenstadt, Treptow, Rixdorf—the ring of *Vorstadt*
neighborhoods was where newcomers first settled, where they
revealed the stretch of their ambitions, and where they
learned to live with the disappointments that ultimately made
them more alike. For Victor Hugo, it was the outskirts that
best told the story of the city:[58] "To observe the *banlieue* is to
observe an amphibian. End of trees, beginning of roofs, end
of grass, beginning of paving stones, end of ploughed fields,
beginning of shops, the end of the beaten track, the beginning
of the passions, the end of the murmur of things divine, the beginning of the noise of humankind." Again and again, the eyes
of city chroniclers rested on the *Vorstadt* that surrounded
Paris or Berlin. Artists and writers such as Heinrich Zille,
Hans Baluschek, Georg Hermann, and Max Kretzer also
felt drawn to Berlin's edges. Zille, for example, repeatedly
sketched his characters against open fields, construction
fences, or the firewalls of another newly erected block of tenements. The widow, too, watched the sidestreet rather than the
main street.

To observe the city through the fortunes and misfortunes of
the *Vorstadt* was to apprehend what made the metropolis distinctive from other social milieus. The proletarian *Vorstadt*

revealed as many contrasts and finely shaded patterns of work and sociability as did the more affluent *Tiergarten*. Far from being a uniformly grey precinct, the suburb was full of life and energy. The Vorstadt was also a mutable form; the expansion of the city and the addition of thousands of newcomers each year insured that the metropolitan border would be a turbulent, perpetually changing zone. It was this fluctuation that most attracted the newspaper's metropolitan eye.

Visitors who took the streetcar all the way to the last stop could follow the tracks of workmen and the horse-drawn wagons carting timber or catch sight (as did Zille's camera) of a stooped figure collecting firewood from the diminishing forest. This muddy, scarred acreage spread beneath a slate-grey sky fascinated Georg Hermann, author of *Kubinke*, a widely admired Berlin novel which first appeared in serial form in the pages of the *Berliner Tageblatt* in summer of 1910. Kubinke was a young hairdresser who lived "weit draussen" (far out), an enterprising "little man" without roots or family who embodied the brand new city. The novel recounts his downfall in the "Hinüber und Herüber" of Berlin:[59]

> where the streetcars now rattle until three in the morning, that is where the beautifully lonely, deep-rutted field-path once lay. . . . One fine day, sand was deposited and then streets laid out . . . at one corner, a building was erected, then at the opposite corner, another. And there they stood half-finished. Court cases were launched, hearings scheduled, titles prepared, money loaned, money made, money lost . . . horses were abused, workers fired, craftsmen cheated. Buildings changed hands three times before they were completed. . . . Where there is a cheese shop today, there will be a shoe store tomorrow, and electric lamps in the window the day after.

With newly arrived families and often enough an additional *Schlafbursche* (boarder) crowded into two-room apartments

that were stacked in five stories around a series of dingy courtyards—Meyers Hof on Wedding's Ackerstrasse had six—the
Vorstadt was also the place where new city people created a
distinctive metropolitan culture. Popular newspapers were especially attentive to the rhythms of city life on the outskirts.
In bold colors they painted portraits of Berliners at work and
at play, introduced readers to new customs and leisure activities, and always accented the hectic movement of city scenes.

In good times, especially when the building trade boomed,
"Groschen added up to Groschen, rounded up to Marks, and
soon you could calculate in Talern," Talern which were tallied
against the fortunes that migrants hoped to make, perhaps by
buying into a corner tavern, by endeavoring to be the best
plasterer on the job, or by carrying bags across town between
the Anhalter and Stettiner railway stations, like Karl Sie-
brecht in Hans Fallada's *Ein Mann will hinauf.*[60] Reporters
for the *Berliner Tageblatt* traveled out to the Schillingsbrücke
in southeast Berlin to see the thousands of workers going to
work in factories along the Spree River, "the blue or brown
enamel coffeepot in the hand of every man, woman, and
child."[61] The *Berliner Illustrirte* went to Gesundbrunnen,
Warschauer Strasse, Hermannsstrasse, and Frankfurter
Allee to see "people, people, and more people" on their way to
work, "lunchpail under their arms, the distinctive colored coffeepot in their hands." At the end of the day, after the factory
whistles had sounded, the scene was bright with color: women
and children waited at the gates to accompany husbands and
fathers home, a happy family picture that reminded readers
that the Berlin worker was really a *guter Kerl,* a good fellow.[62]
A carnival atmosphere prevailed each Saturday afternoon, on
payday, when families shopped together along the crowded
stalls of the markets: "today, provisions are heaped two or
three times higher than normal." Cafés and taverns were

busier still: "Almost everywhere, you notice the joy that tomorrow is a holiday, that hard work will be interrupted by a
day of rest."[63] The picture presented here is all warmth and
cheer, leaving out the poverty and strain of industrial work.
Imperial Berlin was thereby made accessible and friendly. At
the same time, metropolitan portraits showed the city stamped
by a distinctive culture that gave Berlin its rhythm and character.

Long before Billy Wilder's 1929 documentary, *Menschen
am Sonntag*, *BZ am Mittag* and the *Morgenpost* observed
ordinary Berliners at play. Makeshift ice-skating rinks or
amusement parks *(Rummel)* dotted the outermost neighborhoods across Berlin whenever an enterprising operator rented
an empty lot in the *Vorstadt*, cut an entrance into the wooden
construction fence, and set up shop. These enterprises not
only provided a garish contrast to the red-brick tenements
and factories but also heightened the tentative nature of city
institutions. Around the corner one week, gone the next, the
Rummelplatz constituted the bright-colored fringe of the city.
In addition to these, three pages of sports news in *BZ* recounted Sunday activities at a half-dozen suburban stadiums.
Ullstein's reporters also accompanied a social club on a *Krem-
serfahrt* (wagon ride) through the Tiergarten, joined a picnic
in the Grunewald, and, one summer night, strolled among
merrymakers at Café Josty and along Kurfürstendamm:
"wicker chairs, ice coffee . . . ice-cream soda."[64] One Sunday
every month, Berlin N. invaded Berlin W. A popular illustrated commented on this "twenty-five-pfennig Sunday" at the
zoo: "Today, the real Berliner sets the tone! Little people with
bag and baggage, and wrapped sandwiches and big hair with
all sorts of pins and needles sticking out."[65] Although neither
BZ am Mittag nor the *Morgenpost* neglected the finer arts
shown in Berlin's theaters, operas, and concerts, both news-

papers always reported on the new metropolitan amusements in the Grunewald, sports stadiums, and *Rummelplätze*, and also in Berlin's numerous varieté theaters, cinemas, and circuses.

Luck sometimes ran out on the city folk. A real-estate developer went bankrupt, a bad injury kept father from working, a scheme to sell door-to-door fell through. Then the downpayment on the sewing machine had to be retrieved by carting the machine off to pawnbrokers on Rosenthaler Strasse. During hard times, children's clothes and Christmas presents would be purchased in the second-hand market, "the department store of the poor."

If misfortune lingered, families moved to more modest apartments. On *Ziehtag*, or moving day, which always fell on the first day of April and the first day of October, Berlin's streets filled with wagons and handcarts stacked high with furniture. Choreographing so publicly the variable fortunes of metropolitans, moving days elicited much comment from local papers: "Every step up the ladder and every step down is accompanied by a move," the *Berliner Tageblatt* pointed out.[66] *Ziehtagen* stories were typical of the attitude major newspapers adopted toward Berlin's deep pockets of poverty. Unless misfortune could be described in aesthetic terms of circulation, movement, or variety, it was not very interesting to write about. Moving days did provide that very mix, and so did more exotic expressions of big-city poverty that threw strangers together, such as the Schrippenkirche on Ackerstrasse, faith-healers in the Friedenstrasse, or the municipal *Warmehalle* (winter shelter) near Jannowitzbrücke, all of which attracted the feuilletonist.[67] But most of Berlin's desperately poor people did not enliven public places. One homeworker, "Fräulein G," for example, was up at five in the morning to receive her consignment and labored until twelve at night, "and most Sundays too." A basketweaver's wife reported that she did not get out either. "Hey, I can't take the outdoors anyway. Fresh air comes in and I start coughing and hacking." Besides, "on Sundays, I clean house. Couldn't go out if I wanted to. Who's got fine clothes?"[68] It was left to the Social Democratic Party to investigate the dark cellars and garret spaces in which thousands of Berliners still lived.[69]

With its alternation of misfortune and luck and of work and play, the *Vorstadt* concentrated the emotional intensity of the city. "Nowhere is the sky so dazzlingly blue, so unreservedly blue, as it is over this sandy terrain and these newly built districts," wrote Georg Hermann. And "nowhere will you find the way ahead so mercilessly long as along these brand new tenements."[70] It was in these far-away places of the *Vorstadt* that so many of the tragedies tallied in the columns of local newspapers took place.

Driven to Suicide by Hunger. Albert Burkhardt, aged 32, a worker from Seelbach in Baden, currently living as a *Schlafbursche* at Alte Jakobstrasse 47, committed suicide this morning. After a long spell of unemployment, he reached for his revolver and shot himself with one shot through the right temple.[71]

Desperation. Desperation drove Else Buchholz, a twenty-two-year-old woman from Lebus, to jump into the Spree River near the Schlütersteig. Boatmen came to her rescue and transported her to the hospital. She had only recently arrived in Berlin to work as a buffet lady, but after only finding employment as a waitress and then losing her job, her apartment, and finally her money, grew tired of life.[72]

Mother Murders, Then Kills Self. A horrifying family tragedy took place last night in Rixdorf. Master Shoemaker Jupke lived with his wife and three small children, aged 2 to 7 years, in an apartment consisting of one kitchen and one room on the first floor of a side building at Handjerystrasse 60. For some time now,

Jupke had been speculating in real estate, which brought in enough money for the family to live decently. In addition, the couple enjoyed a happy marriage.

Mrs. Jupke, forty-one-years old, was originally from Wohlau in Silesia, from where a debt of 200 Marks followed her. The loan was to have been paid back today. Her fear of this deadline was so great that she ended up murdering her youngest child and killing herself.

The couple slept with the three children in one room. Around one o'clock in the morning, Mrs. Jupke, having made sure her husband was asleep, arose, strangled two-year Otto with a shawl, and then choked herself with a piece of rope. She strangled herself with such force that the rope cut through to her vertebra.

This letter lay on the table: "Dear Husband! I can no longer go on living. Be a good father to my children. Sell everything to raise the money! Take care and don't abandon the two kids. Otto will go with me. Give my regards to the whole family."[73]

There was something specifically metropolitan about suicides. The language by which they were presented to the reading public—"Tragedy in the Big City," "Big-City Drama," "Defeated in the Struggle for Survival"—emplotted suicide in the uncertain urban economy. Suicides suggested just how infirm the ground really was and how brief good fortune might be and how emotionally charged modern life had become. The story of the big city was composed of countless currents which could bring you up or suck you under, and which made autobiographies as unstable and inconstant as the traffic on Potsdamer Platz. Newspapers found suicides such compelling items because they dramatized so well the fugitive quality to the city.

For *BZ am Mittag*, the *Morgenpost*, and the *Lokal-Anzeiger*, tales from the *Vorstadt* recited the story of Berlin itself. They set a vast stage for the incursions of city into countryside, introduced a broad range of nonbourgeois characters who spoke in loud and unabashed voices, and provided the pulse of the metropolitan heartbeat: going to work in the morning and returning in the evening, shopping on payday and entertaining on Sunday, the boom season and the stringent period of unemployment, moving into the *Vorderhaus* or back into the *Hinterhaus*, the expectant arrival of the newcomer into Berlin one afternoon, from Wohlau or Seelbach, and the gruesome late-night departure of an indebted mother and her youngest son. The city of contrasts was best revealed along edges, in the *Vorstadt* and at night, and along Friedrichstrasse or Potsdamer Platz, where the *Vorstadt* confronted the *Hauptstadt*.

To readers of the local press, Berlin was anything but an undifferentiated city of stone, which was an image favored by Realist novelists like Kretzer and even such Expressionist poets as Heym and Stadtler. Local reportage challenged the image of the nineteenth-century metropolis as two cities—the poor (East) versus the wealthy (West), as in Berlin and London—or as completely chaotic and disorderly or simply incomprehensible because uniform. Some years later, when Franz Hessel, flâneur, novelist, essayist, reviewed *Das steinerne Berlin*, Werner Hegemann's diabolical 1930 account of municipal speculation, he pleaded the case for the viability of the motley city:[74] "Maybe it is madness, given this devastating judgment about all the stupidity that has been and continues to be undertaken, but I have the feeling that things will still work out, that we can, in the side-by-side confusion of vulgar and worthy, of solid and fraudulent, build a proper city, today and tomorrow."

Walter Benjamin agreed in a like-minded review. The city was not simply the sorry work of Hohenzollerns and police officials: "No matter how horrible they are to live in," tenements have "windows [that] not only reflect injury and crime but mirror a morning and evening sun which has a melancholy grandeur that can be found nowhere else, and they have fashioned urban childhoods in stairwells and on asphalt streets which are as valuable as those of any farmer growing up surrounded by barns and fields."[75] City life was oppressed by shabby, overcrowded housing, but it was enhanced as well by a rough beauty and the rich pleasures of play and the memory of play. The widow at the window had recognized the same thing.

Newspaper reports on the diverse, sensational, and fast-moving contents of the city revised basic notions about Berlin and Berliners. Accounts of the discontinuity and variability of the city offered a more democratic and inclusive view of its people and challenged the authority of the late nineteenth-century Realist voices. But the focus on diversity and contrast could also overrule other perspectives. The aesthetic fascination with disruptions on the surface—the colorful cast of rich and poor on Potsdamer Platz, for example, or discrete human-interest stories—elided over social facts of poverty or privilege. Newspapers rewrote sociology in aesthetic terms and, as a result, they left readers with an incomplete and overly passive view of the modern city. To simply alternate light and dark tones from the palette of big-city colors was to erase the danger of prostitution, to diminish the hardship behind *Ziehtagen*, to trivialize suicide. In much the same way, portraits of city characters or sociological sketches of the Tiergarten naturalized the city and stiffened metropolitan life into a few identifiable poses. Impoverishment or suicide or matchgirls all too often appeared as natural links in a great chain of metropolitan being.

Nonetheless, to render the city as a city of contrasts allowed readers to breathe life and complexity into a social formation that had been previously regarded as deadening. Berlin N.

was not simply a wasteland of exploitation and impoverishment as so many novelists and urban critics indicated in the 1880s and 1890s, a place from which writers sought escape (at the literary colony in Friedrichshagen, for example), but was described and appreciated as a complex ecological zone that offered all sorts of unexpected niches of prosperity and felicity. The counterpoint to the late nineteenth-century Friedrichshagen generation is the very metropolitan cohort that appeared a few years later comprising Hans Ostwald, Georg Hermann, and Heinrich Zille. By collecting the incidental debris and exploring the various points of exchange in the metropolis, these and other writers stood against the relentlessness with which Clara Viebig or Max Kretzer had propelled the degeneration of their fictional characters.[76] Their contributions to big-city newspapers encouraged readers to repudiate single-minded renditions of the metropolis, to see it as a contradictory and surprising settlement in which anything could happen, and to approach it as an object of desire and imagination. In doing so, metropolitan newspapers invited readers to look with new eyes and to move through the city as consumers, spectators, and collectors.

Well before Benjamin reviewed Hegemann at the end of the Weimar Republic, mass-circulation newspapers at the turn of the century attempted to approximate the experience of living in the modern city. To be sure, they overlooked the larger political forces that acted so deleteriously on the city, which neither Benjamin nor Hessel wanted to miss, but nonetheless they brought to light the public places and amusements that city people had fashioned, charted the manifold rhythms and tentative arrangements of the metropolis, and thereby extended the geographic, social, and imaginative bounds of Berlin. The word city included Berlin N. and Berlin O. as well as Berlin W., and "little people" such as Kubinke at play in the Grune-

wald as well as the nouveaux riches strolling along Unter den
Linden. A city of contrasts emerged from under the typolo-
gist's lens, a mosaic of unexpected abilities and misfortunes
that no single collective noun or root metaphor could encom-
pass. "Berlin Allerlei," the title of the local column in the *Morgenpost*, exploded the military and bureaucratic geometry of
the Prussian *Hauptstadt* into a thousand stories that took
place on a thousand streets.

4
THE CITY AS SPECTACLE

"Die Strassen komme ich entlang geweht"—I move as if brushed along the streets—this fluttering image, which also provided the title for Ernst Blass's 1912 collection of poems about everyday life, summons up the rush of traffic and evokes a lightness of movement—a leaf swirled around in the autumn wind.[1] Brushed along the streets, a man passes a rich variety of sights. Blass fears running into a "skirt," "with words, vile, raw, and illicit"; he hopes instead to meet a "girl friend." In any case, the city is full of chance and possibility, a fullness which Blass's long brushstrokes comprehend. At the same time, the reader suspects encounters with "skirt" or "girl friend" will be fleeting; brushed along, the male urbanite passes on. With these motions, Blass has described the browser, the type who corresponds to the unexpected variety and ceaseless fluctuation of the city. (In a similar fashion, Max

Rychner described Walter Benjamin's gait as "at once advancing and tarrying, a strange mixture of both.")[2]

The browser, like the "cosmopolite" in a 1738 French definition cited by Richard Sennett, moved comfortably in diversity.[3] But what had been a carefully acquired sensibility in the eighteenth century, when most city dwellers lived and worked in the narrow confines of a single neighborhood or *quartier*, had been transformed, by 1900, into a second skin which millions of metropolitans wore unawares. The formation of this cosmopolitan identity has important economic roots. Industrial cities at the end of the nineteenth century circulated and recirculated inhabitants in countless ways. With the increasing specialization of labor, the growing distance between workplace and home, and the everyday use of mass transit, strangers met and interacted all the time: they "crossed paths, walked the same way for a bit, separated, and perhaps met again."[4] However, the constitution of this public space was as much the work of fiction as the function of commerce. The cosmopolitan did not simply set out to see the diversity of the city. Metropolitan encounters were always marvellously aesthetic, and they were guided by the layout of the word city as well as the design of the built city.

The best-explored word cities are the "various intricate and confusing plotlines" of nineteenth-century novels,[5] but the most elaborate, widely read, and informative versions appeared in daily newspapers. With its attention to variety and detail, the newspaper rewrote the city as a perpetually replenished sensation and, accordingly, addressed readers as compulsive spectators and browsers. Full of news about theaters, amusement parks, department stores, demonstrations, and the noise and traffic of the street, *BZ am Mittag*, the *Morgenpost*, and Berlin's other major dailies tilted the city toward the browser. In their pages, Berlin paraded, performed, boasted, and exhibited its fashions. As the *Morgenpost* column promised, Berlin was "allerlei;" the city generated a continuous stream of incidents, events, and impressions. Mass-circulation newspapers themselves quickened the flow of this metropolitan stream. Bold headlines and front-page layouts, opinionated writing and loud-mouthed newsboys, all enhanced the clamor of the city. The big-city daily grabbed readers, showed them any number of windows onto urban scenes, and hurried them along to the next sensation, the next window. If newspaper stories openly invited readers to browse the city, newspaper style surreptitiously taught them how.

It comes as no surprise, then, that observers repeatedly used the image of the newspaper to convey the modern spirit of urban life, particularly the uncensored and ceaseless fluctuation of images and impressions. As we know, Picasso and Braque pasted newsprint onto their canvases, reproducing the quirky syntax of the boulevard. Elsewhere, the daily paper served as a shorthand metonym for the disorderly and haphazard quality of the city. According to the essayist Bernhard von Brentano, street advertisements, appearing in "a continuous edition," composed the largest daily source of news in Berlin.[6] Only wind and rain, noted another observer, edited the ever-changing "newspaper" of colorful notices, posters, and broadsides that appeared on hundreds of *Litfassäulen* (advertising pillars) throughout the city.[7] Stocked with newspapers for all tastes at all hours, the streetcorner kiosk ("a department store that never closes!") stood out as a symbol for the multiplicity of urban sights and sounds.[8] The newspaper packaged and juxtaposed its contents and varied them each day; in a like manner, Simmel contented, city minds took stock of the "rapidly changing and closely compressed" shocks of the metropolis by errant consumption, flipping through, browsing over, looking past.

Emphasizing the movement, contrast, and transitoriness of urban inventory, the newspaper moved away from a textual or narrative organization of reality and constructed a visual or tactile encounter with it. Without photographs and making only slight use of line drawings, lithographs, or half-tones, the boulevard press generated image after image whose selection had been made according to formal properties rather than thematic substance. In this way, the print media anticipated the nonmimetic, purely visual effects of cinema. The "urban spectacle" that is so manifest in Walter Ruttmann's acclaimed 1927 documentary, *Berlin: Symphony of the Big City*, for example, embellished a visual field already prepared at the turn of the century by the publishers Ullstein and Mosse. As readers and thus as consumers, the prewar public approached the city more and more completely in terms of visual pleasure and spectatorship.[9]

The depiction of the city in an endless series of sharp, visually compelling images had important political consequences. By representing Berlin as a vast spectacle which provided pleasure and, at the same time, by rewriting difference and division in aesthetic and otherwise nonpolitical terms, the major dailies invariably falsified urban reality. The preoccupation with exterior forms and surface textures—contrast, discontinuity, surprise—overruled the presentation of socially conscious themes and cogent political analyses of the city. Again and again, critics assailed urban spectatorship for having fashioned a "lazy, passive" imagination (Wordsworth) or serialized the "ever same" (Benjamin).[10] By making the metropolis so delightfully consumable, the mass media—newspapers, advertisements, and later the cinema—laid the foundation for a consumer culture (derailed by the advent of Hitler) that defuses class conflicts and glosses over ethnic differences. Even though neighborhood, Social Democratic, or craft-based circles of sociability resisted this process of mass-formation at the time, the signs of commercialized culture were unmistakable by 1914: crowded streetcars, stadiums filled with spectators, gigantic amusement parks, grand downtown cinemas, gramophone *Schlager* (pop hits), mass-circulation newspapers.[11] In the two decades before World War I, certain class barriers became more diffuse as the spectacle of the city became more irresistible. Spectacle also created a city-wide audience in increasingly homogeneous terms. This is not to say that the rise of urban spectatorship suddenly brought forth a unified vision of the city. Men, women, and children, as well as newcomers, proletarians, and tourists, all imagined the city in different ways. There was no set itinerary by which to see Berlin. Browsers generated multiple versions of the place depending on their inclinations and reactions—there is no single text to this city. What did take place, however, was the formation of a common perspective: that is, various groups routinely encountered the metropolis as an ample field of visual pleasure.

The browser and the flâneur are typically seen as emblematic (though lamentable) incarnations of modernity. They are recognizable derivatives of a process of commodification in which the rapid alternation of images reduced dazzled spectators to the level of appearances and to the immediacy of *Erlebnis* (sensation). What gradually disappeared, as Walter Benjamin suggested in his classic analysis of late nineteenth-century Paris (itself influenced by his upbringing in early twentieth-century Berlin), was the "sanctioning framework of *Erfahrung*" (experience). In modern culture, experience was increasingly accessible only in the diminished vocabulary of incessant actuality.[12] The "soubresaults" (Baudelaire) or jolts that punctuated life in the industrial city made metropolitans more distracted and emotionally indifferent, prone to the blasé outlook that Simmel considered to be the most prominent trait of contemporary urban life. Distracted browsers are commonly identified as the new social type who filled the great cities, flocked to their entertainments, purchased their ready-made wares, and otherwise nourished commodity capitalism.[13]

To engage the city in terms of spectatorship is not all bad. The meandering viewpoint of browsers allowed them to con-figure the city to be in startling new ways. A purely digressive approach challenged official hierarchies and revealed the city to be a place of surprise and inconstancy. Moreover, the browser accepted and reveled in the condition of instability, thereby anticipating the premises of twentieth-century mod-ernism and promoting an intellectual virtuosity that Simmel, for one, cherished. An entirely expedient attitude made sense for the unreckonable conditions of the city: "A man who prides himself on following a straight line through life is an idiot who believes in infallibility," observed Balzac about Parisians.[14] Flâneurs intrigued contemporaries because they did not walk straight lines. Indeed, as Dana Brand points out, no other urban figure "offered the example of a posture of curiosity and tolerance." "Even if it was merely spectatorial," browsing was superior to the "fearmongering and demonization of the other" that occurred as well. What the browser or the flâneur offered was reconciliation with the world of strangers.[15]

This reconciliation is more impressive if one considers Berlin's status as a city of potentially divisive class and ethnic conflict. Already a largely proletarian city, imperial Berlin witnessed a steady influx of Polish and Russian Jews and Polish Catholics in the two decades following 1900. Many of these migrants eventually moved on to Bochum, Hamburg, or Hoboken, but thousands also stayed. The Scheunenviertel, for example, acquired its reputation as an impoverished Jewish precinct only at the very end of the nineteenth century. At the other end of Berlin, Polish was as widely spoken in

Kreuzberg's churches, sportfields, and streets as German. Rather than dwell on the foreignness of these residents in the name of ethnic identity, as did German nationalists and home-grown anti-Semites, the mass media ended up submerging them in common rhythms of metropolitan life. The homogenizing effects of a commercialized popular culture thus offered a plausible alternative to the radical nationalist project.

Browsing created an undeniable zone of safety in which to encounter strangers. Ernst Blass's image of brushing by and passing on established a protective distance among metropolitans. More and more Berliners accordingly followed Blass and wandered through a world of strangers and took pleasure in the stimulation that such encounters produced. As they did so, they served as crucial constituents of a public sphere in which strangers were not only likely to meet but actively exchanged opinions and goods. In this respect, the visual thrills of browsing were an extension of commodity exchange and economic necessity. In style and substance, newspapers carried the message that cities were places where goods had to be efficiently stored, handled, and moved and they also fashioned a democratic space accessible to idlers, spectators, and strangers. However, this arena remained tentative. So long as urban spectatorship was restricted by the protocols of the monarchical state—the case until 1918—the incidental, non-political movements of browsers could have fundamental political consequences. Berlin's press did not simply represent the city in terms of spectatorship but vigorously promoted unrestricted access to city places. In the face of police infringements on the rights of pedestrians, newspapers championed the free flow of both things and people—of sale items and consumers.[16] Even as they remapped the metropolis as a field of visual pleasure, the print media reworked the political face of the German capital: diluting difference into merely formal variation and habituating metropolitans to thrive in a world of strangers and to participate in the restless activity of commerce, while encouraging them to move about freely and haphazardly. Urban spectatorship, consumer capitalism, and democracy thus worked in surprisingly compatible ways.

BROWSING . . . IN THE NEWSPAPER

Browsing requires a variety of goods arranged so that each item promises to produce a predictable effect. The hundreds of different items in a department store, for example, have little in common except their ability to be selected, purchased, and consumed. In the same way, unrelated newspaper stories on the front page can be packaged as commodities designed to attract readers. The looser, more relaxed page layout at the turn of the century plainly revealed how the business of selling had commodified the news. And it was tabloids, which had to be sold every day to passersby, that did the most to make news appealing and sensational. If *BZ am Mittag*, the *Morgenpost*, and even Scherl's *Lokal-Anzeiger* unfurled basically similar maps to the city and city types, *BZ am Mittag* distinguished itself by adding exclamation marks, bold typefaces, and headlines.

To open the pages of *BZ am Mittag* was to riff through a menu to the city. Typeface, headlines, layout, writing style, and pages of advertising in the back were all designed to stimulate readers. From the first day of its appearance on the streets, on Saturday 22 October 1904, *BZ*'s scripted header drew attention to itself and remained the newspaper's signature for forty years. Slanted diagonally to the right, "BZ am Mittag" slashed the static geometry of the conventional newspaper page. The "ornamental upstroke of 'M' in 'Mittag' was pulled across the page and underlined gondola-like the initials 'BZ', as if the time of the day supported the newspaper, which was in fact the case, while, in a parallel stroke, the 'g' of

'Mittag' hung practically in free air."[17] Designed by Carl Schnebel, the header immediately declared its hostility to the strenuous reading that long print columns in most other newspapers in the capital demanded; *BZ* would present the news in a lively, playful way.

Four columns wide, *BZ am Mittag* left room for three or four showcase stories without crowding the front page. While most Berlin newspapers used headlines sparingly, *BZ* generally topped one or two columns with two-line headers large enough to be read by passersby at a distance and soon wrapped the front page with an additional banner headline. Since *BZ* was bundled, distributed, and sold folded along its width, the top half of the paper, with the distinctive title header and headlines, had the bold, economical look of a poster. No other paper—as a glance at streetside kiosks confirms—promised exciting stories presented in such readable form. The rest of the layout was inviting as well. Large typeface facilitated reading while subheads broke up the uniformity of columns of print. In addition, editors left ample room between stories, giving the paper a clean, spare look. *BZ am Mittag*'s front page was designed as a "show window" to entice readers and encourage browsers. To sell the news it literally dressed up the news.[18]

If headlines attracted attention, fetching subheads caught the reader's eye again and again as it wandered down the column:

> According to One of the Injured
> An Awful Crash
> Climbed through the Window
> Spared by a Miracle
> "My God, That's Where I Just Boarded"

Subheads like these about a train wreck provided fresh sensations at rapid intervals. They were at once compelling and dis-

Berliner Zeitung

B.Z. am Mittag

Nr. 10
Berliner Zeitung
35. Jahrgang

Verlag: Ullstein & Co. — Redaktion: Berlin SW. 68, Kochstraße 22–25.

1 Uhr
Donnerstag
12. Januar 1911

Der Eisenbahnerstreik in Portugal.

Bedrohliche Ausdehnung des Streiks.

Eigener Drahtbericht.

Lissabon, 12. Januar.

Forderungen der Eisenbahner.

Militärische Maßnahmen.

Nach den Vollmachten streiken.

Minister Almeida will zurücktreten.

Das Urteil im Moabiter Prozess.

Wage und Schwert.

Antirepublikanische Soldatenmeuterei.

Eigener Drahtbericht.

Paris, 12. Januar.

Ein Bombenattentat.

Explosionsunglück in einer Feuerwerksfabrik.

Eigener Drahtbericht.

Paris, 12. Januar.

Börse von heute.

Berliner Anfangskurse.

Caption: Front page, *BZ am Mittag*, no. 10, 12 Jan. 1911.

tracting, inducing readers to stop and look and also driving them onward.[19] Breaking up the story at regular intervals, subheads not only monitored the narrative stream but quickened its flow. By contrast, even the occasional headlines in the *Lokal-Anzeiger* or *Berliner Tageblatt* did little to relieve their uninterrupted columns of small-type print.

Recounting events in the form of drama or suspense, in which aesthetic effect regulated the telling, undoubtedly piqued the interest of readers, but it also encouraged them to take a detached, spectatorial view of the world. Feuilletons reminded one thoughtful reviewer of a complicated optical apparatus displayed in Munich's Deutsches Museum. Figures that moved in front of its distorting lens appeared in miniature, like characters in a puppet show. "It is amusing to watch as one thing after another . . . becomes small, toylike, and then disappears."[20] The window through which the ninety-year-old widow gazed out at the world achieved the same effect. In miniature, the world assumed a panoramic aspect that heightened both the *Schaureize* (allure) of the object and the *Schaulust* (curiosity) of the viewer. Through the feuilletonist's way of seeing things, even outrageous incidents became simply tragic tales, further serializations in a compelling drama. Excursions through nighttime Berlin, for example, invariably took note of poor children selling roses or matches, a detail which enhanced the intensity of the portrait. Even cheerless soup kitchens, asylums, and hospitals dazzled readers by providing a medley of colorful characters. Each item, whether whimsical, outrageous, or pathetic, contributed to the feuilleton's "troittoir roulant." "Poverty and privation" enhanced the magic of the metropolis, wrote the art critic August Endell, who recognized "wonderful, stark beauty" in the "sickly colors" of city children.[21] This gaze in search of impressions had the sure effect of trivializing the conditions of life in the metropolis by presenting them as a theater of color and emotion for the entertainment of urban spectators.

The startling visual effects that each article generated extended to the newspaper itself. Promiscuous juxtapositions on each page made it easier for readers to browse the news and, at the same time, kept them from getting absorbed in any single item. Political articles, murder stories, and other sensational items all tumbled onto the front page. Although *BZ am Mittag* never abandoned political coverage, its front page typically featured a variety of disassociated, dramatic events— assassinations, earthquakes, shipwrecks, mine explosions, zeppelin flights—that had little political consequence or correlation. With one sensational tale next to another, *BZ*'s front page resembled a three-ring circus. Most other Berlin papers assumed a much more reserved demeanor. They attempted to cover parliamentary developments and international frictions in a coherent way and relegated even the most sensational crime stories to the back pages. When thirty Berlin women were stabbed by an anonymous attacker over the course of a single week in February 1909, news which *BZ* hurried onto the front pages—"Das Schrecken von Berlin"—the *Berliner Tageblatt* consigned this, with the other urban mishaps, to the fifth page.[22] Yet it was just this sort of titillating drama that sold papers on the street. On the front page as much as on the city street, surprise depended on curious arrangements and unexpected intrusions. Heinrich Zille's newspaper vendors understood this precisely and anticipated the business day with satisfaction, given that day's offerings: "Heite wird's een Jeschäfft! Acht Prozesse, drei Morde, zwee Bankjehs, zwee Sitte, Spione und Attentate, zwee Flieger jestürzt, een Luftschiff verloofen." (We're in the money! Eight trials, three murders, two armed robberies, two morals charges, espionage,

In der Friedrichstraße
„Müller'n, heite wird's een Jeschäft! Acht Prozesse, drei Morde, zwee Bankjehs, zwee Sitte, Spione und Attentate, zwee Flieger jestürzt, een Luftschiff verloofen –"

"On Friedrichstrasse. We're in the money! Eight trials, three murders, two armed robberies, two morals charges, espionage, assassination, two fliers have crashed, one zeppelin is stranded." Drawing by Heinrich Zille, 1911.

assassination, two fliers have crashed, one zeppelin is stranded).[23] Laid out to grab the attention of casual passersby, the front pages of tabloids were explicitly compared to department-store windows, stacked as they were with as many colorfully diverse and unusual items as possible.[24] Peruse the headlines of *BZ am Mittag:*[25]

MURDER IN BERLIN N

KAISER-FRIEDRICH-MUSEUM ROBBED

ISLOWSKI ON THE POLITICAL SITUATION

Z II IN COLOGNE

HIGHSEAS TRAGEDY IN THE NORTH SEA

CIVIL WAR IN IRELAND?

FAMILY DRAMA IN BERLIN N.

Inside Berlin's popular dailies readers found a marketplace variety of news. In *BZ* (on 24 October 1904) political updates—"War in the North Sea. Russians Destroy English Fishing Boats"—jostled with sensational local stories— "Young Girl Missing" and "Mutilated Body Found"—sports news—"Hamburg's Automobile Race"—and a regular column reporting on "Das Neuste in Berlin."[26] Advertisements crept onto the third page, which also featured weekly programs for concerts, theaters, and cabarets, as well as sports news and humor sketches.

More than half of any big-city newspaper was given up to advertising and classifieds. In these well-designed and often fetching pages, the city appeared as a luxuriant garden of possibility. Ballrooms ("Künstler-Kapellen"), beerhalls, wine houses ("Déjeuners, Diners, Soupers"), night bars, concert-cafés ("lustige Abende"), theaters ("Das muss man seh'n!!"), variety shows ("Monstre-Eröffnungs-Programm"), circuses ("Grosse ausserordentliche Gala-Vorstellung"), exhibition halls, aquariums ("Reichhaltigste Ausstellung der Welt"), ice palaces, sports arenas ("Grosser Preis v. Europa"), and galleries ("Collectiv-Ausstellungen: Paul Cézanne, Curt Herrmann, Edvard Munch") all drew attention to their inventories and novelties.[27]

Advertisements in *BZ am Mittag.*

Equally sensational were the piles of diverse and wonderful and newly improved goods featured in commercial advertisements. Turn to page six or seven of a metropolitan paper and browse what only the original German can properly convey:[28]

> Wunder der Industrie. Unerreicht grossartiger Regulator. Wanduhr in Nussbaum mit fein regulierendem Patentwerk, bewährt, 4,50 Mark.

> "Bade zu Hause!" Die Wellenbadschaukel ist noch immer die beliebteste Wanne für Wellen-, Regen-, Voll- und Schwitzbad. Unverwüstlich. Nimmt wenig Raum ein. Ueber 100,000 im Gebrauch.

Etwa 175,000 neue Schallplatten. Der grösste Gelegenheitskauf, der je existierte. 25 cm doppelseitig, sonst 2 bis 3 Mark, jetzt Serie I 10 Platten sortiert, Tänze, Märsche, Walzer, Gesänge, zusammen 6,50 Mark.

Vergleichst Du die Systeme schärfer, wählst Du bestimmt den Blickensderfer! 150,000 Blickensderfer-Schreibmaschinen im Gebrauch. Inklusive eleganten Verschlusskasten 200 Mark. Orientalisches Modell für Hebräisch, kombiniert mit Deutsch 350 Mark.

This rich selection of goods and services was unprecedented before the end of the nineteenth century. Not until then could department stores and specialty retailers take advantage of the increasingly large public of consumers, filling their needs and stimulating their desires. As a result, advertising space grew dramatically. In Berlin's *Vossische Zeitung*, for which comparative statistics are available, the number of pages of advertising more than doubled in the late nineteenth century, while the number of pages of text remained about the same. More significantly, turn-of-the-century advertisements featured luxury items and fancy goods and, to a lesser extent, clothes; these items almost completely replaced the offers of books and produce that had predominated fifty years earlier.[29] As important sources of business revenue, individual ads had grown larger and their style became bolder and more imposing. Berlin's biggest department stores, Tietz, Israel, Hertzog, Jandorf, Wertheim, and Kaufhaus des Westens, all took out striking full-page ads, often tying their advertising copy to current events such as zeppelin flights or the Köpenickiade—topicality, after all, was part of the spectacle. Whether readers browsed advertised items or news items, they encountered a city in perpetual renewal.

Larger and more spacious ads, bolder lines, and fetching typography—reading the back pages of the boulevard newspaper repeated the kaleidoscopic experience of reading the front pages. Readers glanced over showcases of appealing articles, dipped into a scandalous story or glanced at automobile ads, and turned the page to the sports or business columns. With a rich selection of advertising, various regular columns and weekly supplements, and a front-page assortment of late-breaking news and enticing tales about diverse aspects of contemporary life, these tabloids invited browsing. There was no single repertoire of reading; on the contrary, the paper was designed to be used in a variety of ways. Loosely arranged layout made the city seem more varied and rich. Indeed, the front page resembled nothing so much as the unregulated floorplan of the great department stores, where, as Emile Zola reports in *The Ladies' Paradise*, haphazard arrangements of items boosted sales.

The city that took shape in the boulevard newspaper was a disorderly composition of the casual glances of readers as well as of writers. Mass-circulation newspapers typically travelled with commuters ("almost everybody reads," we have been told) and were unfolded and perused even as streetcars filled up with passengers and lurched from stop to stop. What facilitated this sort of easy reading were headlines, subheads, illustrations, and larger print. Looking at *BZ am Mittag* in the 1920s, Larissa Reisner observed: "You don't even have to chew this news . . . just swallow and you're informed."[30] As a result, Berlin's one-million commuters could easily pick up and put down the paper and skip from one item to another. Boulevard newspapers facilitated a distracted style of reading that corresponded to the ceaseless dislocations of the mechanical city and to the meandering movements of urban spectatorship. That the conservative *Lokal-Anzeiger*, for example, launched a midday edition with a busier look in March 1909 and also filled its front pages with more sensational items

("Marriage in the Future" or "The Russian Zeppelin" or "Berlin Teenagers") indicated how compelling *BZ*'s rapid-fire style had become.[31] Contemporary journalism won a citywide readership by treating readers as spectators who would be dazzled by a rapid alternation of sights and sounds.

Streams of available newspaper copy invited readers to browse among various editions as well. Papers could be found at almost any busy corner in turn-of-the-century Berlin. It is difficult to imagine public places without kiosks or water fountains, advertising pillars, bus stops, flower stalls, and telephone boxes. Yet these amenities embellished the boulevard only toward the end of the nineteenth century. Before then, the city was simply not regarded as entertaining and had not been cut and channeled by the free flow of commodities. As for early newspapers, they did not reach most metropolitans, and those who did read them typically received them at home. With the inauguration of Berlin's *Stadtbahn* in 1882, however, the demand for occasional reading material increased, and one Georg Stilke received a municipal concession to run permanent kiosks inside the commuter stations. The police further eased regulations on street sales in 1904 (a sign that news had become more of a commodity, less of a dangerous political substance), but it had been public indifference more than municipal restrictions that had until then kept street sales minimal and kiosks few and far between.[32] However, once the city appeared as an object of compulsive spectatorship and became the topic of more wide-ranging writing and reading, street sales soared. Ullstein's successes with the *Morgenpost*; the rhythms of commuting; and the media's account of the pleasures of viewing the city all stimulated activity on the streets after the turn of the century. Stilke's Deutsche Kiosk company constructed a total of 90 stands on Berlin's sidewalks in the fifteen years before 1918.[33] Often outfitted

A postcard from Berlin that shows the city's curbside
amenities, including a kiosk and an advertising pillar.

with telephones and benches and tended by quick-witted, well-informed proprietors, kiosks quickly became distinctive city landmarks. Penny-pinching boys and girls gawked at the headlines and illustrated covers on display, and passersby stopped to buy an afternoon or out-of-town paper and perhaps to browse and chat.[34]

At the same time, individual newspaper vendors proliferated. By 1907 they were numerous enough to organize their own interest group and publish a bimonthly trade journal, *Der Zeitungshandel,* with 700 subscribers.[35] When Ullstein founded *BZ am Mittag* in 1904, the new venture sent a battalion of uniformed vendors into the traffic of the streets; Ullstein's competitors, Mosse and Scherl, followed suit a few years later. Both in and out of company uniforms, the men who sold the papers quickly became familiar Berlin characters.[36] "I greet this old newspaper man every morning," explained one child beneath a picture of a big-city scene.[37] Other city people often adopted "their" vendor and mourned his passing when he died or moved on.[38]

The streets teemed with newspaper sellers and echoed with their cries, although municipal regulations in Berlin prohibited vendors from calling out headlines. "Montag Morgen," "BZ, BZ am Mittag," "Nachtausgabe"—"an unmistakable billboard of sound" composed part of what Walter Kiaulehn described as the "sensational allure of the street."[39] Tabloids even infiltrated the pages of Döblin's *Berlin Alexanderplatz*. On page 269, for example: "She went slowly back to the café, Prenzlauer corner . . . On the Alex the newsboys were calling *Montag Morgen* and *Welt am Mittag*. She bought a paper from a strange boy, even looked at it." Turn to page 274: "He stepped into a little café, took a Kümmel, thumbed the pages of the *Vorwärts* and the *Lokal-Anzeiger*." And to page 279: "Franz reads a copy of the *B.Z.* which is lying on the chair."[40]

Metropolitans could literally browse through the newspapered streets of Berlin, reading, glancing, unfolding, tearing out, tossing aside pages from early morning until after midnight. Newspaper vendors brought this city of readers into sharp relief:[41]

He knows newsprint not simply according to the various titles but also by the interior character of the newspaper. He is familiar with the political positions of the dailies and is informed of the groups for which a newspaper or a magazine holds interest. If the *Tägliche Rundschau* is sold out, he will not offer customers the *Berliner Morgenpost*, but suggest instead the *Deutsche Tageszeitung*. He has a talent for judging character and is as expert recognizing big-city life as the taxicab driver or the luggage porter. He knows what sort of people buy film, sports, or men's magazines. If he has a particular speciality, say sports literature, then he knows the field and can give advice and hold up his end of a conversation. What is more, he has good business sense and a feel for the political and spiritual climate in which new magazines have to succeed. . . . He can give information on just about everything—that belongs as much to his profession as the telephone and municipal address book belong to the tobacconist.

BROWSING . . . THROUGH THE CITY

Repeating and embellishing a thousandfold the meanderings of the drifter, tabloids choreographed the metropolis as a marvelous display. Never before had metropolitans experienced such a barrage of sensations and impressions. The modern city seemed to require exploration and invite excursions. Already the German Romantics regarded city streets as sites of uncountable treasure and possibility. Metropolitan geography possessed the fantastic, never-ending aspect of a dream world: streets ended in crooked alleys or wide plazas and doors opened onto hidden chambers, staircases, and courtyards.[41] Christmas, which has so governed Western ideas of sumptuous wonder, was also distinctly urban. Dickens's "A Christmas Carol" or E. T. A. Hoffmann's "The Nutcracker and the Mouse King" (which was later adapted by Tchaikovsky) are not imaginable in anything but the middle of a bustling city. The favorite location of the Christmas feuilletonist was invariably the city within the city, Times Square, Les Halles, Potsdamer Platz. By the turn of the century, however, the dazzle of Christmas suffused the newly electrified metropolis year round. And it was not only the stock figure of the provincial visitor spending "zwo dotzend Grossstadttage" who conjured up magical journeys of light and sound—"Musik Reklame Zeitungsschrei"—while walking through Berlin.[43] Longtime residents marvelled at the city's luminosity. "Let's step across Auguste-Viktoria Platz onto the promenade in the middle of Tauentzienstrasse," invited Leo Colze:[44]

> A sea of light stretches out before us. To the right and left, one show window after another displays luxuries for ladies and gentlemen alike. An elegant stream of people, full of cheer and with all the time in the world, laughs and flirts its way down the street. Strollers, flâneurs. Ahead on Wittenbergplatz, magical lights, rare delicacies, silk, gold brocade, bronzes, ostrich feathers, show windows that are more like jewelry cases: the new department store. Dense crowds rush in without pause.

Turn-of-the-century Berliners, for whom the press of the crowd, the busy traffic in goods, the ceaseless noise and light were still novel experiences (the Wertheim department store opened only in 1894, for example), encountered the metropolis as a place of previously unimagined possibility: "Past the show windows, which beckon pedestrians with their glittering wares, past women, who beckon with glittering eyes," observed at least one contributor to the *Berliner Tageblatt*.[45] To browse the city was to bathe in the sensual gratifications and surprising exchanges that proliferated in its public places, along the grand boulevards—Friedrichstrasse, Leipziger Strasse, Tauentzienstrasse—in department stores (especially Wertheim and Kaufhaus des Westens), in the cafés and restaurants open late into the night, and also on city buses, streetcars, subways, and in the dancehalls and carnivals of the *Vorstadt*.

The big-city newspaper played a major part, introducing but, more importantly, enhancing the theatrical nature of the metropolis. It did not simply describe; it represented the urban world as ready-made for browsing. Rich descriptions of cafés, kiosks, *Litfasssäulen* (advertising pillars), display windows, and street advertisements provided a public roominess that was ideal for the spectator. At the same time, the constantly changing stories and the hurried tone of reportage pressed readers to move on, to turn the page, to see the next sight. If posters, kiosks, and water fountains invited metropolitans to stop and linger, streetcar schedules, *Normaluhren*, and the movement of traffic along the streets distracted and urged them to move on. Pedestrians were constantly being taken up, deposited, and retrieved by the city.

A fascination with windows onto the city revealed the newspaper's awareness that looking at the metropolis had become part of the metropolis. Countless reportorial "window shots" in which the "frame" remained clearly visible did not so much provide views on the city—although they certainly did, in rich variety and discrete detail—than announce the secret pleasures of viewing. The stress was on the verb. In several remarkable exercises in self-referentiality, newspapers drew attention to their own generation of narrative and came to address readers as reporters who themselves might view and encounter the city as if they were looking for stories.

Image after image in the paper depicted the prevalence of urban spectators. In what became a staple of big-city reportage, stories about the *Litfasssäule* at once stimulated pleasure in the reader (by telling a story) and depicted the stimulation of pleasure for the reader (by showing the telling of a story). As a result, newspapers projected their own surveillance of the city onto the city itself. Two meters taller than anyone in the crowd, topped with a green crown of wrought iron, plastered with the striking colors of *art nouveau* posters, *Litfasssäulen* caught the glances of city people again and again. Conceived by Ernst Litfass, a Berlin printer who received the permit to erect them in the 1850s, the pillars were designed to arrange in an orderly way the posters and notices that littered city fences and sandstone facades. Litfass thereby entered history. He died in 1874, leaving a legacy of 150 advertising pillars; by the turn of the century there were 1,500 of them, and the press welcomed municipal plans to increase their number by several hundred more.[46] Along the way, however, the original function of *Litfasssäulen* changed. The order they had once imposed on the Prussian capital had given way to disorder, as poster designers experimented with new typefaces, attention-getting layouts, and bright colors. One Berliner tried to remember the "hapless arrangements of letters," the subdued tone that had once prevailed: "And if a red patch ever disrupted this innocent harmony of white, it seemed as though the thick belly was bleeding, red blood screaming for revenge: a police notice." But the blood-red colors reserved for an extraordinary murder had long since been adopted by promoters of boot polish, variety theater, and new-age messiahs. The fabricated quality of sensation wrecked any sort of hierarchy among the items and occasions of the boulevard. As a result, Litfass' pillars came to upset the demeanor of the streets: they stood out like giant "exclamation marks,"[47] they "screamed," their "thick letters" danced a "never-ending Cancan."[48]

The "masquerade" *(Mummenschanz)* of *Litfasssäulen* offered gallery portraits of the chaos of the city.[49] To this day, the pillar remains a favorite image to depict the clashing voices of modernism.[50] For one turn-of-the-century feuilletonist, the pillars caught "the debris that otherwise floated aimlessly in the ocean of the street." Stuck between neat theater and concert notices and well-designed advertisements for shoes or chocolate less tidy scraps could be found: small "poison-green" or "bright red" rectangles promoting "nightspots with charming waitresses from Bohemia, Hungary, and Poland"; cheap-paper broadsides announcing "Germany's Collapse," the "Reichstag's Final End," or simply the wisdom

"100-Mark Reward." Four boys crowd around an
advertising pillar in this turn-of-the-century postcard.

of "Der Führer Johannes"; and (still) disconcerting police notices offering "100-Mark Reward" for information regarding
an unsolved murder. This disorder was the allure of the *Litfasssäule:* "Whoever has time and inclination," gushed the
Tageblatt, "should let himself fall into the dream of these
pillars."[51]

Journalists browsed through the metropolitan miscellany,
spinning fantasies for their readers about the private dramas
behind the public notices. "Mauritius" at the *Morgenpost*
went so far as to script a heart-wrenching tragedy out of the
single line on a posted handwritten note: "Otto H! Come back,
we found the one-hundred Mark bill in the apartment!"
Thus:[52]

As day breaks, the parents realize to their horror what happened
last night. They run anxiously to the police. One more time they

had turned the household upside down, and—look!—there the lost bill lay among the papers, messed up by a nervous father. Heartsick, the unhappy family tries the last thing available in this huge city. A few hours later, the small announcement broadcasts from the pillars. Will the desperate boy see it? Is he sick to death? Will he find courage to pull the trigger?

This sort of story became commonplace in the press. The *Lokal-Anzeiger*, for example, mentioned a handwritten notice "Kurt! Come back!" in 1899. It was Gertrude's turn in 1906: "Come back immediately. All is forgiven."[53] These notices may have been large part legend and only small part fact, but whatever their veracity, their retelling in the newspaper encouraged passersby to linger and to read the *Litfasssäulen*. Tacked onto "the last romantic herald," according to Edmund Edel, the paper scraps about ordinary people—Otto, Kurt, Gertrude—brought human interest to city streets.[54]

And by all accounts, passersby did in fact make a habit of perusing the *Litfasssäule*, forming as they did an impromptu circle of readers around the pillar:[55]

Women from the aristocracy, these shapely matrons hold lorgnettes in front of their blue eyes, and together with their slender blond daughters study the theater and opera programs; a gentleman in top hat and a light high-collared coat, his silver tipped cane under his nose, flits his eyes from the Deutsches, Lessing-, Residenz-, Wallner-, to the Friedrich-Wilhelm-Theater before resting them on the Viktoria-Theater . . . Here comes a petty-bourgeois family. It's Papa's birthday, and since pretty much all Berliners know that the best way to celebrate such an occasion is to go to the theater, he lets his wife and daughter decide between the Adolf-Ernst- and the Zentraltheater. Frau Mama is for Belle-Alliance since the streetcar connections are so convenient. . . . Several workers in blue shirts stand around as well. It is unlikely they are deciding among sixteen theaters. Maybe they're interested in the notice announcing the opening of training courses for carpenters and bricklayers. Or the large poster, unmistakable in the screaming colors of the God of War, calling up various age groups for military service? No, the pillar has other announcements: roofers, bricklayers, and plasterers are being called to union meetings.

What is so striking about this description is not simply that readers from various social stations encounter and use texts in self-revelatory ways, but the way this story identifies with the tableau style of representation. The account suggests that the city is quite plausibly and wonderfully encountered by browsing, by reading occasionals like notices, advertisements, and newspapers.

Readers browsed through the city in other ways as well. Along the busiest streets, passersby were constantly handed handbills promoting fortune-tellers, cafés, and nightclubs. A newspaper story about a "handbill" offered readers a pretext to explore the exotic services that a card reader offered and, thanks to the framing device of the handbill, rehearsed them in the motions of browsing.[56] Similar stories recalled for readers the sudden encounter with extra editions, the distracting bright colors of public posters, and the outsized advertising figures painted on exposed walls.[57] "All of Berlin is one big placard by [the illustrator] Lucian Bernhard," mused Max Brod after a visit to the city in 1911. "Doesn't the purple knight with the orange beard fall to his knees on every street corner? Don't prolific hordes of thin greyhounds, lime-green monkeys, cigar-smoking goblins, and tender Gibson girls fill the streets?"[58]

Of course, added the *Berliner Tageblatt*, "whoever doesn't have the energy to read through the bookcases of the street can find amusement in its colorful showcases." The forsaken, dangerous streets that Max Kretzer had described in his

novels were hard to locate in the geography of the big-city
newspaper. To be sure, "bread earned on the street is hard
and often mouldy," the *Berliner Tageblatt* conceded; "the
street does not nourish its guests, but it certainly does provide
generously for their entertainment." The popular press introduced Berlin as a city of windows, in the first instance of marvelous commercial display windows, but also a place that provided continuous pleasure if viewed through the newspaper's
front-page "windows." The loving attention to metropolitan
windows confirmed spectatorship as the most accessible and
dominant mode of encountering the city. Even the most ordinary windows offered viewers moving and intriguing dramas,
as the *Tageblatt*'s look behind the plateglass of a store selling
shirt collars reveals:

> A small, well-crafted automated man watches as a white collar is
> dunked into ink. Dressed in an elegant grey suit, he opens his
> mouth, moves his chin, and makes an inaudible pitch from behind
> the window pane. First the collar goes into a soap bath and when
> it emerges—imagine!—it's all clean and white. It's a scream to
> watch the man's hair stand on end; his top hat takes such a de-
> lightful little jump.

Pedestrians stopped and stared in astonishment, the *Berliner
Tageblatt* noted, making sure that readers identified with the
spectators.[59] After watching the fun three or four times, most
people moved along Friedrichstrasse, down Leipziger Strasse,
perhaps to the next set of fancifully decorated windows, a feature which earned Berlin the playful sobriquet, "City of Show
Windows."[60]

Metropolitan newspapers attentively reviewed fetching displays as a matter of course—the *Vossische Zeitung* even featured a regular column, "Schaufenster und Ladenschau."
They also loudly protested police regulations proscribing

public displays on Sundays, which left the streets looking like a disheveled *Lappenparade* (rag parade) of shuttered store fronts.[61] "People are born with a desire to gaze," explained the everyman's *Morgenpost*, yet the "people" only have Sundays "to stroll and look about," the very day of the week municipal authorities inhibited them from doing so.[62] Once these regulations lapsed in May 1910, however, the city's transformation into a magical landscape of wares was nearly complete. The show quality that characterized Berlin was made explicit during the city's "Show Window Contest," an annual promotion first organized by a local business group in September 1909. Proprietors piled their wares to the ceiling, invented amazing mechanical mannequins, and carefully dressed each window for a parade of shoppers that enthusiastic Berlin newspapers reported was three or four people deep.[63] The *Lokal-Anzeiger* even came out with a lavishly illustrated supplement to accompany the contest.[64]

The wandering viewpoint of spectators in front of shop windows encompassed the city itself. Even the most fleeting glances and nimble encounters, newspaper readers learned, offered the possibility of visual pleasure. The Berlin writer Hans Ostwald compared pedestrians to wares in a department store: crowds in the Kaiser-Passage, he exclaimed, are "as colorful as the murals and the displays of the show windows."[65] As they were watched by metropolitan newspapers and as they read and, in turn, watched themselves, Berliners easily slipped into the parts of virtuoso spectators: the widow at the suburban window, the family around the *Litfasssäule*, bystanders in front of the collar shop, passersby in the arcade. Of course, the assumed spectator whom newspapers addressed was usually male. Readers recognized the experience of browsing or being the objects of browsing:[66]

Tens of thousands pass each other. Glances meet, or pass cooly over the passing figures. There, what a wonderfully sweet creature! White cashmere, and a black feather hat on top of a rosy-fresh blond head. Ten steps further. Oh, what a proud beauty! Well-shaped, with a pair of fiery eyes underneath curls so black I imagined for a moment I was on the promenade in Seville. A half-glance to the splendid woman in the green velvet dress, then my eyes take in a slinky seventeen-year-old, slender as a reed, with eyes bright as life itself. . . . The streets fill up. Fat people and thin people and slender people and meaty people and small people and big people all glide, walk, and march past. They are well-dressed or not, and they all seem quite amused and animated.

However, the roles of men and women could be reversed, which had important implications for the different ways the paper might have been read. In a scene described by one reporter in Berlin W., a "charming turbaned beauty" on Tauentzienstrasse was flirting with one young man, but at the same time stole glances at others coming down the street. She was no different from other strollers: "they are all searching for the happiness that lies on the street!"[67]

Imagined encounters among strangers on streets and in arcades charged the city with erotic possibility. In a sketch that must have appealed to male and female readers alike, the *Morgenpost* defended these meetings and dismissed their dangers. The scene this time was set in Berlin N: "As the setting sun streaks the grey city red one fine evening in autumn, a fresh young girl makes her way through quiet neighborhood streets." A young man passes by, the eyes of two city people meet and "catch fire." All the attempts of the man to talk to the woman are fruitless, however. Despite her interest, she refuses his polite request to walk her home: "My father forbids me to make acquaintances on the street." Fear and prejudgment kept these two young people apart, but the *Morgenpost* spoke in favor of accidental big-city encounters such as this one. "We have to emphasize that with taste, intelligence, and a modicum of psychological judgment, everybody, whether male or female, should be able to decide, after a short encounter, if they are dealing with an honorable person." Too often the street was demonized, the editors concluded: "Men on the street or in the café are really not different people from the men to whom one is introduced in salons and parlors."[68] Indeed, Berlin folklore thrived on the promise of anonymous encounters. "The captain with the moustache / How he caught me in his stare," reminisced the organ grinder's song throughout the city's tenement courtyards.[69] Somewhat later, recollections of glances stolen on streetcars and subways qualified as a distinct genre among Berlin feuilletons.[70] Baudelaire, too, in one of sonnets in *Fleurs du mal*, "To a Passer-by," had drawn attention to the passions fleetingly aroused in the crowd: "I am so suddenly reborn from your swift glance." "The delight of the urban poet," Benjamin remarks, "is love—not at first sight, but at last sight."[71]

Did strangers actually exchange glances and meet? Newspaper feuilletons are clearly not reliable, but we do read in the local stories about murderous rages, lonely suicides, and marriage swindlers that the principals, often enough, had met quite by chance at a dance, in the park, or in a store. According to Max Marcuse, a Berlin doctor who investigated illegitimate pregnancies, it was the lure of metropolitan sensation which endangered young women.[72] He paraphrased the city's part in the seduction:

> At last it is closing time, and what do they have to look forward to? an impoverished home, family scenes, bedtime, and next morning's commute to work. Day in, day out, this does not add up to a very amusing week, particularly if the way to work passes by well-lit beer palaces and cafes, by theaters and concert halls.

And this in the years of sexual awakening when desire tickles every nerve. Is it surprising that girls want to enjoy the wonders of the big city on display? . . . And aren't thousands of young clerks and hundreds of students ready to take out some young thing rather than remain alone—and a prostitute isn't quite the same. . . . One fellow sweet-talks the salesgirl, accompanies her part way home, and makes a date for the next evening. Before you know it, the little girl has fallen in love. The informal "Du" and the first kiss follow. A few more dates, and she anticipates the last request with burning desire.

The doctor disapproved, of course, but nonetheless made plausible links between the dazzling plentitude of the metropolis and a heightened possibility of transgression, something which undoubtedly intrigued many more Berliners than just the unfortunate girls in Marcuse's report.

To read the newspaper was to consume the city and also to see oneself as a consumer or spectator. "Just looking" described the basic urban encounter. The shift from reader to spectator and back again was facilitated whenever the press cast the city in explicitly theatrical terms. Court proceedings were the most commonplace spectacle. What did "the season in Moabit" (the neighborhood that housed the Prussian courts) hold?[73] *BZ am Mittag* previewed the coming attractions, informing readers in November 1904 that "a sensational profiteering trial will open on Monday the 7th and should prove to disclose most astonishing revelations."[74] A slew of theatrical metaphors (tragedy, last act, main role) enlivened day-by-day coverage of trials. The performances of judges, prosecutors, and attorneys were also closely scrutinized: Landgerichtsdirektor Kanzow, for example, was "an aesthetic pleasure to watch as he playfully controlled the situation, trapping the accused in a spider's web."[75] Careful mention was always made of spectators who filled the visitors gallery, occasionally with opera glasses in hand.[76]

The overdramatized reporting at crime scenes, the flurry of extra editions, and the crowds of bystanders who inevitably gathered were also all of a piece. Events were at once choreographed by and reported in the newspaper. From time to time, crime dramas absorbed all Berliners, making the city of readers correspond very nearly to the city of spectators. When Rudolf Hennig, a suspected murderer, eluded police by escaping over the roofs of Prenzlauer Berg and stayed on the loose for weeks, *BZ* had a field day. Its front page provided minute-by-minute reports on police activities and possible sightings. Phone calls and telegrams from readers fanned a brushfire of rumors. Encouraged by a 1000-Mark reward offered by the *Morgenpost*, citizens looked sharply at their fellows on streets and streetcars, eager to nab anyone vaguely resembling Hennig or wearing his clogs or his green cap, vastly complicating the efforts of the police. As over one thousand policemen endeavored to deal with innocent suspects and locate Hennig, *BZ* sustained the comedy by publishing this imaginary "interview" with the fugitive:[77]

I spoke to [Hennig] just fifteen minutes ago. On Friedrichstrasse, right near the arcade. Since he wasn't wearing clogs or a green cap, I recognized him immediately.

"Let me ask you," I began, "isn't it a bit crazy for you to be running around Friedrichstrasse?"

He looked at me, astonished: "What do you mean? There is a policeman on every corner. What can happen to me?"

"Herr Hennig," I said, "you have it in your power to change someone's life."

"How so?" he inquired curiously.

"It is a serious decision," I continued, "an opportunity to do good which will perhaps never come again. . . . Find an obscure, low-paid detective, a family man, and introduce yourself to him. Just think of his career, his promotion. He'll be set up for life."

He shook his head.

"Herr Hennig," I raised my voice, "I know a man who has eleven living children."

He retorted: "That man can't be helped." He laughed and disappeared into the crowd.

For the full story of Hennig's crime, Berliners were better off reading the fifth page of the *Berliner Tageblatt*, which also provided reliable details about the police manhunt. But it was thanks to *BZ*'s uninterrupted and sensationalized front-page coverage that Hennig became such a popular citywide figure. Apparently, "everyone" talked about Hennig's daring escape. Quick-witted promoters sold "Hennig" postcards and "Hennig" songs and even tried to screen a "Hennig" movie. In the Scheunenviertel, delinquents mocked police by dressing like Hennig, and boys all over the city played "Catch Hennig," which resulted in the accidental shooting death of one thirteen-year-old.[78] It was typical of *BZ am Mittag* that after one breathless "Hennig-Week," the newspaper found the story tiresome and stopped reporting on it. Although briefly returning Hennig to the front pages when he was arrested five weeks later in Stettin, *BZ* quickly dropped him altogether since his "appearance shatters all preconceptions . . . Hennig has a pale, pointed face and is of medium-build; his pathetic figure simply seems to hang in his brown jacket."[79]

BZ am Mittag had the opportunity to script other shows for the city, reporting on its front pages the felonies of the *Messersticher*, a knifer who terrorized Berlin women in February 1909, and also the delightful October 1906 story of the "Hauptmann von Köpenick," in which a thoroughly unremarkable drifter bought a Prussian captain's uniform in a second-hand shop, commandeered a troop of passing soldiers, arrested the startled but compliant mayor of Köpenick, made off with 4002.37 Marks, for which he left a signed receipt, and forever amused the world with a reminder of how much Germans respected a uniform. Hennig, the anonymous knifer, and the "Hauptmann von Köpenick"—each story revealed the central elements in the newspapers' composition of the metropolis as a field of visual pleasure. The press achieved its spectatorial effects not simply by providing rich descriptions or deploying theatrical metaphors; again and again, the metropolitan newspaper reported on events as if it was watching people watch. Editors addressed and even enrolled readers as spectators. This doubled mediation made reading the newspaper much like reading about a film that depicted the news. Text was therefore first and foremost spectacle.

A NOTE ON SPECTATORS

The rapid rise in the circulation of newspapers around the turn of the century, the acquired habit of reading afternoon as well as morning papers and perusing them while commuting on streetcars or sitting in cafés, and the increasingly busy traffic in the city center provided the background for the new city type, the browser. It is clear that Berliners were using the city more deliberately and more self-indulgently. They crowded department stores, cafés on Potsdamer Platz, and the carnival grounds at Lunapark. It was the metropolitan daily papers that made the novelties of the great city available for consumption and taught their readers the ways to enjoy them. Newspapers also encouraged readers to watch the city. And there is every reason to believe that the rhetoric of the paper, which so often spoke to readers as spectators, reinforced a pleasurable and increasingly visual relation to the city. Indeed, one of the joys of reading the local paper was the very familiar staples about Sunday in the Grunewald, crowded streetcars, shopping at Wertheim, all stories which allowed readers to observe themselves.

By all accounts, the city was filled with sightseers on Saturdays and Sundays, the busiest days for the "Grosse Berliner." Metropolitan browsing was decidedly not limited to the dandy or the aesthete. The overwhelmingly working-class population of Berlin participated as eagerly in the rhythms of urban spectatorship as did middle-class families. In the Wilhelmine era urban workers prized their Sunday suit of clothes, which they wore in public on weekends and holidays (and strike days). "On any fine Sunday in spring," reported the *Morgenpost,* "what you will see if you wander through the Eastside, the Southside, or through the streets of Rixdorf and Rummelsburg" (the proletarian quarters of Berlin), are "men wearing festive clothes. Their suits are not always the best or the newest, but they clearly indicate the desire to elevate oneself above the quotidian by appearing neat and clean." Indeed, fancy clothes made it easy to mistake a bricklayer's apprentice for an "assistant judge" or a "lieutenant in the reserves." "One thing is clear," the paper concluded, "the blurring of visible distinctions between classes represents a real step toward democracy."[80] (Evidence suggests that those who could not afford suitable clothes in fact preferred to stay at home.)[81] With their bowler hats and dark jackets, workers, merchants, and employees increasingly constituted an outwardly undifferentiated public of spectators.

The itinerary of Berliners was not so different from that of tourists. Guidebooks and incidental newspaper reports all indicate that what attracted visitors were distinctively metropolitan as well as grandly imperial sights: the busy streets, the department stores, and the elevated *Stadtbahn*. Everyone's destination is "Potsdamerplatz, Leipziger Strasse, and Friedrichstadt," the *Morgenpost* reported one Sunday in April.[82] The guidebook *Berlin für Kenner* returned visitors to the same downtown geography again and again: "Dinner at Kempinski" (day 1); "lunch at Rheingold on Potsdamer Platz," "coffee at the Piccadilly," and, at night, "strolling" around Friedrich-strasse (day 2); "Apollotheater" (day 3); "movie theater on Potsdamer Platz" (day 5); "stroll through Friedrich- and Leip-ziger Strasse" and "Wertheim" (day 6); "dinner on Potsdamer Platz" (day 7); "coffee in the Fürstenhof or at Piccadilly on Potsdamer Platz" (day 8). "This unbelievable movement of people, lights, and cars," the guidebook added, "this is Berlin!"[83] Guidebooks thus recommended that tourists adopt the *Bummelschritt* (stroller's pace) that Berliners themselves had expressly designated.[84]

What intrigued sightseers in particular were shop windows, which was precisely why regulations requiring stores to draw curtains on Sundays grated so. The city's museums and impe-rial sights could not compare to those in Paris or London. The Siegesallee, the stone parade of Hohenzollerns that was the kaiser's contribution to metropolitan culture, "is nice and white, but you can't walk through it more than three times a day," and coffee at Bauer's, sausages at Aschinger's—"well, that doesn't fill the day either," satirized the *Berliner Tage-blatt*. "What else to do?"—naturally, "a stroll through the great department stores and a review of the display windows on Friedrich- and Leipziger Strasse."[85]

Wertheim certainly figured on any boy's or girl's treasure map to Berlin. Young Hans Fallada and his friend Hans Fötsch would walk all the way from Luitpoldstrasse in Schöneberg, along Martin-Luther-Strasse, across the Land-wehrkanal, up Potsdamer Strasse, to Wertheim. Flanking "a corpulent lady," the two boys always managed to slip in and elude the long-armed doorman who was instructed to keep un-accompanied children out. Once inside, Fallada and Fötsch explored

the book displays, of course, and the toy department. But what I liked best was the relatively empty linen department . . . I loved the sight and smell of the stiff red, blue, and striped bed ticking; I loved the big crates with a glass front which displayed the various feathers, from the finest eiderdown to roughly spliced chicken feathers. It made my day to watch that big machine clean the bed feathers and send feathers and dust in a turning, dancing swirl.[86]

The two boys were certainly not alone. Wertheim was a tourist attraction from the day it opened in 1894. On the two Sundays before Christmas, the so-called *silberne Sonntag* and *goldene Sonntag*, when prohibitions on Sunday shopping were lifted, the "Massenwanderung" and "Menschengetümmel" of gawking Berliners in the city center grew so dense that police occasionally had to cordon off Leipziger Strasse and temporarily close the department store. "Packed shoulder to shoulder, crowds pushed, bag and baggage, up the street to catch a glimpse of the wonderful, fairy-tale illumination of the blazing show windows," reported the *Lokal-Anzeiger* in December 1910.[87] Even on a cold and wet November day, before the Christmas rush, "well over one-thousand people" could be counted strolling among the shops and peering in the curiosity cabinets of the crooked Kaiser-Passage arcade.[88] Every year thousands of Berliners also took an "Ausstellungsbummel" (exhibition stroll)—the term is *BZ*'s—to the annual automobile show (25,000 on a rainy Sunday, 4 November 1906), the sports convention (40,000 on Sunday, 28 April 1907), or the agricultural exhibition (exactly 118,229 on Sunday, 17 June 1906).[89]

Nighttime illumination completed the transformation of Berlin into a fantastic display. The urban proscenium at Potsdamer Platz hovered above onlookers—"advertisements soar up to and hang over the roofs," wrote Robert Walser.[90] As Karl Aram stepped out of Potsdamer Bahnhof, from the roof across the street, "a thick, blinding burst of light shot into my eyes, smashing into me like a grenade."[91] The effect was disorienting, but thrilling. On special occasions, the municipality and the chamber of commerce worked together to illuminate Friedrichstadt. The most famous attempt to light up Berlin and reproduce the city as a series of sheer surface effects occurred in 1928, but Berliners enjoyed winter light shows already before the war. Spectators crowded the main streets in February 1906.[92]

> Building after building was ablaze in Leipziger Strasse, in Friedrichstrasse, and Unter den Linden. Once the Bengal lights were illuminated on Leipziger Platz, on the Gendarmenmarkt, from the Lehrter Bahnhof, Brandenburger Tor, and the Rathaus, the sky turned red as if it had been set on fire by a gigantic torch. Red and green flames burst into the night out of the eight balconies of the Reichstag, which shone bright as day.

The city was also illuminated on the occasion of the kaiser's birthday, 27 January. Well before the 1920s, the decade so much associated with speculation and ballyhoo, the garish spectacle of promoters and consumers, tourists and browsers, had captured the sober Reichshauptstadt: the residence of the Hohenzollerns, well-built garrison for their armies, center of Prussia. What emerged was a distinctive municipal map on which Friedrichstrasse, Leipziger Strasse, Potsdamer Platz, the Tiergarten, and Tauentzienstrasse constituted the main thoroughfares and which showed the locations of Moabit, the Kaiser-Passage, and department stores, cafés, and theaters. By contrast, the imperial city, from the Stadtschloss *unter den Linden* to the Brandenburger Tor, faded almost completely from view.

A QUESTION OF CURIOSITY

The Reichshauptstadt faded almost, but not completely from view, for the all-Berlin public of browsers and spectators came

under repeated attack whenever the Reich attempted to recast
the metropolis into a straight-lined imperial parade ground.
Prussian law had traditionally been hostile to the idle flâneur.
The Lustgarten, for example, the landscaped square between
Schinkel's Altes Museum and the castle, was reserved exclusively for officers until the beginning of the nineteenth century. And in the reactionary pre-1848 period, the King of
Prussia went so far as to prohibit the leisurely habit of
smoking on Unter den Linden. Nearly a century later, bourgeois observers continued to chafe at the king's insistence on
laying out the big boulevards and squares in the newly built
Westend as parade routes first and commercial thoroughfares
second.[93] If nothing else, the names of schools, hospitals, and
streets served to remind Berliners each day that it was a king
and emperor rather than a parliament or cabinet that deter-
mined the future of the nation. "There is a Kaiser-Allee, a
Friedrichsplatz, a Friedrichshain, a Friedrichsberg, and a
Friedrichsstrasse, a Kaiserin-Augusta-Strasse, a Königin-
Augusta-Strasse, a Kaiser-Passage, a Kaiser-Wilhelms-, a
Karl-August-Platz. You can find a Königsstrasse, a Neue
Königsstrasse, a Königsplatz, a Königsallee, a Königstor, a
Königsbrücke, a Königschaussee . . . And they say that there
are Germans who supposedly don't know the history of the
Hohenzollerns!" joked Jules Huret.[94] In this spirit Traugott
von Jagow, the police chief of Berlin who served at the kaiser's
pleasure, insisted on treating boulevards as corridors of imperial power in which the ambitions and amusements of citizens
had to be closely regulated.

Jagow's conception of Berlin as an imperial backdrop obstructed the free movement of browsers. Parades and other
court ceremonies took the streets for the exclusive use of the
court and often left the city literally sliced in halves. Speaking
in the name of metropolitans and their business, the major

newspapers fumed at police orders which closed the main thoroughfares of the city for hours at a time. "Yesterday" [6 November 1905, the day the King of Spain arrived to visit Wilhelm II] "the police had another fun day. They could cordon off, cordon off to their heart's desire." On this occasion, Potsdamer Platz as well as Unter den Linden were off limits: "Everyone who was not sitting in a royal carriage or did not have a feathery plume stuck on his helmet found it easier getting to the North Pole than reaching Kranzler's from the north or the Viktoria-Cafe from the south."[95] (Revealingly, for *BZ am Mittag*, what hurt most was that boulevard cafés had been rendered inaccessible by the emperor's parades.) A few years later, when the King of Sweden came to visit, court ceremony appropriated the bridge over the Landwehrkanal at Belle Alliance Platz for an entire Monday morning, blocking traffic on Friedrichstrasse and disrupting a dozen streetcar lines. For bourgeois observers, it was inconceivable that commercial traffic could not have been permitted to pass in stages between the parade groups.[96] The police even assaulted individual pedestrians who tried to cross the parade route when the street was empty, incidents which created a public scandal.[97]

Evidently not everyone liked a parade. The idea that "all Berlin" lined up to watch the kaiser *BZ* found preposterous; most people were kept unwillingly behind cordons. "It would be more accurate to say half-Berlin, since it was mainly the finer sex that was represented among those who waited for hours and willingly let themselves be pushed and shoved in order to catch glimpses of a little bit of silk, lace, or gold embroidery." Long waits and interrupted vantages made watching imperial spectacles on Unter den Linden rather different from browsing at Wertheim.[98] And officious ceremony diminished the joy of those Berliners who came willingly. "Only once they have been removed quite some distance from . . . the kaiser can the hearts of spectators beat faster at the sight of white pants on parade," quipped the *Berliner Tageblatt*.[99] The press was quick to point out that frequent use of cordons not only blocked traffic but inhibited watching. The Reichshauptstadt repeatedly obstructed the views of even royalist Berliners.

Police attempted to regulate the rights of citizens on the streets in other respects. For Jagow, electric lighting on Behrenstrasse was too bright and street noise too loud. If the street regulations he drafted were put into effect, Mosse's editors satirized, police would have to confiscate the bells on Bolle's milk trucks, proscribe newspaper vendors from calling out the evening edition in anything but a whisper, and require officers and soldiers to parade on tiptoe. What "would happen to a city in which one could throw nothing out of the windows, neither dust nor noise?" the paper asked, a question that revealed a rather remarkable conception of the metropolis as a colorful, confusing, contradictory place that frustrated regulation from above.[100]

Streets belonged to citizens and would therefore be littered with the dusty, noisy, and even offensive business of citizens, including those Social Democratic citizens whose right to march for electoral reform Ullstein and Mosse (though not Scherl) consistently defended.[101] What really galled boulevard opinion, however, was less Jagow's opposition to Socialist street demonstrations than his broader contention that "the exclusive function of the streets is to serve traffic," and his official warning to all street-bound "curiosity-seekers" in a notice posted on *Litfasssäulen* throughout Berlin in February 1910, just days before a scheduled Socialist march. Jagow thereby shifted the terms of the political debate from questions of public order, which had concentrated on the Social Democrats, to the right of any and all citizens to wander the streets. "Citizens build the streets, but have no right to them, on the contrary, the police determines who may use them," concluded the *Berliner Illustrirte* increduously.[102] It was precisely the rights of "curiosity-seekers" to walk about as they pleased that the boulevard press defended most energetically; indeed, most of Jagow's "blood-red" proclamations had been ripped down just a few hours after they had been posted.[103] Metropolitan newspapers spoke out loudly for the city-browsers, decrying police cordons and other imperial obstacles, defending the disorder of the boulevard, and even pleading the legitimacy of casual *Strassenbekanntschaften*, the street acquaintances that fathers warned against. On the political front, the metropolitan press actively engaged imperial authorities and offered its vision of the metropolis instead of the imperial capital: a place in which city people appeared as consumers, spectators, and strangers, and encountered the city as a warehouse of possibility and pleasure.

5 ILLEGIBLE TEXTS

"Strolling" *(flanieren)*, Franz Hessel explained, "is a way of reading the street whereby faces, displays, show windows, cafés, tram tracks, automobiles, and trees all become . . . letters which compose the sentences and pages in an always-changing book."[1] Heaps of words and piles of goods circulated in the metropolis and could be idly browsed, but could they be read and interpreted as elements of a coherent story? Hessel, a Weimar-era flâneur, thought that their meanings were necessarily fleeting and provisional. Other Berliners also found the words in the street jumbled and the sentences and pages they composed unintelligible. Some advertisements confused turn-of-the-century viewers. "On that building over there," one sightseer pointed across Potsdamer Platz, "huge electric letters crawl up, one after the other . . . then the letters crawl back down to the ground with the same haste, even before the eye has been able to make out the word that all this creeping and crawling is supposed to spell out." Signs along Leipziger Strasse and Friedrichstrasse were just as unreadable. "Words appear phantomlike and disappear again, red, yellow, green, mottled, completely mixed up," a confusion that extended to the city itself: "the whistle of the policeman shrieks across the square . . . the streetcar screeches along the curved tracks." The commotion of metropolitan words insinuated the unsettling confusion of metropolitan sensations, which amounted to "a genuine *Höllensabbat*" (witches' sabbath). What made Berlin so hellish was that the "red, yellow, green . . . poison to the eyes" did not simply offend but actually incapacitated the senses.[2]

Essayist Joseph Roth reacted with likeminded censure to the unmonitored stream of words in the city. "Take a look at a *Litfasssäule*," he wrote soon after arriving in Berlin in the early 1920s: "Every day an unbidden motley crew [*Unzahl Unberufener*] discusses the Hereafter, God, Philosophy, Infinity."[3] Until this "Unzahl Unberufener" was stopped, Berlin's *Litfasssäulen* would offer nothing but a "random" assortment of notices—"magicians next to fly trainers"—which left readers bewildered rather than uplifted or informed. The city Roth perused was not intelligible because it was not edited according to any hierarchy of values.

Pages and pages of billboards, placards, and signs also covered the facades of city buildings. Advertising murals, three- or four-stories high, looked down on passersby, offering gigantic Manoli cigarettes, shoe wax, or razor blades, at once turning inside out and enlarging the private universe of the consumer. The metropolitan outlook did not heed distinctions between private and public or trivial and important, and placed the effects of each realm side-by-side-by-side. Any turn-of-the-century photograph of Friedrichstrasse revealed how little room there was to put up even one more placard: "Each [store] with its own display, its own illumination, its own mechanical noisemaker . . . appears to step out of the entryway, to scream at passersby, and to forcibly pull him inside"—a "bewildering mess."[4]

The indifferent veneer of advertising went so far as to impede the view of many of Berlin's landmarks or block it altogether. It gave the city a radically improvised look, which frustrated historical reading and orientation. Pushing against the "Linden" on two sides and surrounding totally the splendid eighteenth-century Gendarmenmarkt, metropolitan commerce steadily stripped the city center of its aura of architectural venerability. Plastered over the old buildings, advertisements overturned old values, a problem that curators frequently raised, though they did so in vain. Indeed, the very idea of value appeared questionable. From all sides, advertisers rushed to replace existing products with newer, better substitutes. At the same time, real-estate developers tore down elegant Frederician palaces along the Tiergarten in order to put up office buildings and retail stores. There was no better example of the "decline of distinction" that Simmel first recognized in modern Berlin than this relentless process of commercialization. Toward the end of the nineteenth century, a mature money economy had created the conditions of unmanaged exchange that aristocratic notions of refinement had hitherto excluded.[5]

City sounds were as incoherent as city words were disordered, producing for any number of metropolitans a cacophony which disrupted clear lines of thought. The metropolis assaulted the ear of philosopher Theodor Lessing:[6]

Hammers roar, machines rumble, the wagons of butchers and the carts of bakers roll past the house before daybreak. Countless bells wail uninterruptedly. Thousands of doors are slammed shut. Thousands of hungry people haggle and scream, they scream and argue beside our very ears and fill the streets of the city with their business and their trade. The telephone rings. The automobile horn honks. The streetcar screeches. A train rolls over the iron bridge. Straight through my aching head, straight through our finest thoughts.

The "letters" Hessel collected on his city walks, the "random assortment" of public notices that Roth condemned, the indiscriminate advertising on Friedrichstrasse, and "thousands" of disorderly screams described a city flooded with words in constant motion, haphazardly rearranging and recombining themselves. The patterns and contrasts that had so fascinated city viewers and allowed them to discern various metropolitan settings could also disorient and bewilder. There were many different responses to the surplus of city texts, and the analysis that follows, which explores how writing about the city enhanced the fugitive nature of the city, should not be considered any more authoritative than that of other metropolitan encounters. Indeed, the problem of legibility underscores the plurality of readings in the word city. Words, sentences, and texts could all be interpreted in myriad ways. As a narrated form, with heteroglossic insertions and daily editing and a basically unstable tension between imposed design and self-interpretation, the word city was open to readers from any number of entryways and along any number of causeways.

As I see it, the act of reading the entire city as a complete work was overwhelmed by the larger, ongoing process of just rereading and rewriting. Again and again, texts interrupted and obliterated each other. Every attempt to create a legible description ended by compounding overall syntactical confusion. Even as pieces of detail remained clearly in place, the newspapers' focus on the endless series of abrasions—the differences, movements, and surprises that broke apart the metropolitan surface—had the effect over time of rendering the city chaotic. Big-city dailies aggravated the crisis of meaning by fastening on what was extraordinary and astonishing about each day, reproducing the clash of urban sensations in adventurous front-page layouts, and miming the speed by which impressions appeared and disappeared with late-breaking morning, midday, and evening editions. Words themselves were legible, but, often enough, the sentences and pages they formed proved to be unintelligible. What seemed to be missing was an encompassing or identifiable sense of design.

The illegible city is central to twentieth-century modernism which disputed the transparency with which eighteenth-century observers had viewed the world. The turbulence of rapidly alternating impressions challenged the nexus between "Sehen" (seeing) and "Erkennen" (recognized) and thereby represented an assault on sensibility. While it was easy to participate in this new urban world of flickering images and circulating things, it was much harder to find one's way or retain a sense of permanence or stability. Capitalist circulation and technological innovation, Dana Brand points out, lead to "a surplus of signifiers and a dearth of signification" in the city.[7] This uncertainty about the possibility of seeing clearly or representing authoritatively is the foundation of modernism; it is also the reason that the city became such a congenial setting for modernist experimentation. Avant-garde writers at the turn of the century, for example, transformed concrete metropolitan elements such as streets, squares, and windows into purely mnemonic devices, encounters which splintered the asphalt city into innumerable dreamscapes and shattered a knowable, socially recognizable geography. The most famous version of such an interiorized city is the Paris that fills Rainer

Maria Rilke's *The Notebooks of Malte Laurids Brigge* (1910). However, the proliferation of private cities enforced a melancholy sense of disconnectedness. An emphasis on fluctuation and contingency left the metropolis without shared landmarks or common history. The word city was in danger of becoming illegible because it had taken on such inconvertible forms.[8]

The revelation that there was no syllabus of texts to read the modern city in an orderly way is also at the heart of Alfred Döblin's *Berlin Alexanderplatz*. "Layering, piling, rolling, pushing . . . serial production on an assembly line"—these were the collage techniques Döblin identified by which writing could be true to the metropolis. To maintain the fiction of the red thread of narration that made its way through the urban labyrinth would "cut through," as Döblin scholar Harald Jähner puts it, "the real connections among events and would obstruct the free play of associations."[9] Excessive details, interrupting voices, and eye-catching inscriptions demonstrated "the priority of the principle of contradiction without resolution." Döblin's city is a place that challenges the entire project of narration and representation.[10]

The mediated spectacle of the city fascinated modernists like Döblin and provided them with the layered roominess in which to explore the contingency of order and the discontinuity of narrative. But the very disconnectedness of these inconclusive versions of a purportedly real city also prompted discussions about the "unreal" nature of the print media and the importance of maintaining distinctions between trivial sensations and consequential events. The big-city newspaper quickly found itself at the center of Wilhelmine debates about dangerous voices on the streets, which supposedly threatened the moral hygiene and political order of the monarchy. Without closer regulation of reading and writing, the argument went, the effect of the mass-circulation press was to disorient and mislead city readers. What is striking about this debate is the extent to which both modernists and their critics agreed that the press had indeed created an extraordinary city of words. If the former reveled in the mutability of the real, the latter condemned its persistent falsification.

The disagreement, then, revolved around the nature of perception. Did the city exist apart from the word city? And if so, could the word cities composed in the newspapers be revised to conform more nearly to the built cities? These questions anticipated aspects of the much more focused debate over mass culture in the second half of the twentieth century. But early detractors of the boulevard press generally confined their commentary to the threat posed to cultural authority. They accepted the nonhierarchical, even subversive aspects of the media spectacle, an issue which has become the most contested point in culture studies today. Left more or less unconsidered was the connection between metropolitan spectacle and commodity capitalism, to which Walter Benjamin, Guy Debord, and others have since drawn attention. In this later view, city people were far from disorderly, and they entered the public sphere more and more in the passive roles of docile consumers who were enthralled by the spectacle of commodities and fashions. This massive transformation, which occurred after the turn of the century, obscured and consequently subordinated in social life other, more fractious metropolitan relationships —between tenants and landlords, debtors and creditors, employees and employers—and thus gave broad cultural legitimacy to the capitalist economy.[11] However, this very neat portrayal of mass culture has never been completely persuasive. Students of "social history from below" have indicated how emancipating and self-revelatory the culture of display could be, particularly to previously marginalized groups such as women or ethnic minorities, and at the same time, how unstable and destructive capitalist exchange had in fact become.[12] Likewise, it is the corrosive nature of commercial exchange that captured the imagination of both German modernists and German conservatives in the years before World War I. Their readings of the word city emphasized the instability and even the unintelligibility of the metropolis. Where the two groups parted company was in the welcome they extended to this leveling process.

THE DISHEVELED WORD CITY

Jacob van Hoddis's 1911 poem "Weltende," which opened this book, pointed to the lively part the press played in fashioning our precarious world. We know because "we read"—van Hoddis says parenthetically—about shinglers plunging, tides rising, and locomotives dropping. The disheveled universe the poet implies is the one headlined on the front pages. If we did not read the newspaper, our surroundings would not appear nearly as astonishing or apocalyptic. What van Hoddis draws attention to is the way description turns event into spectacle.

Roland Barthes made a similar connection between *faits divers*, random newspaper items like those van Hoddis recounts, and a view of the world in which the disharmonious, the contingent, and the precarious stand out. "'The Palais de Justice has just been cleaned,'" Barthes notes. The cleaning itself is insignificant, he explains, but cleaned "'for the first time in a century.' That becomes a *fait-divers*" which teases the reader by providing information as astonishment, coincidence, or paradox. To report that "a judge vanishes in Pigalle" or a "police chief kills his wife," Barthes argues, is "to preserve at the very heart of contemporary society an ambiguity of the rational and the irrational, of the intelligible and the unfathomable."[13]

The front page operated in a world of *faits divers* by presenting an eventful newsday each and every day. Newspapers have their origins in the seventeenth century as fascinating reports about faraway events. Hometown matters were ignored because they were known to readers. Even when they expanded their local coverage, newspapers continued to flourish through contrasting the known and the unknown, the expected and the astonishing, this valley and the deep blue sea. They "see only the New, the Unknown, the Rare, the Heroic, the Disrupted, the Wonderous, the Criminal through the eyeglasses of the Old, the Known, the Prosaic, the Usual, the Average . . . that is to say [they] see everything in contrast."[14] By their very nature, then, as the eyeglasses of the marvelous, newspapers reported on a world that was not uniform or predictable.

It was this daily argument against coherence that liberal minds found so intolerable. In the years before World War I, the unmistakable ascendancy of mass culture—movies, variety shows, and especially tabloids—prompted an extensive debate about cultural authority.[15] Mass-circulation newspapers posed the real possibility that readers would be left to cobble together a worldview from a variety of unauthoritative sources. Under these conditions of ongoing improvisation, readers could entertain all sorts of irrational and subversive ideas and, as a result, endanger the rational order that liberals cherished. At stake was not so much political stability or even moral well-being, which police censorship might have been able to enforce, but the stability and organization of meaning itself.

Turn-of-the-century critics were especially vexed by the way mass media seemed to rewrite the observable world, turning it inside out, garbling the ordinary into the extraordinary. The result was as baneful as the most incendiary political tract or pornographic postcard. "Certain newspapers in

the big city," explained one observer in 1906, two years after
the appearance of *BZ am Mittag*, "cultivate sensation as a
genre and thereby paint a picture of life that does not correspond to reality . . . they describe how a perfectly decent
virgin meets and then seduces the friend of her fiancé, they detail the suicide of a bon vivant on his honeymoon, they depict
the interior thoughts of morphine addicts, burglars, and baby
killers as if the world was populated only with this sort."[16]
Even before the war years made certain that each day had its
share of sensational and battle-scarred events, bold-faced
headlines and extra editions proliferated and gleaned the most
astonishing and unprecedented items from among incoming
telegrams, sports finals, and police blotters. This lack of dis-
crimination disturbed critics accustomed to a hierarchy of important events which only occasionally merited emphasis.[17]
According to a lead article in the industry's trade journal, *Der
Zeitungs-Verlag*, front-page layout should accurately reflect
the political temperature; a responsible newspaper should
therefore maintain its composure in the face of all but the most
eventful news.[18]

To the critics, the fashionable metropolitan layouts in *BZ
am Mittag* had the deleterious effect of needlessly agitating
readers day after day. "Lines and pictures disrupt the text,"
Hans Traub complained in 1928: "The human eye is deflected
from its natural setting and is 'caught'" by the "eyecatching"
elements of modern layout.[19] With its Cubist-like design, the
front page impaired natural sight. Similar charges were also
leveled before World War I, when sensation-mongering newspapers were repeatedly assailed for being "disquieting."

A daily diet of headlines and exclamation marks threatened
to corrupt readers by leading them into a fabricated landscape
of the extraordinary. "How are people supposed to come to
the right decisions and do the right thing," asked one of the

leading liberals, Wilhelm Foerster, in 1910, "if minds are constantly informed about the abnormal, which on close inspection only composes a small part of what happens in the world, and if, as a result, judgments are made according to misleading and often abnormal conclusions?"[20] According to Foerster, the "real" world had been rendered unintelligible by the big-city newspaper, although he implied that more responsible journalism would clarify matters and thereby lead readers to the "right decisions." A few years earlier, the Social Democratic critic Jakob Julius David made the same point with a different metaphor. The world in the modern newspaper was too loud and had therefore become inaudible.[21] The boulevard newspaper distorted the world beyond recognition by making readers' surroundings seem inordinately precarious, endangered, and strange. It is striking how closely these charges corresponded to van Hoddis's insight about modern reading and twentieth-century apocalypse, although the poet was thrilled with this disorder whereas the liberal was appalled.

All newspapers contributed to the crisis of realist representation by treating long-term processes as isolated events. The habit of reading more newspapers and proportionally fewer books fragmented nineteenth-century lines of perception. "Unlike the linear development of a plot or an argument in the book," suggests Donald Lowe in his study of bourgeois perception, "the concurrent reporting of news from different parts of the world made newspapers a mosaic of unrelated events." The reader's "perception of the present became more disconnected," particularly since more and more news items—fully three out of four by 1906, according to one scholarly analysis of German papers—were published as a single episode without any follow up in subsequent editions.[22] At the same time, the intellectual fashion at the turn of the century of writing small essays, impressions, and aphorisms presented the public with a diversity of points of view, augmenting the number of subjective, playful, and questioning voices at the expense of authoritative ones. *Kleinkunst* was essentially kaleidoscopic.

Articles in the metropolitan dailies were generally not moored to any context or connected to similar stories on previous or subsequent days. Only the momentary, the *Augenblick*, was present on the front page. As a result, the newspaper appeared to contract time to the instant and to erase everything else. In the half-century between 1856 and 1906, the proportion of articles that reported on events that had occurred within the previous twenty-four hours increased from 11 to 95 percent.[23] Obviously, this dramatic change was the result of technical innovations in the transmission of news. But telegraphs and telephones only facilitated, they did not themselves create the newspaper's relentless topicality. By the beginning of the twentieth century, national newspapers appeared every day of the week and some, like the *Berliner Lokal-Anzeiger* or the *Frankfurter Zeitung*, published three daily editions. Large press empires such as Mosse and Ullstein in Berlin offered separate morning, afternoon, and evening newspapers plus extra editions. (This appetite for current news reached its apogee in 1914; after that year the mounting costs of paper limited what had often amounted to nearly "live" coverage.) By not respecting continuity and by allowing the past to nearly disappear from view, the newspaper had the effect of fragmenting time into pieces of an ever-changing present. In the wake of this "triumph of simultaneity," the lasting impression for the reader was constant fluctuation.[24]

Big-city newspapers boasted of their completely up-to-date, all-new editions. Journalism's romance with speed all but banished any item more than a day old from newspaper pages. Proud to be the "most up-to-date newspaper," *BZ am Mittag* would not report the news that had occurred the day before, after the paper had come out. "From the beginning . . . *BZ* reported on only the newest news," explained one Ullstein editor.[25] In a famous poster plastered on Berlin's *Litfasssäulen* in 1913, *BZ am Mittag* promoted itself as "the fastest newspaper in the world:"

12:10—First quotation of stock prices in the Berlin exchange.

12:12—The quotations are telephoned into the offices of *BZ am Mittag*.

12:14—Last news telephoned into the composing room of *BZ am Mittag*.

12:15—Presstime. The last page of *BZ* is laid out. The page matrices are stamped on the Hercules presses.

12:16—The plates are poured.

12:17—The plates are attached to the cylinders of the rotary presses. *BZ am Mittag* is in print.

12:18—Distribution begins. The huge parking lot fills with delivery trucks, automobiles, motorcycles and bikes.

Only eight minutes have elapsed from the arrival of the last news to the distribution of the first copies in Berlin.

The rush to put out the paper did not stop at the pressroom. If vendors did not receive *BZ* by 2 o'clock, they could not sell it by 4, when the first evening papers appeared. At noon, divisions of motorcyclists and bicyclists assembled in the courtyard of the Ullsteinhaus on Kochstrasse ready to hurry *BZ* throughout the city. "Pale guys with windchapped faces and balloon caps," the newspaper bicyclists quickly became familiar city sights, modern-day versions of older Berlin types such as *Eckensteher* (day laborers) and *Schusterjungen* (cobblers' apprentices). Ullstein's fastest pedalers even found fame and fortune on Berlin's bicycle tracks, and thousands of spectators turned out for the annual race that *BZ* sponsored among newspaper bicyclists during the Weimar years.[26] From the beginning, speed was the watchword at *BZ am Mittag*, and it was the nearly "live" coverage of news that city readers found so appealing. Speed became a valued commodity as newspapers made up their front pages with a litter of late-breaking telegrams, rushed extra editions into the streets more often than necessary, or predated editions so that *Der Montag* appeared on Sunday, *Nachtausgabe* in the late afternoon, and *12-Uhr-Blatt* already at 11 o'clock. "To be a journalist," concluded Ernst Wallenberg, *BZ am Mittag*'s editor-in-chief in the 1920s, "means to internalize tempo." The only way to put out a paper was "push and shove, again and again."[27]

Yet the mechanical and organizational mastery that produced the paper every day at presstime was dismissed as "black magic" (Peter de Mendelssohn) by its detractors, who found that the newspaper's obsession with speed invited superficiality and unaccountability. The pressure to sell denied the boulevard paper the time to ponder the consequence or context of news. According to Karl Bücher, only an editor of a "subscription newspaper" with long-term subscribers rather than impulsive buyers was able to "educate and inform his readership and steer public opinion to make the right choice."[28] Mass-circulation newspapers, by contrast, were assailed repeatedly for catering to the fashions rather than enlightening the minds of their huge readership. The question was whether editors abandoned analysis and reflection when they filled the front pages with telegrams and telephone reports, all written up in a clipped syntax and exuding the "glare of the present."[29] Telegrams, published with increasing frequency because they designated the newspaper's topicality, created wholly isolated events that lacked explanatory context.[30] The desire to include as much late-breaking news as possible also forced editors to cut, cut, and cut, red-pencil strokes that resound through any description of the newspaper business. Short articles and short sentences enhanced the breathless and incomplete nature of news.

The scene condemned readers as well as editors; unregulated browsing aggravated the sins of unregulated writing. The bold headlines and tabloid layouts encouraged already entrenched bad habits of metropolitans to read cursorily. By glancing, browsing, and skipping through the paper, readers had become dilettantes and thereby slipped the authority of writers and educators. Perusing newspapers, smoking cigarettes instead of cigars, and drinking beers at Aschinger's, where the bottled-beer merchant (and later Foreign Minister) Gustav Stresemann reported that "the constant hurrying and scurrying, coming and going, barely leaves anyone time to even sit—one downs a beer standing up and with a glance at the watch rushes on"—Berliners felt completely in the thrall of speed.[31]

In the liberal ideal world, newspapers were to be the grand institutions of mass enlightenment. Not only were journalists supposed to provide readers with expert commentary and surefooted guidance, but the sobriety and length of their essays lent reading a pace and method that tended to honor the authorities of high culture. In the twentieth century, however, the patrician republic of readers disintegrated. Critics repeatedly lamented the loss of the thoughtful reader. In contrast to an allegedly more wholesome past, city people began to read less attentively and more promiscuously, moving quickly from one article to the next, riffing through the pages, merely glancing at the paper on the streetcar. Subscription papers, which were usually read at home and had a less agitated front page, might be read more carefully, but even these, observers admitted, had adopted the tone of the competition.[32]

That newspapers were disposed of so quickly seemed to confirm the cursory way they had been read. The perishable nature of written words suggested how unstable and merely transitory their significance had become. "The black letters of the newspaper are still damp with the sweat of the composer," noted Bernhard von Brentano in the 1920s, when "readers have already finished and thrown it on the ground."[33] With up-to-date evening, late-night, and early-morning editions, the potential readership of any given paper evaporated within a matter of hours, whereas in the eighteenth or early nineteenth century, newspapers retained value for several weeks.[34] In their disposable form, modern newspapers resembled other street texts, handbills, advertisements, and *Litfasssäulen* notices, mere fragments that failed to provide a lasting or coherent image of the city.

The crisis of reading that critics deplored was part of a larger crisis of cultural authority at the beginning of the twentieth century. The interior and hallucinatory voices of modernism, Belle Epoque's enchantment with primitive and "Oriental" cultures, and the alienation of urban proletarians from middle-class values challenged the uniform perspective of liberalism. Hierarchies of value and standards of judgment no longer enjoyed public consensus. New readers, new styles of reading, and new contents upset the liberal literary "republic."[35] In the face of this shock of pluralism, energetic attempts were made to re-regulate reading and writing.

The most serious attempt at regulation was the effort to license journalists in the same way as doctors or lawyers. "In every profession one has to fulfill exact requirements," noted the kaiser in 1906; "except the journalist, who neither has to study nor take final examinations." Wilhelm II had, of course, suffered the sharp criticism of the press, but his frustration had a long pedigree. Already Richard Wagner had chided journalists for their lack of university training.[36] Even *Schaubühne*, a forum for the theatrical avant-garde, excoriated journalists as "sterile parasites" and "foggy brains" who made up for a lack of education with "ein Notizbuch oder einen Zettelkasten"—with hastily jotted scribblings or academic pedantry.[37] The repeated emphasis on lack of education signaled considerable frustration with journalists for defying intellectual authority and thus threatening social values, a criticism that spoke in the name of a vanishing high-culture consensus.

The issue of licensing journalists divided the industry throughout the Wihelmine and Weimar periods, although most observers agreed that it was desirable for reporters to have some university education. The more ambiguous suggestions for certifications of "moral" health indicated the deep fears that a polyphonic press had generated, but these offered little practical guidance to editors.[38] Newspaper publishers also tried to promote industry standards, but they did so by simply excluding from their trade group the unwelcome tabloid press (until 1901), and writing off the thousands of city readers who "can't be fed enough sensationalization."[39]

In the end, self-regulation was successful only by acts of commission rather than omission. On the eve of World War I, each of the three press empires in Berlin offered the public a sober newspaper of opinion. August Scherl, who had offended the literary establishment when he published the mass-circulation *Lokal-Anzeiger* in 1883, twenty years later founded the loss-leader *Der Tag*, which published high-brow feuilleton and commentary. Mosse consistently won the accolades of educated readers for the well-written *Berliner Tageblatt*, and Ullstein, publisher of Berlin's most popular newspaper, the *Morgenpost*, felt it necessary in 1913 to acquire the small but venerable *Vossische Zeitung*, which indicated its stately eighteenth-century origins with the cumbersome "by appointment to his Majesty" subtitle, "Königlich privilegierte Berlinische Zeitung von Staats- und Gelehrten Sachen." On the other hand, the *Morgenpost*'s experiment to eliminate the sensation-alist column "Aus dem Gerichtssaal" cost the paper thousands of readers, and even bone-dry Social Democratic papers felt it necessary to compromise their rigorous standards, "because you don't go the newspaper vendor to buy sleeping pills," as SPD-speaker Otto Braun reminded the party.[40]

The Wilhelmine critics' ideal newspaper invariably spoke in an authoritative and masculine voice. It was heavy on cul-tural reviews and political commentary and only briefly re-ported on the trials and crimes and occasions of everyday life. It would avoid sensationalism, which was invariably labeled an emotional, feminine weakness, and one way of achieving that was to limit the place of women in the paper: first, by cut-ting down the number of women journalists, and then, by throwing into the back pages or eliminating altogether serial novels, *faits divers*, and other gossipy items.[41] Idealists also thoughtfully provided their imaginary newspapers with prop-erly trained readers who had the "tranquil mind to read a newspaper as it should be read," although one aspiring pub-lisher hoped to restrict circulation to 100,000 souls, beyond which number the educated public transmogrified into a big-city mass.[42] As it was, in *Verdorben zu Berlin*, Otto Hellmut Hopfen's inferior but revealing 1914 novel about the attempt to establish a "quality" newspaper, the demands of adver-tisers and vulgar expectations of city readers eventually cor-rupted the venture, sensationalized its pages, and induced the hero to abandon Berlin for Bavaria.

The shrill cries of condemnation mounted as the number of mass-circulation newspapers continued to increase. Neither the regulation of journalists nor the launching of serious pa-

pers appeared to restore the press to the deliberate and privileged role it had supposedly once assumed. As Alan J. Lee
concludes for turn-of-the-century Britain, "the vision of an
order in which the press enjoyed an enduring and unchanging
role was fast disappearing."[43] After 1900 diverse styles of metropolitan reading flourished unregulated, as both the literate
and leisured public and the available technology expanded
dramatically.

Nonetheless, the critics of the mass media cannot be simply
dismissed as antimoderns. Their frustrations are suggestive of
the new world the mass-circulation press had created. Hans
Traub and Wilhelm Foerster, as much as Alfred Döblin or
Jacob van Hoddis, had begun to trace the outline of a second-
hand looking glass that overlay the original metropolis and
governed encounters with it. With its stress on visual pleasure,
contrasting images, and constant movement, newspaper reportage had the effect of making the city look more precarious
and fragmented.

In a highly regarded feuilleton that appeared in the *Frankfurter Zeitung* in 1932, Siegfried Kracauer compared living in
Berlin to reading the newspaper. Existence in the city, he
wrote, "is not like a line but a series of points; it is new every
day like the newspapers that are thrown away when they have
become old." In this word city almost anything could happen.
Events took place with great energy and then disappeared as
suddenly as they had appeared. Not surprisingly, Kracauer
noted, many city people "experience precisely this life from
headline to headline as exciting; partly because they profit
from the fact that their earlier existence vanishes . . . partly
because they believe they are living twice as much when they
live purely in the present."[44] "Headline to headline," the startling, inherently unstable paper version of the world was also
used to great effect by a generation of modernist writers and

painters who wanted to challenge nineteenth-century certainties about vision and representation.

THE FUGITIVE CITY

Caught in the media's "glare of the present," the imagined city was an indeterminate place. No street or location remained undisturbed, no person or character appeared true, no single itinerary could be repeated. This "Fugitive City" was in part a fabrication; the print media constantly revised the city to fit the visual requirements of spectacle. But the imagined place was not completely fantastical either. Media images corresponded to the tremulous rhythms and fluctuating, subversive orderings of the modern city. The front-page alternation of stories, each disconnected and discontinuous, resembled in miniature the thoroughly mobilized urban landscape. Crowds of strangers and warehouses of goods moved through the city as well as through the newspaper, and every day brought new arrangements and combinations. Indeed, the newspaper was the basic document to report the city's changing physiognomy, its tables of contrasts, and its loss of coherence.[45] As Kracauer observed, the daily newspaper was most like the fugitive city, and the one heightened the effect of the other.

For over one hundred years the root metaphor for comprehending Berlin has been the image of ceaseless movement. The last words of Karl Scheffler's well-known 1910 summary of the city condemn Berlin always to become ("immerfort zu werden") and never to be ("niemals zu sein"). Scheffler's Berlin will always be in transition and his Berliners will always be resident nomads rather than recognizable bearers of culture and tradition. If modern rootlessness had geography, it would look like Berlin and would include the following elements: Potsdamer Platz, tenement buildings, construction-site fences, and Friedrichstrasse.[46]

No location in Berlin had as many people and goods circulating as did Potsdamer Platz, which was why it attracted so much press commentary. With the Tiergarten angled on the north and the main freight yards to the south, the square served as a vital passageway for almost all the city's east-west traffic. Despite efforts at regulation, including the construction of traffic islands, the enlistment of traffic police, and the erection of Europe's first traffic signal in 1924, Potsdamer Platz remained badly overloaded. For the half-century from 1890 to 1940 it drew sightseers and tourists and journalists eager to take stock of the tremors of the city. *BZ am Mittag* invited its readers: "Let's place ourselves on Potsdamer Platz— we can even go to Café Josty and work sitting down—and let's count, just for a one single hour." According to results tabulated for one hour in October 1905, "416 streetcar wagons, 146 omnibuses, 564 carriages and automobiles, 538 other vehicles, 54 coaches und 138 three-wheelers" crossed Potsdamer Platz. To make the three-figure numbers look more impressive, more commensurate with a world city, *BZ* multiplied them by the eighteen busiest hours in a day (for a total of 33,048 vehicles), the thirty days in a month (991,440), and the twelve months of the year (12,000,000). It was not simply eight-digit numbers of cars and wagons but the ever-changing pictures they produced that fascinated city observers: "they come from the left, from the right, from all sides, every second a new picture."[47]

The kaleidoscopic city had its dark sides, too. For the novelist Paul Gurk, the street, which had once stood for order, "dignified, stiff, and latched . . . like the leather attaché case of a privy councillor," had exploded into "a place of collision and confrontation, poisoned by gas and exhaust." The nature of the street was "explosion," concluded Gurk: "Not even for a blink of the eye does it hurl at us the same picture."[48] According to Gurk, the fugitive city had destroyed any meaningful sightfulness.

The explosive quality hovered over the crowd as well. The rapid circulation of city people made social identities difficult to determine. Innumerable crime stories in *BZ am Mittag*, the *Morgenpost*, and the *Lokal-Anzeiger* confirmed just how uncertain metropolitan identities had become. Not only did thousands of newcomers enter the city each week, but inhabitants changed places of residence and employment at an astonishing rate. An inadequate housing stock created varieties of nomads. Wilhelmine Berlin's homeless shelters registered nearly one-million overnight stays every year. Thousands of single men also lived with working-class families as *Schlafburschen* who rented the corner of a room, an unused daytime bed, or even the top of a wooden wardrobe. Poor families spared expenses as *Trockenmieter*, moving every six months into the cold and damp rooms of newly plastered apartments that otherwise would have stood empty. Once they dried the walls with the heat of their bodies and the small amounts of coal they might afford, they were charged rents commensurate with the now livable apartments and made way for the wealthier tenants for whom the buildings had been constructed in the first place.

Every six months, on the customary moving days *(Ziehtagen)* of April 1 and October 1, *Trockenmieter* resumed their pilgrimage across the city. A reflection of untamed real-estate speculation as well as sheer industrial poverty, the annual turnover rate for apartments hovered between 43 and 65 percent between the years 1879 and 1894.[49] These figures suggest that more than half of all Berliners grew up in and experienced the city from constantly shifting vantages. Just before the turn of the century, Albert Südekum, Social Democrat and doctor, questioned one proletarian woman about her various households:[50]

At first they found lodgings with a brother of the husband in Lich-
tenberg, at that time a rather insignificant village. Then they
moved for two years to Pankow, where the husband had found
good work on a road crew for two years. Finally, they arrived in
the city itself. The sick woman couldn't even keep straight the
streets in which she had lived, didn't even know in which apartments her last two living children had been born. She could only
say that the family moved every six months. She had lived in some
fifteen different apartments.

Because of this proletarian *Nomadenleben*,[51] people lacked
stable landmarks and to anchor even their memories.

The past vanished as well in the rapid turnover of jobs and
positions. Young women from the countryside streamed into
the city to work as maids. But after only twelve months, more
than half of all ordinary household maids had switched employers. A number had found husbands, better-paying factory
work, or more pleasant conditions in other households. But
many other young women had been let go or perhaps needed
to support illegitimate children. Some slipped out of house-
work altogether and made ends meet as prostitutes.[52] Of the
1,689 prostitutes registered with the police in 1900, for example, 1,026 had formerly been maids. Waitresses were not
much better off. Although newcomers to Berlin found easy employment in the city's restaurants, cafés, and bars, they could
be fired easily, and they subsisted mainly on meager tips. As a
result, restaurant help rarely stayed in one place for more
than several months. In 1893, according to one sample of
1,108 waitresses, 732 had changed places of work more than
six times in a single year, 200 more than ten, and 63 more than
twenty.[53] Waitresses, we are told, also frequently enhanced
their incomes as part-time prostitutes.[54]

For their part, employers found the high rate of turnover
unsettling because it was difficult to oversee the past history of

employees. After the robbery and murder of one couple by their maid's brother, the *Berliner Tageblatt* realized: "We live in our apartments with girls and the only thing we know about them are their first names. Who among us knows where they come from? Is there a father? Who is the mother? Do they have brothers in the city? Do they have lovers with whom they go out?"[55] The uncertainties brought up in stories about city strangers were compounded in streets and cafés where different types of people gathered.

Given the rapid turnover of apartments, the proliferation of boarders, and the blurred distinctions among city people, residents in Berlin's crowded tenements never quite knew among whom they were living. After the murder of a landlady by one of her *Schlafbursche* on Skalitzer Strasse in 1899, the *Morgenpost* drew attention to the untrustworthiness of deceptively well-mannered tenants.[56] Just how dangerous poor people's quarters could be was made clear by the gruesome 1904 murder of nine-year-old Lucie Berlin, who had learned to trust the familiar faces of neighbors in her tenement courtyard on Ackerstrasse and fell victim to pimps and criminals. Detailing the most improbable metropolitans living cheek-by-jowl, the press's exhaustive front-page coverage of the subsequent murder trial illustrated the unsettling instability of metropolitan identities.[57] Again and again, narratives of murder and suicide recounted the unexpectedness of encounters and temporariness of fortunes of city people, charging the urban landscape with excitement but also cloaking it with uncertainty and dread.

Blocks of new buildings were as unmappable as crowds of strangers. In the push for urban development between 1860 and 1910, the city transformed itself several times. To native Berliners the metropolis grew more unfamiliar, and to strangers it appeared unfathomable because improvised. It was in the *Vorstadt* especially that the transitoriness Baude-laire identified as the iridescent skin of the modern shimmered most brightly. The suburbs that had once been rural villages, faraway destinations for weekend outings—"all the way to Steglitz!" recalled Auguste Heinrichs, the oldest woman in Berlin—merged with the outskirts of the city to form a stone sea of tenements and factories and ruler-straight thorough-fares that stretched far into the plains of Brandenburg.[58] Ste-glitz, for example, with a population of 1,899 in 1871 mush-roomed in the next forty years and counted 83,366 inhabitants in 1910. The population of Wilmersdorf exploded from a few hundred villagers to 109,716 city people in the same period. When the Reich was founded, Charlottenburg was a mid-sized town on Berlin's outskirts; a generation of industrial develop-ment left it a proper city of 305,798 in 1910.[59]

Not surprisingly, the *Bauzaun*, or construction fence, was one of the most recognizable features of Berlin's urban land-scape. The proletarian figures sketched by Heinrich Zille and Hans Baluschek made their way along fences enclosing the construction site that doled out wages and opportunities, fences erected by a regime of law and property that did not protect them, fences that charted as well a ceaseless upheaval of things and values. Dozens of feuilletons chronicling the transformation of Berlin began with the *Bauzaun:* "And one day, the grey construction fence grew out of the ground," wrote the *Berliner Tageblatt* in 1906.[60] Then the terrain was captured by *Fangarme,* "the tentacles of the big city," and forever annexed to an empire of restless change.[61] "Next to the brand new row of villas there is still a remnant of 'forest,' thin stands of pine in barren soil," recounted Max Osborn:[62]

It is already fenced in. Tomorrow it will be a construction site, day after tomorrow there will be buildings. A *Rummelplatz* has established itself between the firewalls of tenements. Next week it will disappear; the bricklayers are already on their way. Over there is a bicycle track, but the rows of buildings are advancing relentlessly . . . In the distance, you can make out plywood fences, telegraph poles, a few solitary trees, newly laid streets . . . sand heaps, dry grass, construction shacks.

In similar fashion, Anselm Heine tells how a garden allotment full of "pumpkins and melons . . . bird cages, aquariums, pigeons, chickens, and, above all, children" becomes a construction site. "After a few months all this loveliness is destroyed . . . the owner develops his lot. He erects a *Bauzaun* and while he waits for necessary building licenses or for the ground to thaw he leases the enclosure for a season as a *Rummelplatz*, a bicycle track, or an ice-skating rink." Invariably, "a few weeks later, several men arrive with string, they measure, they make notes," and from one day to the next these sites of entertainment are dismantled, just as the *Laubenkolonie* (garden plots) had been, and resettled farther away on the next empty construction site. Soon enough, wagons deposit stones and lumber, workers arrive, and across the street "a tavern opens, a cinema, cornerstones already announce the names of the streets. And Berlin has been enriched by one more raw, uniform block of houses."[63]

Bauzäune, Laubenkolonien, Rummelplätze, and other fleeting forms of the metropolis—all attentively reviewed by the big-city daily—kept receding to the distant suburbs. Indeed, Karl Scheffler described the extensive transformation of Greater Berlin as a work of colonization that deserved comparison with the American frontier. Outermost Berlin W. was even labeled WW, for "Wild West," an open space of hot real-estate speculation and development. The city never stopped as Jules Huret drove through the Tiergarten, down the "endless Charlottenburger Allee" and the Kaiserdamm: "Eventually

The skating rink operator: "Hey, that's only a dime, it costs a quarter to get in!" *Girl:* "But I only have one ice skate." In this Heinrich Zille drawing, the firewalls of newly constructed tenements look down on a makeshift skating rink, which will invariably give way to further development.

there are no houses anymore. However, the street is already paved, the gutters are laid . . . after a while, the pavement ends. The car sinks into the wagon ruts that make their way between sand embankments, piled-up concrete and iron pipes, heaps of bricks; between ditches, barracks, and wheelbarrows." Then suddenly, twelve kilometers from the Tiergarten, "the lane simply stops in front of a dense stand of trees."[64]

Far beyond the city limits, Paul Gurk's itinerant bookseller still felt surrounded by Berlin: "His shoe knocked against pavement, that barren stone; the white-chalked kilometer markers appeared at regular intervals out of the dark . . . all this had been surveyed . . . the ring of a bell could be heard . . . and when the bicyclists passed he heard fragments of conversation or the tunes of the latest hit—from the city."[65] On the periphery the sharp contrast between city and countryside was lost. Both Huret and Gurk made a point of the blurred geography and vague definition of the fugitive city.

The renovation of the city center was as thorough as the development of the periphery. In the decades since 1871, Berlin's main railway stations—the Stettiner, the Schlesischer, the Anhalter, and the Potsdamer—had thrust into the city like the advance outposts of an invading army that brought with it hotels and restaurants and amusement palaces to service visitors along with freight yards, depots, post offices, and streetcar and subway lines. By the turn of the century, *Bauplätze* churned up the built city around Alexanderplatz and between Hallesches, Potsdamer, and Oranienburger Tor. Commenting on all this "ditch digging" and "hellish noise," the *Berliner Tageblatt* announced in May 1905 the outbreak of "war in time of peace."[66] "Berlin is in the process of exploding!" agreed Hermann Konsbrück; a conflagration that was "at once horrifying and electrifying."[67] Every spring, newspapers reported on new construction sites and continuing subway tunneling that turned elegant boulevards into alpine wilderness.[68] On Tauentzienstrasse, "the mountains tower on high and between them yawn deep ravines." Nollendorfplatz was "a jumble of iron rails, arcs, bridges, and steps."[69]

The Promethean proportions of Berlin's modernization could not hide a tragic, Faustian aspect. The city had lost its familiarity. The feuilletonist Arthur Eloesser rebuked the founding generation which had proudly anticipated "intoxicatingly great times and was a particularly appreciative audience whenever there was something to be leveled or carried off," as the "old Bürgerstadt" was torn down street by street.[70] "Throughout Berlin, the goal is to 'clean up,' to create room for something new," observed Anselm Heine. "Berlin is intoxicated by the New."[71] City chroniclers, particularly Max Osborn at *BZ am Mittag*, kept track of the gradual disappearance of the vestiges of old Berlin. Nostalgic accounts of the last *Kremser*, the horsedrawn wagons that used to bring merrymakers into the Grunewald or to Tegel; the last *Pferdeomnibus* (the horse-drawn bus of line 4c, Stettiner Bahnhof to Hallesches Tor); the last *Droschke*, the horse-drawn cabs that finally disappeared in 1928; or the Krögel, the sole surviving (until 1935) medieval alleyway—these were all typical newspaper items that took the pulse of the transitoriness of the city.[72] Without ever examining the process of urban transformation itself, these *Abschiedswörter* (parting words) in the daily newspaper produced a motion picture of hundreds of endings and closings, one after the next. "Again and again, the places where old Berlin laughed and lived and drank are being torn down," went a typical story in *BZ am Mittag*. That time it was the Pilsener Bierstube, Unter den Linden 13, that was scheduled for demolition to make room for a modern office building.[73] "Even the Wilhelmstrasse"—where new department stores threatened the most stately Prussian street.[74] "The destruction of old Berlin is proceeding briskly," the paper concluded.[75] "Spreechicago," Walther Rathenau summed up at the turn of the century, had killed "Spreeathen."[76]

What made the city so difficult to read was not so much the destruction of old Berlin (Rathenau's Athens-on-the-Spree) and its replacement by a new Berlin (Chicago-on-the-Spree)

nor the rapid tempo of modernization, but rather the ceaseless transformation of everything, even of newly built precincts. The tempo, like the incessant actuality of the daily
newspaper, gave inhabitants the dizzying sense of living constantly in the present. There no "piety," as observers invariably put it, toward the remains of Baroque or Biedermeier
Berlin; indeed, there was no piety at all. What Simmel had
defined as values of refinement and "distinction" *(Vornehmheit)* had disappeared altogether in the capitalist economy of
the twentieth century.[77] *Bauzäune* were put up around old
one- and two-story buildings and also around those simply
considered "not modern enough."[78] Time had evidently
speeded up. "Developments in the city center, which our fathers had built," wrote Hermann Konsbrück, "make way, as
tumbledown junk, for grandiose new structures."[79] By the
same token, the brand-new structures of the present had to be
considered purely provisional, a concept that would culminate
in the prescription of Martin Wagner, Berlin city-planner in
the 1920s, to rebuild Alexanderplatz every twenty-five years.

   The modern city was a process rather than a place, and it
therefore held no monuments or landmarks. Berlin "draws
the traveler into a labyrinth of uniform streets and cripples his
imagination," complained Scheffler, "because Berlin does not
have natural points of reference or a dramatic physiognomy."
"The highs and lows that give a city charming and lively differences of altitude are completely missing," he continued.[80]
Except on the *Stadtbahn* or along the *Landwehrkanal* it is
difficult to gain perspective even in today's reunified Berlin.
Without major architectonic punctuation, without pauses and
breaks, the imperial city was nothing more than "a heap of
buildings,"[81] "a gigantic improvised structure," "a stony labyrinth,"[82]—an endless iteration of grey broad streets that was
disorienting, even unreadable.

The effort to remake imperial Berlin into a *Weltstadt* left the city looking ever more improvised. Wilhelmine splendor was carved in ornate sandstone facades that were simply bolted onto the red-brick fronts that previous architects, following Karl Friedrich Schinkel, had preferred to leave bare. Sandstone allowed extraordinary stylistic variation. "And then it started," lampooned Max Osborn as he described the gaudy style of Wilhelm II: "The time when elaborate, heavy ornaments decorated newly erected buildings which staggered through all the styles of the past; the time when sumptuous houses sported false pillars, fake pilasters, alcoves, towerlets, rows of gables, bogus 'Palazzi' facades and pompous phrases over the portals of tenements, office buildings, and government structures."[83] Sandstone allowed Berlin to give itself ever grander, more modern facelifts that erased the past and repudiated any distinctive city style. As a "sandstone city" Berlin was infinitely renewable.[84]

The fluctuating face of Berlin delighted Robert Walser, an enthusiastic newcomer from Switzerland. "The wonder of the city," he wrote in 1907, his first year there, "is that any particular bearing or behavior is drowned by all the thousands of variations, that opinion is completely fleeting, that while judgment is pronounced quickly, everything is forgotten as a matter of course."[85] Surrounded by new facades and new fashions, city people moved restlessly forward and did not give a second thought to the past. "What did we pass," Walser asked, "a facade from the Second Empire? Where? Back there? As if someone were going to stop, turn around, and look at the old-fashioned style one more time. Why? Move on, move on."[86] But if observers did turn around, they saw the sight of the once modern (the Second Empire) in decay, a startling reminder that the attractive novelties ahead ("move on, move on") would also soon grow old and wither and that their charms were entirely temporary.

Wilhelmine observers such as Robert Walser had anticipated Siegfried Kracauer's acclaimed meditation (1932) upon
the city's transitoriness. The Kurfürstendamm, a "Street
without Memory," Kracauer wrote, was not built or even rebuilt for eternity. It merely held "emptily flowing time in which
nothing endures." A never-ending train of new shops, new
fashions, and new facades effaced the memory of what had
been: "The new enterprises are absolutely new and those that
have been displaced by them are completely extinguished."
Once the prewar sandstone ornaments themselves became "a
bridge to yesterday," they were simply knocked down.[87] In the
throes of ceaseless renovation, the Kurfürstendamm stood for
a city that lived without the past. Berlin was less modern than
eternally transitory. Like so many turns on a child's toy kaleidoscope, renewable facades and ever-changing shops withdrew
from city viewers stable points of reference and coherent
vistas.

Once the splendid location of Germany's youthful ambitions, by the 1920s busy Friedrichstrasse—even more than the
Kurfürstendamm—summed up the impermanence of what
was once valued. It is a distinctly modernist street because its
decline revealed that transitoriness brought with it premature
endings as well as an ever-changing present. Friedrichstrasse
was the longest street in central Berlin, stretching from Oranienburger Tor, across Unter den Linden, past the precisely
laid out blocks of the eighteenth-century Friedrichstadt, to the
Rondell, the circular drill ground at the city's southern gate.
Long and broad, it accommodated the parades of Prussia's
soldier kings but had been mainly a residential street, lined
with barracks, beer halls, and the two-story homes of Prussian officials and nobles, including Adalbert von Chamisso,
who lived in a garden villa at number 235. Once Berlin was
made the capital of the newly unified Reich, however, Friedrichstrasse was transformed into an imperial showcase.

Railway stations, grand hotels, and dozens of restaurants, theaters, and cafés made it a bustling commercial boulevard. One by one, the old eighteenth-century townhouses were torn down to make way for the latest-style buildings with elaborate façades and electric-light advertising. It was Friedrichstrasse which made credible Berlin's claim to cosmopolitan status. At the corner of Behrenstrasse it boasted the iron-and-glass Kaiser-Passage, modeled on arcades in Paris and Milan. The arcade housed specialty stores, restaurants, a concert hall, and a wax museum. All accounts of late-nineteenth-century Berlin celebrate Friedrichstrasse as the principal thoroughfare on which to see and be seen.

With its entertainment palaces, neon lights, and splendid display windows, Friedrichstrasse embodied that quintessential Wilhelmine value, the "colossal." But the most modern street of Berlin did not survive the twentieth century. Even before World War I, Friedrichstrasse had grown shabby in comparison to the elegant streets of Berlin W., Tauentzienstrasse and the Kurfürstendamm. The street's bright nighttime glamour looked suspect to Hans Modrow, who remembered that around 1900 Friedrichstrasse was already "played out," "overaged." "Like a woman who sees her first wrinkles, Lady Friedrichstrasse put on more and more makeup, dollied herself up, trilled a little song, and became a nighttime street. . . . If her charms had faded by day, they still had all manner of effects in the artificial light by night."[88]

"Her glitter is gone," agreed the *Berliner Illustrirte Zeitung* at the end of war.[89] Friedrichstrasse has become one big construction site of wooden boards and heaps of sand: "The only thing that remains are the side streets, at the corners of which street vendors stand peddling chocolate, shoe wax, pancakes, shoelaces, cigarettes, sandwiches, an endless chain along the building fronts from Belle-Alliance Platz to Weidendammer

Brücke." Berlin's grandest sandstone boulevards were carved out of sand.

"Friedrichstrasse had a difficult old age," concluded Walter Kiaulehn, a fate which was as much a sign of the transitoriness of the modern as was the "unhappy youth" of the Kurfürstendamm, Kracauer's "Street without Memory."[90] No wonder Siegfried Kracauer found Berlin to be so much like the newspapers that flooded its streets every day. The city's attractions and fashions were as ephemeral as the events reported on the front pages, its sandstone buildings and revamped streets as disposable as the morning edition at midday. Like any newspaper, Berlin shook off its yesterdays, and its urban physiognomy was without the permanent features or remembered landmarks that would make it more memorable or intelligible.[91] As such, the city embodied the paradox of modernism that Walter Benjamin had identified in his essays on Baudelaire: the always-different blurred into the ever-same, fabulous alternation slipping into endless iteration.

6
PLOT
LINES

At the end of the nineteenth century, one of the remarkable characters roaming aimlessly in the word cities that novelists constructed was the stranger. Without background or family ties, this shadowy figure eluded social designation. One Berlin novelist, Hermann Conradi, called them *Uebergangsmenschen*, anonymous, indecipherable people who prospered by manipulating the money economy. They showed up again and again in newspaper items about potentially dangerous newcomers and hustlers, *Schlafburschen*, and maids. Like the last man in Edgar Allan Poe's London crowd, the face that "does not permit itself to be read," they illustrated the city's illegibility and threatened its moral stability. Anonymous, faceless men, masked or painted women, and the detectives and journalists who followed their tracks—they composed a new literary cast that exemplified the unpredictable and often terrifying nature of the modern metropolis.[1]

The dynamics of urban crowds intensified the uncertainties that fleeting encounters with strangers had first raised. Not only was the milling crowd the perfect milieu for strangers; the crowd itself appeared as vague and menacing as the unaccountable people who were part of it. According to literary scholar Burton Pike, both the figure of the alienated individual and that of the obscure crowd corresponded to a kaleidoscopic, fugitive conception of the industrial city.[2] Big-city newspapers enhanced this effect, exploring dark and exotic corners in the city, introducing strangers and strange incidents on the front page, and repeatedly rearranging these with each new edition. Every day presented readers with an entirely different version of the metropolis. But as inconstant as the composition of the crowd (or the front page) was, the patterned movement of the crowd, day after day, retrieved the coherence of the streets. The daily sale and distribution of metropolitan newspapers, for example, was based on the assumption that the reading public would continue performing its hundreds of thousands of repetitious and equivalent actions. The vast majority of Berliners read daily newspapers, and newspapers appeared with absolute regularity—"Every morning I see . . . the newspaperman on Perleberger Strasse." The formal production of the word city imposed an unmistakable routine on the built city.

It took time to become aware of this routinization. Alfred Döblin's encounters with Berlin for some forty years before his exile in 1933 show a gradual shift in perspective. In his early writings, Döblin recognized little about the city that was systematic. In October 1896, for example, he noted his impressions of Leipziger Strasse in a closely observed, French-flavored piece:[3]

A pêle-mêle of all trades and professions crowded the trottoir. A society lady inspected the products of the hat industry and, wrinkling her noise, pointed out the unsuitable form of this or that elegant bonnet to her friend. With a critical gaze, a man, obviously an expert, looked over her shoulder at the decoration and arrangement of the wares. With a self-satisfied air, he blew the smoke of his cheap cigar right in the face of the lady, who indignantly left the scene. Pretty salesgirls rushed by arm-in-arm, laughing, pushing, nonchalantly looking each passing gentleman in the eye. A banker trotted by, a big leather case under his arm; messenger boys for well-known companies; flâneurs, with a long cigarette in one hand and a thin cane twirling in the other; people who stood and stared at each show window; reservists; soldiers—all these types ventured out onto the trottoir. In the press of the crowd, no one pays attention to anyone else . . . in front of some stores the press became rather dangerous. At Wertheim each step was a conquest. Ladies had a particularly difficult time in this commotion and barely risked crossing the street. And then, all at once, a hay wagon which had been loaded to the breaking point got stuck at Dönhoffplatz. One after another, the streetcars stalled all the way back to Friedrichstrasse. What noise!

A street-level vantage, which closes by focusing on a single incident—the stuck hay wagon—served to reveal the confusion and ill-design of the city. At every step, Döblin noticed some friction that impeded traffic. Rather than flowing or streaming, city people shoved and pushed, each a distinct individual who controlled his or her surroundings by appraising hats, blowing smoke, looking passersby straight in the eye. There is no hint of any power to monitor and regulate either inhabitants or vehicles.

Some thirty years later, in *Berlin Alexanderplatz*, Döblin saw far more orderly, more uniform, and much less colorful streets, which he described in a stripped-down, almost colorless prose. He assumed first the point of view of a policeman, then that of an airborne observer:[4]

> As soon as he jerks around, there is a rush across the square in the direction of Königsstrasse of about 30 private individuals, some of them stop on the traffic island, one part reaches the other side and continues walking on the planks. The same number have started east, they swim towards the others, the same thing has befallen them, but there was no mishap. . . . The faces of the eastward wanderers are in no way different from those of the wanderers to the west, south, and north; moreover, they exchange their roles, those who are now crossing the square towards Aschinger may be seen an hour later in front of the empty Hahn department store. Just as those who come from Brunnenstrasse on their way to Jannowitz Brücke mingle with those coming from the reverse direction. Yes, and many of them turn off to the side, from south to east, from south to west, from north to west, from north to east.

Döblin hovers over Berlin and depicts city people moving in interchangeable and scheduled streams. For all the complicated maneuvers "from south to east, from south to west, from north to west, from north to east," there are no jams or blockages. The city appears to work seamlessly. By the same token, however, its inhabitants have lost their independence. Döblin no longer distinguishes separate individuals promenading on the "trottoir," each with an identifiable demeanor, colorful garments, or idiosyncratic habits. Döblin's city people have grown to look more alike; they have a more collective identity.

What accounts for this shift from a curbside to a bird's-eye view? At first glance, neither vantage point disqualifies the other, and the two readings can be put side-by-side as equally plausible alternatives. Indeed, Döblin experiments with any number of perspectives in *Berlin Alexanderplatz*. He follows Biberkopf, reads the newspapers and advertisements, and hovers over the traffic, only to interrupt repeatedly the sight-lines he has assumed. Precisely because Alexanderplatz invites so many dissonant, tentative readings, the place resists summation by a single governing narrative. The multifacetedness of the city is Döblin's plot. Elsewhere, however, Döblin authorizes the shift in perspective that no longer recognizes the "pêle-mêle." "We experience the collective and the uniform," he explained in an important 1924 *Neue Rundschau* article, "more so than in earlier periods."[5] Walter Benjamin seems to have agreed, comparing "Poe's passers-by," who "cast glances in all directions which still appeared to be aimless," with "today's pedestrians [who] are obliged to do so in order to keep abreast of traffic signals." Modern technology, Benjamin concluded, "has subjected the human sensorium to a complex kind of training" and evidently regulated previously undirected movements.[6]

Likewise, the daily habit of picking up a paper, repeated uncountable times in households, cafés, and streetcars, created similar dispositions. Even without standard itineraries or identical responses, Berliners became conscious of approaching the city in like-minded ways as streetwise pedestrians and as spectators and consumers. Again and again, readers discovered themselves to be constituents of a common metropolitan public. This process of discovery was accelerated and encouraged by the big newspapers themselves. In the first place, readers saw themselves reflected in attentive press accounts that identified and tracked movements of the crowd: the streetcar commute to work, beers at Aschinger's, Sundays in the Grunewald, the first school day each autumn. These stories inserted individuals into broader rhythms. The newspaper also physically assembled its readership on the street by choreographing huge city-wide events that attracted hundreds of thousands of sightseers. The memorable car races, zeppelin flights, and aviation rallies that Ullstein and Sherl sponsored in the years before World War I helped fuse together a popular metropolitan culture. In part, the word city organized the city by creating an increasingly like-minded readership. To read the great text of Berlin for the plot is to realize that as readers encountered the city, they became increasingly self-conscious of themselves as a city-wide public. It was not so much newly kindled nationalist feelings or old-fashioned civic virtues as the pleasures of urban spectatorship that created a tentative, but unmistakable unity in a shifting environment.

THE MACHINERY OF THE NEWSPAPER

Newspapers fashioned designs for the city simply by talking about it. Selecting elements from the vast array of metropolitan contents and introducing and framing these, local coverage tended to standardize stories. Every New Year's Day, for example, the papers commented on the traditional *Sylvester Unfug* on the streets, and every year they gave the same spin to the previous evening's events: "Alles nur halb so schlimm" (only half as bad)—an "ironic, friend-of-the-people" tone that elided over outbursts of class hostility and tended to integrate pranksters and other merrymakers into a wholesome all-Berlin public that would recognize itself (rather than leer at the "other") in the press coverage.[7] Items about suicides or swindlers had the opposite effect, since they typically referred to the precariousness of metropolitan life. In each case, a unique event was fitted into a standardized format that applied to the several stories about the city.

The business of producing the newspaper exposed the design of the city more completely than did narrative strategies. As a material object rather than as a medium, the daily paper exemplified the machinery of the city. It was published and delivered every day within exact schedules: *BZ am Mittag* appeared at precisely 12:18, six days a week; pedestrians observed the newspaperman at the same time on Perleberger Strasse; and accordingly, readers developed their own routines. "I couldn't imagine breakfast without a newspaper," conceded one reader.[8] The loose newsprint pages that disappeared after only a few hours in the streets could be reimagined as serrations in a machinery extending over the entire city and beyond. Far from being an evanescent, utterly disposable novelty, the newspaper served as a daily index to a powerful system in which all movement, whether the delivery of the morning edition to a half-million subscribers, the cutting and pasting of the front page, or the exchange of telegram messages from points around the world was carefully synchronized and calculated. Images of the newspaper in fiction repeatedly attested to the capacity of the press to organize the realm of its readers, and their ominous names—"Moloch," "spider," "world power"—indicated omniscience and purpose. Many contemporary critics saw the press as a frightening, tentacled, but coherent whole.

The metropolitan newspaper was a harbinger of the age of machines and machine-fitted collectivism—an age that Döblin, for one, recognized. The publishing industry was widely regarded as the last word in the organization, automation, and distribution of goods. Where better to see the "world city, roaring, burning, pushing, being pushed," asked A. H. Kober, than in Berlin's newspaper quarter, the three-square blocks around Koch- and Zimmerstrasse that housed Scherl, Mosse, and Ullstein. Night and day, messengers arrived, telegraphs hummed, telephones rang, charging the district with energy. At the center, on Kochstrasse, stood the Ullsteinhaus, "a building glowing with the hot breath of furious rotation machines, of hastily scurrying people, haunted and tormented by the demons of modern technology."[9]

The machinery that produced the papers fascinated observers. Rotary presses appeared in major city films, such as Max Mack's *Wo ist Coletti?* and Walter Ruttmann's *Berlin: Symphony of the Big City*, and figured in nearly every novel about newspapers or journalists. "The machines clasp at rolls of paper, heavy as boulders, as if they were mere balls of cotton," wrote Martin Kesser in 1915:[10]

> They spray steam to make the paper suitable for printing and pull it through freshly inked cylinders, on which the metal imprint of the page has been stamped. Arrayed in groups of three and fastened to the floor, the rotary presses look like a battery of gun embankments. . . . When they are in operation, the building shakes like the engine room of an overseas steamer.

In 1912 Ullstein boasted the largest and most advanced printing technology in Germany, including 32 giant linotype machines, compared to 26 at Scherl and 20 at Mosse.[11] When Ullstein moved its printing works to Tempelhof in 1925, the new machine room was outfitted with plate glass windows allowing visitors, as a prospectus promised, to "immediately get a sense of the scale of the entire operation."[12] Ullstein even offered tours of the printing plant. These were held in the late morning so that sightseers could get the thrill of watching *BZ am Mittag* on press.[13]

The finely tuned Ullstein machine did not stop after the rapid-fire printing of *BZ* had taken place and the visitors' tour was disbanded. "As soon as the machines begin to stamp and drone, shaking the house with their gigantic pace, filling the air with their roar," exalted Gustav Kauder, "they start throwing the mysteriously folded newspapers into uniform catchments, sorting the bundles, and preparing them for delivery. In the middle of all this noise and excitement, you can make out the orders" that mobilized battalions of "delivery men, messengers, drivers" who distributed the paper.[14] During the 1920s it took just one half-hour for motorcycles and trucks to deliver *BZ am Mittag* to kiosks and branch offices across Greater Berlin and to load the bundled newspapers onto trains and Ullstein's two motorboats and three airplanes which deposited the noontime paper in Halle by 1:15, in Leipzig at 1:40, and in Chemnitz no later than 2:20.[15] Over 4,000 employees were in charge of delivering Ullstein papers (the figure for Mosse was 2,900, for Scherl about 2,000 in 1928).[16] Ullstein's mammoth organization reached its zenith during the Weimar years, the "golden age" of the German press, but the efficiency of the system was manifest before World War I. As early as 1905, for example, *BZ am Mittag* offered a specially delivered "Baltic" edition for vacationing Berliners, and by 1912 the paper reached readers in far-off Oldenburg, Mainz, Heidelberg, Munich, Danzig, Oppeln, and Görlitz on the day of publication.[17] *BZ am Mittag* was itself an outcome of Ullstein's efficiency: one reason the midday paper existed at all was because the company wanted to keep the machines working; otherwise they would be idle after the nighttime publication of its morning flagship, the *Morgenpost*.

The Ullsteinhaus was at the center of a far-flung network of reporters and stringers. Cables from around the world arrived at Kochstrasse at all hours. "I felt that I was sitting right in the navel of the world," remembered Vicki Baum, an editor at Ullstein in the 1920s; "life streamed by in thousands of photos, hundreds of people, in the voices of the entire globe."[18] For Hermann Diez, the mythological creatures with hundred eyes, hundred arms, and hundred breasts had come to life in the big-city newspapers of the twentieth century.[19] Indeed, more and more news was published in the form of telegraphed reports, most of which were prepared and circulated according to international agreement by the main German news agency, *Wolffsches Telegraphenbüro*. In the *Frank-furter Zeitung*, for example, cables constituted fully 48 per-cent of news space in 1913, up from 22 percent in 1888.[20]

Their capacity to collect, rearrange, and distribute thou-sands of separate items in a given time slot made newspapers embody the advance guard of the modern spirit. They demon-strated the superlative energy and rational tendency of the twentieth century. According to Werner Sombart, who under-took a comprehensive investigation of modern capitalism, ec-onomic life had reached its fullest development with the met-ropolitan press: "As valuable as the contents of the daily newspaper are," he explained, "this pales in comparison to the wonder and astonishment that grips us when we see and hear and imagine the technology and organization necessary to produce a modern newspaper."[21]

Sombart urged contemporaries to see beyond the often shabby news product and focus instead on the organizational finesse that delivered it. By the same token, the capacity and rationality of the press empires informed the way metropol-itan newspapers approached the city. As the industrial might of Ullstein, Mosse, and Scherl swelled after the turn of the cen-tury, so did their ability to shape a distinctive metropolitan culture. Neither the size of the city nor the mass of its people diminished the confidence of the metropolitan press in an or-derly, manageable, and productive urbanity. The future of Berlin, for which especially Ullstein's *BZ am Mittag* and the *Morgenpost* and Mosse's *Berliner Tageblatt* spoke, was clear. Its millions of residents would govern themselves in demo-cratic fashion; its officials would organize the city in a rational way that provided basic public services and facilitated the efficient movement of goods and people. As in modern busi-ness enterprises, responsibility and prosperity went hand in hand.

THE MACHINERY OF THE CITY

Being one of the most efficient enterprises in town, the news-paper actively encouraged city people to calibrate themselves to machine rhythms. Simply by subscribing to a paper on a weekly or monthly basis, a transaction which involved filling out a form and dropping it off at branch offices that Mosse, Scherl, and Ullstein maintained throughout Berlin, metropol-itans became part of the press operation. Regular subscrip-tions and regular reading habits were an important first step, and the big dailies repeatedly linked their expanding reader-ships with busy commercial exchanges and fast flows of traffic. Regarding themselves as the most modern institution of the age, newspapers had a crucial stake in the free exchange of goods and services. And the more city people inserted them-selves into this larger composition, the more efficient the op-erations of the city and the more successful the newspaper business. The press repeatedly referred to the governing frame of the crowd and regulatory rhythm of traffic, pro-moting an "inner urbanization" that gradually achieved a more exact correspondence between newspaper readers and modern metropolitans.[22]

"Until very recently, the umbrella predominated," observed the *Lokal-Anzeiger* in winter 1889. "In the last 72 hours, how-ever, the ice skate prevails throughout Berlin." Described in this way, the city took on the aspect of a mass settlement, shaking off the quiet and forbearing aspect of a provincial city:

> "That will never come to pass!" I hear a gentleman in a tasseled plush cap exclaim over his *Vossische Zeitung*. He is the same sort who complains to the police when Bolle's [milk truck] bell rings . . . or the mailman knocks twice if the door is not immediately opened. But rest assured, honorable gentleman in the plush cap, it will indeed come to that.

Sudden disruptions and large-scale movements increasingly composed the big-city picture. The *Lokal-Anzeiger*'s jibe at the *Vossische Zeitung*, at the time a small highbrow daily, was an assertion of a distinctly metropolitan culture over a more elitist one. It recognized that more and more Berliners were moving about and using the city in crowds and turning to the plain fare of papers like Scherl's.[23]

New ways of using the city accompanied new styles of reading. Mass culture (ice skates prevail), the browser's ease in the city (noise doesn't bother him), and mass-circulation newspapers (the *Lokal-Anzeiger*) were all of one piece. By the turn of the century most Berliners moved according to factory and streetcar schedules and could hardly be disturbed by loud knocks or Bolle's bells. As newspaper excursions into Berlin N. and Berlin O. made clear, Berlin had become first and foremost an industrial capital in which able-bodied proletarians had long since displaced the "dangerous classes" of the old *Vogtland* and in which quick-witted shopgirls were more typical than prostitutes. Even the city's nightlife was functionalized in press commentary. Mass amusements restored the ability to work; Sunday "ins Grüne" made Monday on the shopfloor more productive. In summer, to be sure, "the powerful machine runs at half-speed." But then newspapers electrified their city descriptions with images of batteries and transmissions, circuits and terminals.[24] What hindered the full development of industrial Berlin, however, were poor traffic habits and anachronistic imperial politics. As long as Berliners were not comfortable in the crowd and Hohenzollerns were not comfortable with the crowd, the city remained a place of unnecessary friction.

Traffic fascinated observers because it showed how crowds moved according to regular schedules and sequences, which indicated that the city worked far more efficiently than previously imagined. Potsdamer Platz, chaotic at first glance, revealed pattern and design upon closer examination. When newspapers talked about traffic in a scientific vocabulary of averages and variations or embellished their reports with statistical series and graphs, they revealed how the city was put together. There was something inexorable and incontestable about these numbers. Every year newspapers commented on the annual business report of *Grosse Berliner Strassenbahn*, typically tallying the total number of passengers (393 million in 1905), noting the increase over the previous year (28 million), recalling the busiest day (a Sunday in June) or the slowest (a Friday in July), looking back on the numbers of injuries and accidents, and finally preparing bar charts which showed the number of streetcar passengers hour-by-hour over the course of an entire day at selected points: Potsdamer Platz; Schönhauser Allee, corner of Gneiststrasse; Hermannplatz; and Königstrasse, corner of Klosterstrasse.[25] Other tabulations counted the numbers of automobiles crossing Potsdamer Platz, circling the Kaiser-Wilhelm Memorial Church, or passing the famous intersection of Friedrichstrasse and Unter den Linden.[26] During the Weimar years traffic statistics often appeared in feuilleton pieces and metropolitan verses as a sign of the "new sobriety," which likened the output of the city to that of a factory or a machine. "In order to depict the complete reality of the big city," asserted Döblin in the introduction to a 1928 book of Berlin photographs, "I would have to transcribe the city's statistical yearbook page by page."[27] But even before World War I, graphs and statistics visually summarized the rationality of the city.

Traffic flows determined more and more the way people should move. Mass-transit schedules were "lessons in exact time," in the words of Lothar Müller, though city humorists noticed small discrepancies between metropolitan and personal clocks.[28] Was it not always the case that the streetcar moved too fast for commuters rushing to catch it and too slowly for those already aboard? Arthur Eloesser made a similar distinction between the subway and the *Stadtbahn.* "When I rush down the stairs to the subway, it has just left," he asserted, but "if I leisurely walk up the steps to the elevated it is still there."[29] Commuters did not always succeed in catching the streetcar or the subway, but they did observe the necessities of synchronization. As Georg Simmel pointed out, city people typically carried pocket watches, which allowed them to time their arrivals and departures with precision. Hundreds of daily rendezvous beneath the *Normaluhren* on the Spittelmarkt, Potsdamer Platz, and in front of Bahnhof Zoo testified to the "synchronized experience" of the city as well.[30] "The closer the minute hand moves to nine o'clock, the more crowded it gets," observed Erwin Alexander-Katz one summer night in July 1912.[31]

Images of synchronization compared metropolitans moving in traffic to machine parts calibrated by punctuality, alertness, and quick response. "With each crossing of the street," maintained Simmel, "the city sets up a deep contrast with small town and rural life with reference to the sensory foundations of psychic life." Simmel posited the existence of a distinctive metropolitan intellect that allowed urbanites to function inside "the threatening currents" of the external environment.[32] In a study of modern life, Richard Hamann came to similar conclusions: "Crossing Potsdamer Platz or even walking through Friedrichstrasse on a busy day requires that presence of mind which makes do with only imprecise impressions and vaguely seen pictures to make adjustments. Those who need to look around and take their bearings would be lost in this commotion. The prerequisite to walking across a busy metropolitan street is the ability to make quick judgments on the basis of minimal signals."[33]

Of course, no one was born a quick-witted pedestrian. Signals had to be internalized and the art of street crossing learned. And there were apparently still a great many apprentices among Berlin's pedestrians at the turn of the century. "The traffic through the main commercial streets . . . is really stupefying," noted one woman. "The streetcars and trams combine to form a single uninterrupted line; wagons of all kinds, hundreds of carriages and two- and three-wheelers drive in front, behind, and often enough into each other. The horns of vehicles, the rattle of wheels, assault our ears . . . and torment visitors from the provinces." "Frau Beulwitz," the city diarist continued, "reported that [visitors] fell into each other's arms upon safely reaching the traffic island in the middle of Potsdamer Platz."[34]

Traffic terrors were not overcome without practice. What city people needed to do was to perform the "art" of crossing metropolitan streets flawlessly every day. Metropolitan newspapers endeavored to "train" city people to adjust to the pace of Potsdamer Platz. When busy traffic functioned well, it had all the melodious order of a symphony. "Fanatical metropolitans that we are," one paper exclaimed, "we love to watch the traffic at Potsdamer Platz:"[35] "Omnibuses and streetcars, car after car, hour after hour . . . carriages, cabs, automobiles, delivery trucks, bicycles enter the flow of traffic from six, seven streets and various angles; in between these the swarm of pedestrians from all directions, going in all directions. Big-city traffic—the busier, the better." Suddenly—"did you see that?"—a woman stepped out of order: "Just one false move and [she] would have been run over by a cab!" For the *Berliner Tageblatt*, the incident was worth some reflection:

> Once again we caught sight of something that occurs every day, every hour on Potsdamer Platz: . . . the foolish and wrong-headed

behavior of a pedestrian in the middle of the street. Once again we saw how a grown woman hoping to cross the busy square did not look carefully in all directions but simply kept her eyes on a passing streetcar and, as a result, would have been run over by the cabman's horse had a policeman not pulled her out of harm's way at the last minute.

The only way to avoid similar incidents was to proceed in a straight line and deliberately cross each stream of traffic. Building a pedestrian bridge over or a tunnel under Potsdamer Platz would be a mistaken solution. The problem would resolve itself "if metropolitans were trained for the metropolis, trained to be attentive and remain prudent in the face of electric rails and diagonally crossing cabs!" The *Berliner Tageblatt* repeatedly opposed technical solutions that would keep the public from disciplining itself. The present-day division of Unter den Linden into parallel one-way lanes, for example, or proposals to establish crosswalks merely spoiled city people who needed to learn "the most vigilant alertness and attention"; besides, editors added, the streets were not for "dreaming."[36] In this illustration of what Gottfried Korff has termed "inner urbanization," people had to adjust to the city, not the other way around. Poor Frau von Beulwitz.

The automobile was cited as the best model for pedestrians to follow. "Any day, any hour," the *Berliner Tageblatt* recommended in 1907, "observe how the automobile quickly and responsively follows the most exact signals [of the traffic policeman], how quickly it brakes, and how easily it accelerates and flits down the street when the all clear is given. More than any other vehicle, the automobile facilitates the quick and smooth flow of traffic."[37] Streetcars, by contrast, ran along fixed rails and moved slowly. They were as unresponsive to changing circumstances as the foolish pedestrian on Potsdamer Platz and as such earned widespread censure from the press.[38] Even at the onset of the twentieth century the private car was setting standards of efficiency for the management of ever larger magnitudes of traffic. In this case, "inner urbanization" manifested itself as automobilization. These notions guided the disposable, transit-oriented city center envisioned by Martin Wagner in the 1920s and culminated after World War II, when post-1945 reconstruction in West Berlin appeared to replace pedestrians with drivers altogether.[39]

New urban protocols outfitted city people with the signals, brakes, and gears by which automobiles already negotiated the flows of traffic. Once the commands were learned, individuals could slip into the crowd without resistance. "Tempted by the warm vapors of humanity," *BZ am Mittag*'s Max Osborn moved expertly in the mass: "A broad stream picks me up and takes me along. I am simply being pushed and don't even think of pushing back. I don't want to. I want to be carried along. I want to lose my individual responses and become a part of the mass into which I have fallen." Moving with rather than against the mass heightened the enjoyment of the city because passing sights appeared as though viewed through a colorful kaleidoscope. At the same time, the short-lived pleasures of browsing the city regulated the flow of sightseers and made the city available to all. In the crowd "everyone can only nip and taste, no one is allowed to push forward."[40]

The city worked best when its people subordinated themselves to streams of masses and flows of traffic. Berlin's workers had learned these lessons long ago, Osborn claimed.

> In the economic and political struggles of the day they learned the importance of the mass and its laws . . . they learned to subordinate themselves, to be considerate and patient, and to keep their cool. This was already plain to see years ago, at the time of [Wilhelm] Liebknecht's funeral. And we've seen the unbelievable discipline of the electoral-reform demonstrations . . . the ability to

calmly wait for the Stadtbahn or along the streets of the working-
class quarters or in summer beer gardens or at the coat-check of
the people's theaters or at political demonstrations.

City observers were fascinated by the patterns made by
workers as they commuted to work, journeyed "ins Grüne" or
to Lunapark, and especially as they mustered themselves in
the long columns of Social Democratic marches. The organization of millions of workers on the streets was an accomplishment no less impressive than the production of metropolitan
newspapers: "People, people, people! Thousands, thousands,
thousands! . . . Masses, masses, masses!" wrote the *Morgenpost* on the occasion of the funeral of Paul Singer, beloved Social Democratic Reichstag deputy from Berlin.[41]

Unfortunately, Osborn pointed out, Berlin's middle classes
only reluctantly observed urban protocols, preventing the city
from running smoothly. "You can see remnants of the primitive wildness with which the individualism of the so-called educated classes reacts to events," Osborn noted, "you can still
see the bestial behavior of 'refined' audiences after the end of
a concert . . . and in the elbow matches at Westend streetcar
stops." In the long run, however, "the teeming metropolis will
cultivate even our bourgeoisie. Already the subway has been
successfully training passengers." Thanks to the calibration
that streetcars and subways required, a mass culture untrou-
bled by particular individuals was coming into sight. When it
matured, all the inhabitants would find it pleasurable "to observe the internal mechanical laws which regulated the movement of crowds and to be a properly functioning part of the
mass."[42] Less than twenty years later, in 1929, Döblin arrived
on Alexanderplatz and reported on the smooth operation of
this urban machinery.

It is clear that Osborn's vision of the city as a machine and city people as machine parts, published on 7 February 1911, was written under the impression of the mammoth funeral for Paul Singer, which had taken place two days before. Without explicitly saying so, Osborn had borrowed the organization and discipline of the Social Democrats and transposed those qualities onto the city as a whole. Like so many other bourgeois observers, both before and after World War I, he admired the political achievement though not necessarily the political program of the Socialists, and he linked future prosperity to the adoption of these collective forms.[43] The challenge for Berlin, in this case, was to reconvene the masses under nonsocialist auspices, to display mass culture and political power in the industrial city without adopting proletarian economics. The great Ullstein papers, the *Morgenpost* and *BZ am Mittag*, played crucial parts in this effort.

CHOREOGRAPHING MACHINES AND MASSES

Mass circulation newspapers not only reported on but helped assemble the metropolitan crowd on the streets. When publishers promoted spectacular events such as automobile races and aviation rallies, they clearly swelled the number of their readers and added to the prosperity of their business. By gathering together hundreds of thousands of spectators the press also redefined the public and transformed a passive readership into an active metropolitan culture. As Berliners lined the streets to cheer the arrival of Ullstein's entry in an around-the-globe automobile race, to welcome Germany's extraordinary lighter-than-air zeppelin, or to send off the first generation of aviators on a month-long rally around the country, city people lost some of the social and ethnic differences that divided them. Under the shared banner of "nation" and "folk," they became more alike. To an enthusiastic press, these spectacles of technology anticipated a machine-tempered nationalism that would resuscitate German power in the twentieth century as much as the patriotic levée en masse had revived revolutionary France in 1792. But it was not simply the victory of national over class loyalties or German over French might that excited Berlin newspapermen; it was also the disciplined constitution of the urban crowd, something which critics of mass society, from frantic antisocialists to old-fashioned liberals, had not believed possible. The orderly movements of masses affirmed a thoroughly commercial and democratic metropolis. Dramatizing the city as spectacle, describing the movement of crowds, and assembling readers on the streets, the press played a vital part in the formation of a consumer public.

Exuberant city-wide spectacles showed that metropolitans composed a coherent entity. Of course, Berliners still remained divided by competing allegiances to class, trade, ethnicity, and religion. In the years before World War I, massive Social Democratic demonstrations and smaller nationalist rallies underscored the basic divisions in Wilhelmine Germany. At the same time, however, partisans reassembled as spectators who read about and looked at and used the city in increasingly similar ways. Readers had not become indistinguishable, but they had grown more alike, and their identification with the displays of consumer culture tended to undercut the authority both of the Wilhelmine state and of the embattled Social Democratic movement. On the street, whether window shopping on Potsdamer Platz, strolling at Lunapark and in the Grunewald, or joining celebrations of German technology, Berliners recognized each other as sharing the experience of the razzle-dazzle of the industrial city.

Ullstein and Scherl spent millions of marks staging huge rallies around technological novelties. They thereby reversed the process, putting the event before the reportage, reproducing the sensationalism of the front pages on the grand boulevards. Being in the city was becoming much like reading about the city. *BZ am Mittag*, for example, jumped at the opportunity to join a consortium of newspapers that included *Le Matin* and the *New York Times* to sponsor an around-the-world, New York-to-Paris automobile race in 1908. Ullstein purchased and "with hundreds of hands working day and night" outfitted a 40-horsepower Protus touring car, hired a veteran driver and a mechanic, and assigned travel reporter Hans Koeppen to cover the race. Although Koeppen did not actually drive the Protus, he became identified as the primary contestant, while the actual chauffeurs faded from view. *BZ am Mittag* introduced the race and racers on its front pages and organized a huge send-off rally in front of the Ullsteinhaus on Kochstrasse on 26 January, a Sunday when most Berliners had the day off. Thanks to publicity in *BZ* and the *Morgenpost*, thousands of city people joined the fanfare. "That was some uprising yesterday morning in the Kochstrasse!" reflected *BZ*. "By the light of Sunday's dawn, people arrived from all directions on foot, by bicycle, by streetcar, and by automobile, as if the street and our offices were the destination of half Berlin." Many more thousands of readers followed Koeppen's telegraphed reports on the front pages, which described the progress of the race through North America, by steamer to Russia, and westwards across Siberia toward Berlin and finally over the finish line in Paris.[44]

Happily for Ullstein, the German team had taken the lead and on 23 July 1908 approached Berlin as clear winners. The company mobilized its resources to welcome the victorious drivers. The penultimate stage of the race, before the final Berlin-to-Paris leg, monopolized Ullstein operations, which breathlessly headlined Koeppen's progress across eastern Prussia, published extra editions once Koeppen was sighted on the city outskirts, and provided an exact itinerary of the race route once the car entered Berlin: from Frankfurter Allee over Alexanderplatz, Unter den Linden, and Friedrichstrasse to the "Hause der *BZ am Mittag*" on Kochstrasse. *BZ* left no doubt as to its ability to choreograph the spectacle. "Everyone walking to work this morning," the paper observed on 24 July, "held our extra edition, eagerly studied the itinerary . . . Never before has Berlin been so enthusiastically engrossed in geography, both big and small." Newspaper vendors were particularly delighted since the race sold so many additional copies of *BZ am Mittag*, "one of our best and most quickly moving items."[45] Thousands of Berliners followed *BZ*'s directions to line the parade route. In front of the Ullsteinhaus, "the crowds grow more dense and more colorful by the minute." Other reporters surveyed crowds in the business district, where "automobiles and streetcars, delivery trucks and omnibuses slowly crept forward," and on Unter den Linden: "Here too everybody is crowded three or four rows deep, expectantly waiting." An "11:15 A.M." telegram in the very latest edition of *BZ am Mittag* announced that Koeppen had "just" passed Frankfurter Allee. The news here is almost live: at that very moment, "thousands of eyes are looking toward the corner of Koch- and Friedrichstrasse, where the victorious car is expected anytime." According to subsequent estimates, eighty thousand people had rallied around the Ullsteinhaus; for them, the front page had expanded to become the city itself.[46] The Ullstein weekly, *Berliner Illustrirte*, also serialized Koeppen's book, *Im Auto um die Welt*, and the firm later published it.

BZ am Mittag heralded Koeppen's accomplishment as an impressive technical feat and also as a great nationalist victory. "A country that can build such machines and raise such men," *BZ* underlined, "is not in decline or growing soft, as its enemies whisper: its people have met the challenge of the times and are prepared to accomplish the most difficult tasks that human progress might present."[47] Although the German nation was still young, and thus handicapped during the nineteenth-century scramble for imperial spoils, technological expertise would make up for political immaturity. Moreover, Koeppen's feat was so warmly applauded by the German people because they understood the national importance of "automobilism." Younger people, especially, showed themselves ready "to open their hearts to the New and the Strong." And the thousands of sightseers that Ullstein had assembled were not the disorderly bunch the critics had anticipated. What made this celebration of the German nation so forceful was its popular dimension and technical aspect. Future prosperity rested on this combination.[48]

Just a few weeks after Koeppen's triumphal arrival in Berlin, Graf Ferdinand Zeppelin captured the German imagination with his long-distance dirigible flights. Despite a series of mishaps and explosions in August 1908, Graf Zeppelin had proven the technical viability of airship travel to jubilant and increasingly nationalist crowds in southern Germany, and he promised to display his rebuilt machine over the imperial capital in August 1909. In the meantime, however, Socialist demonstrations for electoral reform in February and supposedly unruly crowds at a zeppelin landing in Munich in April 1909 unnerved the Prussian police and put the desirability of unofficial "people's festivals" into question. To avoid a breach of public order, the kaiser insisted that Graf Zeppelin fly over Tempelhof Field. City people could gather there, but the airship would actually land at the parade grounds at Tegel, where a smaller court ceremony would take place without danger of disruption.[49]

For the popular press, Zeppelin Day—Sunday, 29 August 1909—became a contest between two different kinds of nationalism: the official one expressed by the kaiser and the court, and the popular, exuberant version on the streets. On this day, the *Morgenpost* editorialized, Berliners had to show that they were politically mature and thus deserving of the electoral clout already enjoyed by rural Prussians (the result of outmoded districting). Even in "the highest ecstasy of enthusiasm" the masses were urged to maintain "dignified coolheadedness."[50] Thanks to the "strict and wonderful discipline which our workers have learned on the political battlefield," editors had no doubt that Berliners would pass muster.

As the city's biggest and most popular newspaper, the *Morgenpost* also assumed control of crowd management. On Saturday the paper published three extra editions to keep Berliners abreast of the progress of the Zeppelin, which had landed unexpectedly in Bitterfeld for emergency repairs. In an age without radio or television, extra editions were the best way to inform the public quickly. At Tempelhof, the *Morgenpost* also organized flag signals, raised by balloons, to broadcast the latest telegraph reports so that hundreds of thousands of sightseers could follow the airship's progress: Greater Berlin was divided into square fields, each designated by a distinctive flag; once the zeppelin entered a particular field, the appropriate flag would be raised at Tempelhof. Of course, the system only worked if spectators purchased the *Berliner Morgenpost* (Ullstein's competitors did not organize similar broadcasting systems). Moreover, the *Morgenpost* explained:[51]

> The black-white Prussian flag means that the Zeppelin III remains anchored in Bitterfeld.
> If the black-white-red Reich flag is raised that means Graf Zeppelin has left Bitterfeld for Berlin.
> Should the telegraphic service of the Berliner Morgenpost report an accident en route, a red flag with a white ball will be raised.
> Once the problem has been solved, we will raise a white flag with a red field.

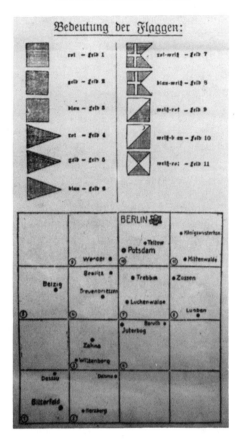

"Unser Signal-Ballon." The *Morgenpost*
explains its system for raising the various
flags over Tempelhofer Field to indicate
the progress of the zeppelin over Berlin.

Clearly, without the *Morgenpost* the spectacle would have been
much less rewarding for sightseers and would have looked
much less organized to police officials.

What could have been mistaken for an Ullstein production
proceeded flawlessly. Until the airship actually crossed Tempelhof, all eyes were focused on the *Morgenpost*'s "signal bal-

loon . . . and as soon as we raised a new flag announcing the
further progress of the zeppelin, a wave of excitement swept
over the crowd."[52] The actual flyover was described by each of
the big papers in flamboyant prose in which adjectives and
verbs tumbled over each other. The poet's sparser language
better caught the image of the city people following the zeppelin's flight: "Berlin has only one single neck today . . . one
cheering mouth, one eye, one heart," wrote Adolf Petrenz.[53]
The sober *Berliner Tageblatt* allowed that Berliners had
never before been seen to participate in such numbers.[54] Indeed, the "Grosse Berliner" sold more streetcar tickets on
Zeppelin Day—over 1.2 million—than ever before![55] One in
every three Berliners was transported through the city; it was
an extraordinary and unprecedented display of civic unity.
More important, millions of metropolitans proved as disciplined on Zeppelin Day as thousands of workers had been on
any May Day. "People of Berlin," gushed the *Berliner Tageblatt*, "yesterday you were simply beautiful the way you presented yourself as mass, as a whole."[56] *BZ am Mittag* agreed.
"Genus Mass" had gained respectability: "The Berlin public,
divided and opinionated as it may be, is unified in that it . . .
can maintain discipline if it must."[57] The masses of Berliners
assembled under the zeppelin symbolized a new Germany, a
nation that was technologically advanced and oriented toward
the future. What newspapers celebrated was the formation of
a popular, patriotic entity beyond the confines of class and the
hierarchies of the monarchy.[58]

The 1911 "Deutsche Rundflug," a month-long airplane
rally across Germany, was almost entirely initiated and organized by Ullstein, who offered the contest's *BZ am Mittag*
"Preis der Lüfte." Both the start and finish of the race produced extraordinary excitement as Berliners gathered to catch
a glimpse of Germany's aeronautical future. As earlier, *BZ am
Mittag* took the lead and published extra editions, appropri-

BZ am Mittag sponsored Germany's
national air rally in 1911.

ately entitled "Extra-'Flug'-Blatt," in addition to a special
aeronautical edition on Saturday, 11 June 1911, the day before the start of the rally. Readers found a helpful program to
the event: there were background articles; a large-type poem
entitled "Volare necesse est" by Karl Vollmöller; a map of Johannisthal, the airfield from which the fliers would take off at
dawn; and details about the special trains that had been
pressed into service (every ten minutes beginning at two in the
morning!).[59] Throughout June and early July, front-page articles in both *BZ am Mittag* and the *Morgenpost* kept readers

informed about the progress of the race and the winners of
various stages; the *Berliner Tageblatt*, by contrast, kept news
of the rally back on page five. The *Lokal-Anzeiger* barely mentioned the city-wide event at all.

Although the race itself was a disappointment because no
single flier completed all stages, the people's enthusiasm for
the race astonished even Ullstein's master promoters. Already
before dawn on the day the race was to begin, Berlin was in a
state of frenzy, as Germany's largest weekly illustrated recalled:[60]

> Countless numbers of sightseers from all parts of the city streamed
> uninterruptedly to the Eastside. A dense column of cars, often
> four abreast, stretched from the city limits to Johannisthal. Al-
> ready at two in the morning crowds had stormed streetcars, omni-
> buses, subways, and the elevated, which pressed extra trains into
> service. The elevated moved the most people. The trains passed
> every ten minutes, one more crowded than the other. I thought I
> was dreaming when I looked at the sight of thousands of passen-
> gers balancing on running boards and sitting on roofs for one-and-
> a-half hours because I never imagined such an event here in
> Prussia.

What astonished the *Berliner Illustrirte* was the outpouring
of popular nationalism in which a wide spectrum of Berliners
participated. This was not something usually seen in the *Re-
ichhauptstadt*'s choreography of imperial parades and Hohenzollern weddings. Thousands upon thousands of Berliners
filled the still-dark streets, and yet they behaved in a completely disciplined way. According to *BZ am Mittag*'s Conrad
Alberti, the crowd's masterly sense of order and boundless
enthusiasm for flying machines revealed the "ethics of the
modern era." As many as 600,000 Berliners from all backgrounds witnessed the early-morning start of the race at Tempelhof.[61] "All sorts of people merged into a colorful crowd on

the green meadow . . . royal princes, officers, elegant society ladies, sport enthusiasts, artists, dignified businessmen, solid workers." Class differences seemed to dissolve in the mass, reported eye-witnesses. The media event turned the diverse readers into like-minded spectators and created the experience, at least for a time, of a tangible city public. "The whole story of yesterday's flight to Magdeburg," Alberti continued, comparing the formation of the crowd to the functioning of an airplane motor, "proves to us how important the least little thing, a retightened screw, a few extra drops of gasoline or oil, is to the success of the mission. That is exactly how a person in the crowd feels, knowing . . . how the success of the whole, the honor of the nation, is so dependent on the loyalty, attention, and energy of even the smallest part."[62] The movement of the masses, in which individuals subordinated themselves into the press of the crowd or the stream of traffic, revealed Germany's mechanical future as much as did the actual flights of airplanes and zeppelins.[63]

The precise form that this new Germany would take was not completely clear. As a first step, however, the patriotic enthusiasm and orderly discipline of the metropolitan public seemed to entitle urban voters to greater political responsibility, which the conservative monarchy had hitherto denied them. In the name of more than a three-quarter million readers, *BZ am Mittag*, the *Berliner Morgenpost*, and the *Berliner Tageblatt* urged the Reich government to embark on democratic reform. Mosse and Ullstein, but not Scherl, demanded a thorough revision of Prussia's antique three-class suffrage system and called for more ministerial accountability to the Reichstag in the wake of the *"Daily Telegraph* affair" of October 1908, when *BZ am Mittag* revealed some careless comments the kaiser had made to an English journalist on delicate matters of foreign policy.[64] Drawing strength from public manifestations of patriotism, and confident that metropolitan culture provided a firm foundation for Germany's future, Berlin's mass-circulation press spoke out in a voice that was robust rather than aggrieved. The emergence of an emphatically urban and increasingly democratic polity seemed inevitable. With the onset of war in August 1914, however, it was not the democratic spirit but the machine-tempered discipline of metropolitan crowds that the German state mobilized. "As far as the eye can see," surveyed Max Osborn in November, "smoke and steam and soot . . . from all directions, hammering, heaving, gurgling, grinding. Columns of workers are in motion, chopping and building, digging and shoveling." This was the sobering picture of Berlin readied for war. "Are the people of this planet aware of this?" Osborn reflected.[65] Three years later, Fritz Koch, employing the literary formulas used by so many observers before the war, wrote with admiration about the tireless energy of Berliners. The synchronized images had not changed, but they were inserted into the grander plotline of nationalist endeavor. "Even in this fourth year of war, the city continues to stretch and strain at full speed," he noted. Koch portrayed wartime Berlin at work and play in a series of literary excursions, "captured," as he put it, "for our grandchildren."[66] Stories of the wartime mobilization of Berlin were evidently to be told and retold. War was the greatest spectacle and seemed, in retrospect, to give purpose to the thousand-headed public that had emerged with such anticipation before the war at Kochstrasse celebrations, Zeppelin Days, and Tempelhof rallies.

13 OTHER TEXTS OF EXPLORATION

All sorts of texts littered the streets of the industrial metropolis. In addition to the newspapers there were books, sold from rickety carts by itinerant peddlers; strange East Elbian names on imperial statuary; sundry notices on Berlin's many hundred *Litfasssäulen*; shoddy handbills which small boys and young men distributed on commercial thoroughfares; postcards depicting notorious or other public figures such as Graf Zeppelin, Rudolph Hennig, and the "Hauptmann von Köpenick"; and oddly angled and shaped advertising placards. People paid attention to the fine print of streetcar schedules, obeyed the posted Prussian regulations and prohibitions, and made use of well-placed municipal clocks, fancifully wrought street signs, and colorful Pharus maps. Metropolitans had to fill out an array of preprinted forms—to register with the police, for example, or subscribe to a newspaper. It would have been difficult to encounter the city or use its services and pleasures without reading and writing. Officials in the imperial capital as well as merchants, agents, and negotiators in the commercial metropolis made extensive use of written records. "Living by the record and for the record," as Lewis Mumford noted in *The City in History*, had indeed become "one of the great stigmata of urban existence."[1]

But if the deep chiselwork of the ancient records from which Mumford generalizes authored a particular or indelible version of the city, the proliferation of advertisements, regulations, and newspapers around 1900 assembled innumerable alternatives. With so many co-authors, this word city made possible a plurality of readings that continuously disorganized and reorganized the metropolitan inventory. It was the very nature of the written word and the way it was edited and published, circulated and deleted, that left the modern metropolis looking so syntactically indeterminate. The newspaper was perhaps the best example of the heteroglossia of modern print culture, because it was both the most ubiquitous record of the city and the most varied in textual forms: telegrams, lead stories, editorials, feuilletons, government notices, advertisements.

This rich textuality produced multiple effects. To some readers, the city acquired a sharp crystalline clarity. The discrete details and contrasting images in story after story added thousands of separate, brightly polished facets to a city once considered grey and uniform. At this close vantage, every colorful character or snippet of conversation could be examined and set at an angle against another to create an intricate urban composition. Although the merely fragmentary accounts in the daily newspaper failed to provide a complete inventory of the city, they easily accommodated new and ill-fitting elements and thus constituted the metropolis as a place that tolerated strangers and cherished difference. For other readers, conversely, the visual enhancement of the city in terms of contrast and discontinuity simply blurred and confused metropolitan matters. Constantly revised daily editions augmented this tentative aspect. Consequently, day after day, as the press wrote and rewrote the word city, the metropolis became more legible to some, and less to others.

If the standard format of stories, the common tropes they employed, and the very regular appearance of the newspaper imposed an unmistakable routine on the city, the attention-calling headlines, the juxtaposition of items on the front page, and the various editions at streetcorner kiosks continuously unsettled metropolitan appearances. The profusion of words in the city assembled legible texts and also replenished judgments and abruptly interrupted compositions. Again and again, the word city resisted an authoritative reading. No two people took up and read the paper in quite the same way.

The unmanageability of the great text of the city, resulting from the uncertain terms of mediation, had the effect of embellishing its fugitive quality. Cities, and the word cities they generated, have thus constituted a congenial topos for modernism. They were repeatedly explored by artists and writers eager to use metropolitan forms to challenge the conventions of representation. Improvised formats such as newspaper feuilletons, "real-life" documentations, and Expressionist brushstrokes all put accent on discontinuity, shock, and fluctuation. Thus the narrative of the modern city and the modernist format of narration reinforced each other in a mutually sustaining relationship summarized elegantly by David Frisby as *Fragments of Modernity*.[2] A look at "other texts on the shelf," at more "canonical" modernist works, indicates just how compelling was the notion of the fugitive city.

No literary product could compete with the metropolitan

newspaper in size of readership, but dozens of texts tried to capture the attention of the reading public. In April 1912, Filippo Marinetti, presumably not satisfied with attendance at public lectures in which he celebrated twentieth-century technology, resolved to combine message and medium and, from an open-air automobile, tossed his Futurist manifestos along Leipziger Strasse until he was stopped from doing so by Traugott von Jagow's policemen. Less fanciful but more accessible were the fifty pamphlet-sized *Grossstadt-Dokumente* edited by the Berlin publicist Hans Ostwald. Deliberately fragmentary and sensational accounts of the big city, Ostwald's volumes went through as many as fifteen editions in the ten years following their appearance in 1904 and found an appreciative metropolitan readership.

True, there were no street outlets for art. The only way Berliners could view the stunning work of Berlin Secessionists, then of the New Secessionists, and, later, of German Expressionists was to push open the doors of posh galleries in Berlin's Westend. Yet newspapers helped: Heinrich Zille was one of only a few important Secessionist artists to gain a genuinely popular audience thanks to his contract work for Germany's largest weekly, *Berliner Illustrirte Zeitung*, and one of its largest corporations, General Electric. Berlin's early-twentieth-century painters—Zille, Hans Baluschek, and particularly Ludwig Meidner and Ernst Ludwig Kirchner—explored the urban setting in enormously suggestive ways. Berlin also supported an impressive number of small literary magazines which became the main venues for the founding generation of Expressionist poets in the last years before 1914, although neither *Pan, Aktion,* nor *Sturm* reached even a fraction of the *Morgenpost*'s or, for that matter, Ostwald's readership.[3] One observer sought to formulate an overview of these diverse artistic endeavors. Himself personally deeply invested in the cosmopolitan attractions of imperial Berlin, and consciously attempting at the same time to fashion a scholarly method appropriate to talking about the modern metropolis, the sociologist Georg Simmel provides the best starting point to discuss the texts of the fugitive city.

Writing around the turn of the century, Simmel was one of the first scholars to theorize how the new psychological combinations and experimental artistic forms had developed out of the terrain of the industrial city. The character of the modern was restless, transfiguring movement for which, according to Simmel, the best illustration was the expansion of the money economy in the big cities. Only in the nineteenth century, with the entrenchment of advanced capitalism, did the circulation of goods and commodities finally begin to dissolve substantial things and honorable ties into entirely functional relationships. A constant process of buying and selling, of destroying, renovating, and reconstructing, had the effect of liquidating the accretion of tradition. These conditions of fluctuation nourished a "culture of indifference" in which city people not only adopted an increasingly blasé, almost defensive attitude toward their turbulent surroundings but also developed a highly subjective sensibility, one that was "indifferent" to distinctions between high and low, fundamental and trivial, and refined and vulgar.

The characteristic modern observer, Simmel argued, was the detached wanderer who cobbled a thoroughly unauthoritative picture of the world by putting together ephemeral pieces in a completely contingent manner, by way of impressionistic snapshots and vignettes. For Simmel, each person delivered on the promise of the very cosmopolitan city in a personal and hence often "undeveloped artistic style."[4] Although the culture of indifference was accompanied by social impoverishment, it nourished a self-stylization of the intellect which

Simmel would celebrate repeatedly in the labile format of the essays he wrote and in the wide-ranging lectures he delivered as a self-described academic *Wanderprediger*, or wandering preacher. This attention to style, or to "the charm of the fragment" as Simmel once put it, corresponded to the diversity and fragmentation of the modern metropolis itself. "The special achievements that I made during these decades," he later reflected, were "undoubtedly tied to the Berlin milieu." By his own admission, Simmel, who grew up on the corner of Leipziger Strasse and Friedrichstrasse, was as much a product as an observer of the city.[5]

The wanderer, whom Simmel called the ideal metropolitan observer can be identified and named: he was Hans Ostwald. After years of rambling through the German countryside as an itinerant craftsman, Ostwald returned to Berlin, the city of his birth, in the late 1890s. What he found in the capital was an urban setting as fresh and unaccountable as the rural landscape he had just left. The city had grown "most modern," its fantastic proportions had become clear only in the "last decades."[6] After completing a novel based on his vagabonding,[7] Ostwald set out to explore the new metropolis with the aimless meander of the *Wanderbursche*. Ostwald's documentary views of the city rested on his marginal status as a vagabond and the itinerant nature of his excursions. The *Landstreicher* (country tramp) had become *Stadtstreicher* (city stroller).

Wandering alongside Ostwald on his *Stadtstreichereien* crossing and recrossing the city garden, readers were introduced to a rich variety of sights and sounds and characters in highly evolved settings. More significant than his introductions however, was the way Ostwald looked at and represented the metropolis. The disorder of the city inspired the absence of narrative continuity in the *Grossstadt-Dokumente*. Twenty years before Döblin, Ostwald collected all sorts of urban debris and stuck the pieces between the pages of his books. He reproduced advertisements and reprinted brochures and flyers handed out along Berlin's streets; he collected paragraphs of barroom conversations, recorded cabaret chansons and dance numbers, and authenticated his texts with slang. Various pamphlets provided long extracts from letters or case studies, an approach that not only recreated the immediacy of social experience but also reproduced the collage effect of the city. Both in style and substance, the *Grossstadt-Dokumente* embellished the fluctuating and kaleidoscopic experience of the industrial city.[8]

Ostwald was exemplary of those turn-of-the-century journalists and writers who experimented with the form of the small essay or *kleine Prosa*, which seemed appropriate to represent the volatile process of urban transformation. If the wonder of the city was, as the novelist Robert Walser put it, "that every attitude and gesture is subsumed by a thousand varieties, that perspective is fleeting, that judgment comes quickly, that forgetting is second-nature," then the city required improvised, detached, and playful interlocutors. These could be found, first and foremost, among feuilletonists, literary dilettantes whose impressionistic vignettes caught the accidental and transitory quality to city encounters. According to the literary critic Eckhardt Köhn, the newspaper feuilleton most suitably brought the metropolis to literary life in the nineteenth century; it was the mainstay for Ostwald's documentations and remained the privileged format for three generations of metropolitan observers, from Julius Rodenberg in the first years after unification to Walter Benjamin and Siegfried Kracauer in the last years of the Weimar era.[9]

The qualities feuilletonists admired—the ability to sketch a scene, to provide local color, to depict contrasts—were heavily indebted to the visual arts, which suggests that the painter had an easier time than the writer: according to Baudelaire, a "rapid . . . speed of execution" is necessary amidst "the daily metamorphosis of things."[10] Given its turbulent rhythms and evanescent constitution, the modern city placed a peculiar burden on metropolitan artists. Indeed, according to Ludwig Meidner's well-known manifesto of 1914, "An Introduction to Painting Big Cities," the primary responsibility of the painter who wished to depict the metropolis was to capture motion. Big cities were not represented by "tonal values," which had been the focus of a now passing generation of Impressionists, but rather by a "bombardment of whizzing rows of windows, of screeching lights between vehicles of all kinds and a thousand jumping spheres, scraps of human beings, advertising signs, and shapeless colors." French Impressionists such as Pissarro and Monet had been wrong to paint cities with the "sweetness and fluffiness" of pastoral scenes. Indeed, it was precisely the artificial, industrial environment that the painter should depict: "tumultuous streets, the . . . iron suspension bridges, the gasmeters . . . the howling colors of the autobuses and express locomotives, the rolling telephone wires, the harlequinade of the advertisement pillars."

Along with amending the painter's subjects, the big city revised his method. Meidner dismissed the whole idea of setting up an easel in the middle of a busy street. Such an endeavor was sure to miss the very essence of the city. "We can't record instantaneously all the accidental and disorganized aspects of our motif and still make a picture of it," he explained. Motion, collision, bombardment were the proper themes of metropolitan painters, but they could not be captured by means of passive observation; artists had to actively search out and reconstruct the "movement of things" in subjectively felt compositions. In other words, the representation of metropolitan disorganization demanded deliberate artistic organization. The job of the urban painter was deletion, exaggeration, distortion; only after these tasks had been accomplished would the city on the painter's canvas begin to correspond to the city under the urbanite's skin.

Meidner would eventually focus on the "splintering, exploding, collapsing quality" of the metropolis to such an extent that his cityscapes became virtual apocalyptic landscapes in which viewers could literally read off the horrors of the coming world war. It would be a mistake, however, to infer that Meidner felt threatened by or alienated in Berlin. Throughout his 1914 manifesto he referred repeatedly to the city in affectionate and breathless terms: "Let's paint what is close to us, our city world!" And night after night, Meidner walked the city streets with his companion, the poet Jakob van Hoddis:[11]

> We used to leave the Café des Westens after midnight and march, straightbacked, quite fast, right ahead through the streets, following our noses. . . . We were twenty-eight at that time and had plenty of stamina; first light found us still marching on, not at all tired, and the early sun was well over the rooftops before we asked each other what part of town we were in. Mostly it was the far north or northeast, but the rows of buildings continued, those cheerfully dismal Berlin apartment blocks, with their dismally cheerful balconies. Here and there were the first eyewitnesses to the coming Berlin weekday, which in those days, for all is homeyness, did not seem plain and banal but beautiful, magnificent, unique, even sublime, and inexpressibly delightful. We were so in love with that city.

Meidner deliberately browsed through the city; he followed his nose and left behind the conventional sightseer's itinerary of the *Hohenzollernstadt* to explore the periphery. And it was there, amidst tenements, construction sites, and excavation pits, that he found the most suitable points of vantage to observe the city in flux. Indeed, Meidner's first urban canvases, painted soon after he arrived in Berlin from Paris in June 1907, detailed a variety of suburban subjects: subway construction in Charlottenburg, a new road in Wilmersdorf, a gasmeter in Schöneberg. To Meidner the city was compelling because it was dynamic, and restless motion became the real theme of his best work. As Charles Haxthausen comments, Meidner's "apocalyptic style" is "grounded in . . . optical experience." To emphasize how the motion of the city required the artist to approach the canvas more deliberately, more brutally, Meidner became more strident and rendered his city in a more fragmentary and chaotic fashion.[12]

Ernst Ludwig Kirchner arrived in Berlin from Dresden somewhat later than Meidner—in 1911—but he quickly came to share his fellow artist's conclusions regarding the representation of the big city. "Objective construction is futile," Kirchner argued, "since a passing taxi, a bright or dark evening dress transforms the entire laboriously achieved construction." The unexpected motions along the metropolitan streets required the artist to convey fields and spheres of force rather than precise trajectories of movement. For that reason, Kirchner believed that "a purely linear scaffolding with almost schematic figures nevertheless represents the life of the streets in the most vital way."[13] Kirchner, like Meidner, worked on the assumption that the altered nature of perception in the big city demanded more labile modes of representation to allow the suggestion of force lines (Kirchner) or bombardments (Meidner). The Expressionists believed in willful experimentalism; it would be misguided to misread, as many commentators have, their accounts of the violent dissociation and discontinuity in the city as commentaries on the violence and alien character of the city proper.[14]

Both the subject and style of Meidner's and Kirchner's canvases drew attention to the ceaseless movement that charged the city center and crumbled its edge. In order to tell their stories, writers and artists returned again and again to the outlying *Vorstadt*. Perhaps the most self-conscious of these observers were the novelist Georg Hermann and the popular Berlin artists Hans Baluschek and Heinrich Zille. For each, the suburbs were not margins of a faraway city center, but rather the most metropolitan place. This was so because these neighborhoods were most decisively stamped with the motions of restless and unforgiving change. "Out here we have the feeling," Hermann wrote in *Pan*, "that with each step our eyes and our senses will make new discoveries." And what was the nature of these discoveries? "Nature, with its old laws, is making way for the city with its new laws."[15] Against a background of wooden construction fences and bare-walled five-story tenements—carefully chosen details which registered the restless motions of urban change—Hermann set his compelling story of the hairdresser Emil Kubinke and Baluschek and Zille drew their melancholy street scenes. Whether in the barroom or the bedroom, the tenement courtyard or the Prussian courthouse, Zille's characters in particular encountered the city in an accidental and usually luckless way. A sense of improvisation pervades his sketches. His quickly drawn lines accent the fluctuating fortunes of his characters' lives, yet they leave room for the appealing humor and self-reliance of his proletarian subjects. Certainly one effect of Zille's focus on children is the wide-eyed depiction of the industrial city as a completely new terrain with strange codes and exotic occasions and also as a place unstable enough to support all sorts of players, pranksters, hustlers, and other whimsical survivors.[16]

Odd juxtapositions, accidental encounters, and nervous spontaneity came to regulate the way a generation of observers

depicted the city immediately after the turn of the twentieth
century. Indeed, the fugitive city seemed to have been discovered almost at once: Simmel published his essay "The Metropolis and Mental Life" in 1903; *BZ am Mittag* arrived on city
streets in October 1904; Ostwald conceived his *Grossstadt-
Dokumente* in the same year; Zille first published his drawings
in Berlin newspapers in 1904 and began work as a fulltime il-
lustrator in 1908; Meidner returned to Berlin for the most
productive years of his career in June 1907; Georg Hermann
published *Kubinke*, his most contemporary Berlin novel, in
1910; and Kirchner left Dresden for Berlin the following year.
Working around the same time, each observer approached the
city with a sense of wonder. Enamored of urban dynamics,
Ostwald, Meidner, and Zille purposefully sought the *Vorstadt*,
a zone of transition which compressed, intensified, and exaggerated that dynamism. There was almost a vengeful search
for disorder in order to rattle complacent bourgeois morals
and to darken the transparent self-satisfaction with which
Wilhelmine burghers judged themselves. Modernists invented
the fugitive city just as much as the city inspired modernism.

No group made better use of the industrial city to over-
throw the supports of epistemological stability than the very
young Expressionist poets who met at the Café des Westens,
and no city appeared to confirm their challenge to the com-
prehensibility of the world more clearly than very new, very
modern Berlin. In the four or five years before the outbreak
of World War I, Jakob van Hoddis, Georg Heym, Alfred
Lichtenstein, and a half-dozen other poets produced an important, versatile oeuvre. Their poetry could be said to constitute a distinctive metropolitan grammar, or rather an anti-
grammar, since the surprises, the flux, and the juxtapositions
of the city infiltrated the verses themselves. Silvio Vietta
draws attention to the formal aspects of simultaneity, serial-

ization, and collage that distinguished the Expressionists and
links these to a uniquely metropolitan perception. The city
provided both an endlessly fascinating experience that challenged the logic and hierarchy of nineteenth-century meta-
physics, and a precise metaphor for the breakdown of perception and the dissolution of the subject. The city of the mind
distorted the links between subject and object and imperiled
the clarifying role of language.[17]

Whereas the Naturalists had conceptualized the big city as
a machinery that heightened the intensity of pathetic, tragic,
or vital elements in ordinary life, the Expressionists explored
the city rather differently, as a qualitatively different universe
in which radically revised laws of nature implicated sight and
perception in new ways. It was therefore beside the point to
characterize the city as oppressive or horrible or alienating; it
was simply not escapable. The city had to be regarded in epistemological rather than sociological categories. While Berlin-
based writers in the 1890s had fled to the lakeside village of
Friedrichshagen, taking the city to be a specific destination
from which one could depart and to which one could return
again, the generation of 1910 regarded it as an unremitting
presence.[18] This was a catastrophic recognition: like death,
the metropolis could not be evaded.

The fugitive city was a distinctly modernist topos, and the
fugitive appearances of the city were heightened by the highly
selective vantages that artists and writers favored. Casual
browsers followed their noses but kept arriving at particular
points of circulation: the tenement courtyard (but rarely tenement apartments themselves); the periphery where the city
collided with the countryside (but not beyond); turbulent
zones of transition in the city center (but not the built-up districts where most people lived); the garish shopping arcades
(but not plainer commercial avenues); dancehalls (but not or-

dinary working-class cafés); twilight (but not midday). Interstitial areas such as these choreographed urban collisions and urban juxtapositions, brought all manner of opposites together, and thereby presented an "always changing, always colorful picture."[19]

The image of the fugitive city tended to fragment and blur the metropolis to the point of obscuring the routine rhythm of factory work and the coherence of broad social classes. To focus on the "clamorous splendor" of Friedrichstrasse and the "always changing picture" of Potsdamer Platz was to disregard the constitution of an increasingly like-minded city-wide public pulled together by attractions such as Wannsee, Lunapark, Aschinger's, and the great department stores. Indeed, the city had become visually compelling, inviting crowds and thus providing the basis for urban spectatorship. Newspaper readers encountered the city more and more as spectators, and as such, they grew more and more alike. Given the emphasis the print media placed on the production of visual pleasure and the transformation of readers into consumers, they anticipated the widespread influence of film and television.

What is remarkable about the formation of a consumer public for city spectacles in the years before World War I is the extent to which big-city publishers such as Ullstein and Scherl were aware of the process and even accelerated it. Ullstein, in particular, actively promoted the urban crowd as a new political subject. The huge rallies the publisher sponsored for the Zeppelin and other technological marvels were harbingers of the popular nationalism that became visible after August 1914. Less spectacular but more consequential were the changing ways in which the city was used. In the prewar years growing numbers of Berliners came to favor explicitly metropolitan entertainments such as Lunapark or the Rheingold restaurant over purely neighborhood entertainments such as *Rummelplätze*. And since Social Democratic demonstrations in favor of electoral reform disbanded after 1910, larger and larger urban crowds assembled to celebrate national achievements. To be sure, this increasingly nationalist public was not the simple-minded creature of Wilhelmine politicians. As we have seen, the crowd resisted the formality and choreography of imperial authority.

The urban crowd was also always a tentative formation, and urban spectacle an evanescent pleasure. After the hardship years of war, revolution, and economic distress, the crowds on Potsdamer Platz and Friedrichstrasse appeared to break up. To be sure, Berliners continued to replenish metropolitan culture during the 1920s. They read the *Morgenpost* to play "Augen auf!"; city people crowded the ever popular carnival grounds at Lunapark and flocked to the movies; they wandered through the nighttime city illuminated by thousands of lights in a gigantic municipal spectacle in February 1928, hailed the return of the zeppelin over Berlin the next year, and celebrated "Iron Gustav," a coachman who, in spring and summer 1928, took the last horse-drawn cab in Berlin all the way to Paris and back before finally retiring.

Nonetheless, the metropolitan crowd assembled less readily than it had before the war. It got drawn into the national arena by new and more compelling media such as film and radio, which lacked a specifically metropolitan focus. Mass broadcasting denied both the city and the text the cultural status they had once enjoyed. As spectators moved elsewhere, the newspaper gradually returned to its former place as a medium of news and opinion. At the same time, metropolitan crowds became more fundamentally divided by politics and economics. The partisan politics of the Weimar era separated and isolated various parts of the public, making chance encounters more difficult and exclusive loyalties to social groups more important. The Sunday suit and everyman's bowler men had worn to stroll through the prewar city gave way to divisive party and paramilitary uniforms or to distinctively proletarian garb, particularly the balloon cap.[20] By the late 1920s, after political tensions between Communists and pro-republican Social Democrats exploded in street battles, neighborhood strongholds such as "Red Wedding" nurtured protective subcultures and pulled working-class metropolitans away from the city center.[21] With the rise of the Nazis, Sundays increasingly became a time of political violence rather than metropolitan leisure. The Great Depression hastened the psychological flight into neighborhoods—Wilmersdorf, Zehlendorf, Schmargendorf, Reinickendorf, Hellersdorf—which were reimagined as idyllic villages hidden in the folds of the dangerous metropolis.[22] At the same time, the stern economies of the early 1930s forced readers to buy fewer newspapers. City people thus encountered Berlin less adventurously. Zille's city became nostalgia even before Zille's death. Even as the culture of mass consumption muted the differences between metropolitans and provincials or between workers and tradespeople, increasingly contentious political subcultures left Berliners more sharply divided.

Spectacles still existed but were re-evaluated. The various lines of difference and scattered points of exchange that had once excited the modernist imagination were increasingly regarded as troublesome. Dancehalls and boulevards, which before the war were interesting for their mixed crowd, now appeared threatening and corrupting to a healthy but beleaguered *Volk*. Nowhere is this shift in the evaluation of difference clearer than in the writings of Hans Ostwald. Ostwald, for whom Berlin had been an exciting journey of discovery in the prewar years and whose *Grossstadt-Dokumente* challenged the pretensions of the Wilhelmine establishment with sympathetic portraits of prostitutes, vagabonds, and other metropolitan marginals, eventually mapped out a fearsome and disreputable cityscape in his influential *Sittengeschichte der Inflation,* "a cultural document," as he put it, of the 1920s.[23] Many of the same characters introduced in the *Grossstadt-Dokumente* reappear in the *Sittengeschichte:* criminals, gamblers, hustlers, prostitutes, musicians, occultists. No longer exotic mutations of the burgeoning industrial city, they are vilified as extraneous parasites. Rather than expand the idea of *Volk* to bring all kinds of city people closer together—the explicit goal of Ostwald's earlier documentaries—the *Sittengeschichte* polices the borders surrounding the *Volk* in an effort to make the core more sanitary.

For Ostwald, the carnival of the city at the turn of the century had collapsed into a house of horrors. The modernist features of the city in 1924 recall those of 1904—instability, mutability, uncertainty—but they are invoked to extinguish rather than celebrate difference. The colorful play on metropolitan identities and metropolitan niches has given way to the grinding work of social homogenization toward a virtuous sameness—the basic thrift and hard work—of the German people. This "displacement of difference" becomes one more version of the word city.[24]

The big city never lost its ability to enchant and surprise, and remained a modernist topos throughout the Weimar era, as the writings of Siegfried Kracauer and Walter Benjamin indicate. But the urban dynamism was never so powerful and attractive as it had been in the first years of Berlin's extraordinary growth, the pre-1914 period, when the experience of the industrial city and the practice of reading were still novel while the dangerous projects of political unity, ethnic homogeneity, and epistemological authority had not yet been realized. In turn, the Weimar years revealed that metropolitan culture was ultimately as fragile and tenuous as the city itself, that urban readerships were as perishable as the newspaper pages that had assembled them in the first place.

NOTES

INDEX

ABBREVIATIONS

NOTES

Introduction

1. On "weak forms," see Franco Moretti, *The Way of the World: The Bildungsroman in European Culture* (London, 1987), p. 12.
2. Anne Querrien, "The Metropolis and the Capital," *Zone* 1/2 (1986), pp. 219–221.
3. Lewis Mumford, *The City in History* (New York, 1961), pp. 97–98.
4. See Mikhail Bakhtin, *The Dialogic Imagination*, Michael Holquist, ed. (Austin, 1981), pp. 6–17, 238.
5. Frederic Jameson, *The Political Unconscious: Narrative as a Socially Symbolic Act* (Ithaca, 1981), p. 48.
6. See, for example, Jameson, *Political Unconscious*; John Bender, *Imagining the Penitentiary: Fiction and the Architecture of the Mind in Eighteenth-Century England* (Chicago, 1987); D. A. Miller, *The Novel and the Police* (Berkeley, 1988); Richard Terdiman, *Discourse/Counter-Discourse: The Theory and Practice of Symbolic Resistance in Nineteenth-Century France* (Ithaca, 1985);

Dominick LaCapra, *History and Criticism* (Ithaca, 1985); and Lloyd S.

Kramer, "Literature, Criticism, and Historical Imagination: The Literary Challenge of Hayden White and Dominick LaCapra," and Roger Chartier, "Texts, Printing, Readings," both in *The New Cultural History*, Lynn Hunt, ed. (Berkeley, 1989).

7. Ernst Bloch quoted in Reinhard Rürup, "'Parvenu Polis' and 'Human Workshop': Reflections on the History of the City of Berlin," *German History* 6 (1988), pp. 234–235.

8. For a brilliant and nuanced statement of the failures of modernism, see T. J. Clark, *The Painting of Modern Life: Paris in the Art of Manet and His Followers* (Princeton, 1986).

9. Simon J. Bronner, ed., *Consuming Visions: Accumulation and Display of Goods in America, 1880–1920* (New York, 1989); and Neil Harris, "Urban Tourism and the Commercial City," in William R. Taylor, ed., *Inventing Times Square: Commerce and Culture at the Crossroads of the World* (New York, 1991). pp. 66–82.

1. The Word City

1. The original reads as follows:

Dem Bürger fliegt vom spitzen Kopf der Hut,
In allen Ländern hallt es wie Geschrei.
Dachdecker stürzen ab und gehn entzwei,
Und an den Küsten—liest man—steigt die Flut.

Der Sturm ist da, die wilden Meeren hupfen.
An Land, um dicke Dämme zu verdrücken.
Die meisten Menschen haben einen Schnupfen.
Die Eisenbahnen fallen von den Brücken.

2. See, for example, Helmut Hornbogen, *Jakob van Hoddis: Die Odyssee eines Verschollenen* (Munich, 1986), p. 69.

3. Cited in Hornbogen, *Jakob van Hoddis*, p. 72.

4. Silvio Vietta, "Grossstadtwahrnehmung und ihre literarische Darstellung. Expressionistischer Reihungsstil und Collage," *Deutsche Vierteljahrsschrift für Literaturwissenschaft und Geistesgeschichte* 48 (1974), pp. 354–373. See also Heinz Rölleke, *Die Stadt bei Stadler, Heym, und Trakl* (Berlin, 1966).

5. Quoted and translated by Eberhard Roters, "The Painter's Nights," in Carol S. Eliel, *The Apocalyptic Landscapes of Ludwig Meidner* (Los Angeles, 1989), pp. 75–77. See also Charles W. Haxthausen, "Images of Berlin in the Art of the Secession and Expressionism," in *Art in Berlin 1815–1989* (Seattle, 1989), pp. 68–73.

6. Quoted in Rolf Lindner, *Die Entdeckung der Stadtkultur: Soziologie aus der Erfahrung der Reportage* (Frankfurt, 1990), p. 102.

7. Hans Brennert, "Gemeinde und Presse," in Brennert and Erwin Stein, eds., *Probleme der neuen Stadt Berlin* (Berlin, 1926), pp. 540, 543. See also Karl Bücher, "Der Zeitungsvertrieb" (1923), in *Gesammelte Aufsätze zur Zeitungskunde* (Tübingen, 1926), pp. 220–221.

8. Hans A. Münster, *Jugend und Zeitung* (Berlin, 1932), pp. 56–57.

9. See the classic study by Peter de Mendelssohn, *Zeitungsstadt Berlin: Menschen und Mächte in der Geschichte der deutschen Presse* (Berlin, 1959).

10. Walter Kiaulehn, *Berlin, Schicksal eine Weltstadt* (Berlin, 1958). p. 26.

11. Anselm Heine, "Berlins Physiognomie," in *Ich weiss Bescheid in Berlin* (Berlin, 1908), p. 3. For the tally of streetcars and other vehicles, see also BZ, no. 240, 12 Oct. 1905.

12. Alfred Döblin, *Alexanderplatz, Berlin. The Story of Franz Biberkopf*, Eugene Jolas, trans. (New York, 1931), p. 5.

13. Lion Feuchtwanger, "Ein Waggon der Untergrundbahn," in Herbert Günther, ed., *Hier schreibt Berlin: Eine Anthologie von Heute* (Berlin, 1929), pp. 235–239.

14. Stephan Schreder, *Der Zeitungsleser* (Vienna, 1936), p. 28.

15. Leonhard Adler, "Die Synthese des Weltstadtverkehrs," in Brennert and Stein, eds., *Probleme der neuen Stadt Berlin*, p. 365.

16. Richard Sennett, *The Fall of Public Man* (Cambridge, 1976), pp. 39, 47. See also Judith R. Walkowitz, *City of Dreadful Delight: Narratives of Sexual Danger in Late-Victorian London* (Chicago, 1992), pp. 16–18; Griselda Pollock, "Vicarious Excitements: London: A Pilgrimage by Gustave Doré and Blanchard Jerrold, 1872," *New Formations* 2 (Spring 1988), pp. 25–50; Deborah Epstein Nord, "The City as Theater: From Georgian to Early Victo-

rian London," *Victorian Studies* 31 (1988), pp. 159–188; idem, "The Urban Peripatetic: Spectator, Streetwalker, Woman Writer," *Nineteenth-Century Literature* 46 (1991), pp. 351–375; and T. J. Clark, *The Painting of Modern Life: Paris in the Art of Manet and His Followers* (Princeton, 1984).

17. Philip Fisher, "City Matters: City Minds," in Jerome Buckley, ed., *The Worlds of Victorian Fiction* (Cambridge, Mass., 1975), p. 388.

18. Köhn, *Strassenrausch*. See also Egon Friedell, *Ecce poeta* (Berlin, 1912).

19. Lindner, *Die Entdeckung der Stadtkultur*, pp. 21, 44–45.

20. Cited in Uwe Böker, "Von Wordsworths schlummerndem London bis zum Abgrund der Jahrhundertwende. Die Stadt in der englischen Literatur des 19. Jahrhunderts," in Cord Meckseper and Elisabeth Schraut, eds., *Die Stadt in der Literatur* (Göttingen, 1983), p. 35.

21. Walkowitz, *City of Dreadful Delight*.

22. Paul Gurk, *Berlin* (Berlin, 1934 [1927]), pp. 256–257, 275, 355–356.

23. Manfred Schlösser, Afterword to Gurk, *Berlin* (Berlin, 1980), pp. 357–358.

24. This debate is rehearsed and analyzed in Patrick Brantlinger, *Bread and Circuses: Theories of Mass Culture as Social Decay* (Ithaca, 1983).

25. Brantlinger, *Bread and Circuses*; "Introduction" to James Naremore and Patrick Brantlinger, eds., *Modernity and Mass Culture* (Bloomington, 1991); Richard Hoggart, *The Uses of Literacy* (London, 1957); and Miriam Hansen, "Early Silent Cinema: Whose Public Sphere?" *New German Critique* 29 (1983), pp. 147–184.

26. Richard Terdiman, *Discourse/Counter-Discourse: The Theory and Practice of Symbolic Resistance in Nineteenth-Century France* (Ithaca, 1985), p. 118, and generally pp. 118–138.

27. See the helpful analysis of Klaus R. Scherpe, "The City as Narrator: The Modern Text in Alfred Döblin's *Berlin Alexanderplatz*," in Andreas Huyssen and David Bathrick, eds., *Modernity and the Text: Revisions of German Modernism* (New York, 1989).

28. Döblin, "Berlin und die Künstler," *Vossische Zeitung*, no. 180, 16 Apr. 1922.

29. Philip Fisher, "The Novel as Newspaper and Gallery of Voices: The American Novel in New York City: 1890–1930," in Thomas Bender and Carl E. Schorske, eds., *Budapest and New York: Studies in Metropolitan Transformation, 1870–1930* (New York, 1994), p. 333. See also Marshall Berman, *All That Is Solid Melts into Air: The Experience of Modernity* (New York, 1982).

30. Lewis Mumford, *City in History*, (New York, 1961) pp. 448–449.

31. Arthur Eloesser, *Die Strasse meiner Jugend* (Berlin, 1987 [1919]), p. 7.

32. Karl Scheffler, *Berlin. Ein Stadtschicksal* (Berlin, 1910), p. 267.

33. For a recent example, see the afterword to Michael Bienert, *Die eingebildete Metropole: Berlin im Feuilleton der Weimarer Republik* (Stuttgart, 1992), p. 212.

34. Gottfried Korff, "Mentalität und Kommunikation in der Grossstadt. Berliner Notizen zur 'inneren' Urbanisation," in Theodor Kohlmann and Hermann Bausinger, eds., *Grossstadt: Aspekte empirischer Kulturforschung* (Berlin, 1985), pp. 343–361; and idem "'Die Stadt aber ist der Mensch . . .'" in Reinhard Rürup and Korff, eds., *Berlin, Berlin. Die Ausstellung zur Geschichte der Stadt* (Berlin, 1987), pp. 643–663.

35. This quote is highlighted and expertly discussed in David Frisby, *Fragments of Modernity: Theories of Modernity in the Work of Simmel, Isracauer, and Benjamin*, (Cambridge, Mass., 1985) pp. 46, 67, 72. See also Gianfranco Poggi, *Money and Modern Mind: Georg Simmel's Philosophy of Money* (Berkeley, 1993).

36. Georg Simmel, "The Metropolis and Mental Life," in *The Sociology of Georg Simmel*, Kurt Wolff, ed. (New York, 1950). pp. 413–414.

37. Georg Simmel, "Soziologie des Raumes," in *Schriften zur Soziologie*, Heinz-Jürgen Dahme and Otthein Rammstedt, eds. (Frankfurt, 1983), p. 88, cited and discussed in Lothar Müller, "Die Stadt als Ort der Moderne. Ueber Georg Simmel," in Klaus Scherpe, ed., *Die Unwirklichkeit der Städte: Grossstadtdarstellungen zwischen Moderne und Postmoderne* (Reinbek, 1988), p. 21.

38. Müller, "Die Stadt als Ort der Moderne," in Scherpe, ed., *Die Unwirklichkeit der Städte*, p. 26.

39. Simmel, "The Metropolis and Mental Life," p. 418.

40. Harry Liebersohn, *Fate and Utopia in German Sociology, 1870–1923* (Cambridge, Mass., 1988), p. 136.

41. The very usable terms "city matters" and "city minds" have been adopted from Philip Fisher's brilliant essay, "City Matters: City Minds," in Buckley, ed., *The Worlds of Victorian Fiction*, pp. 371–389.

42. Michael W. Jennings, *Dialectical Images: Walter Benjamin's Theory of Literary Criticism* (Ithaca, 1987), p. 18; and Charles Baudelaire, "The Painter of Modern Life," in his *The Painter of Modern Life and Other Essays*, J. Mayne, ed. (London, 1964), p. 13.

43. Richard Hamann, *Impressionismus in Leben und Kunst* (Cologne, 1907); and Susanne Hauser, *Der Blick auf die Stadt: Semiotische Untersuchungen zur literarischen Wahrnehmung bis 1910* (Berlin, 1990). For a magisterial overview of modern sight, see Martin Jay, *Downcast Eyes: The Denigration of Vision in Twentieth-Century French Thought* (Berkeley, 1993).

44. Bernt Engelmann, *Berlin. Eine Stadt wie keine andere* (Göttingen, 1991), p. 74.

45. Marianne Thalmann, *Romantiker entdecken die Stadt* (Munich, 1965), p. 7, a sadly neglected, brilliant book. See also Donald Fanger, *Dostoevsky and Romantic Realism: A Study of Dostoevsky in relation to Balzac, Dickens, and Gogol* (Cambridge, Mass., 1965), pp. 21–27.

46. E. T. A. Hoffmann, *Des Vetters Eckfenster* (Stuttgart, 1980 [1822]), p. 37.

47. On Goethe, see Rolf Engelsing, "Die Perioden der Lesergeschichte in der Neuzeit," *Archiv für Geschichte des Buchwesens* 10:2–3 (1969), pp. 951, 978.

48. Thalmann, *Romantiker entdecken die Stadt*, pp. 30–31, 34–35, 39.

49. Klotz, *Die erzählte Stadt*, pp. 15–16.

50. Philip Fisher, "City Matters: City Minds," in Buckley, ed., *The Worlds of Victorian Fiction*, pp. 386–387. See also Hartwig Iser-

hagen, "Die Bewusstseinskrise der Moderne und die Erfahrung der Stadt als Labyrinth," in Cord Meckseper and Elisabeth Schraut, eds., *Die Stadt in der Literatur* (Göttingen, 1983), pp. 81–104; and Steven Winspur, "On City Streets and Narrative Logic," in Mary Ann Caws, *City Images: Perspectives from Literature, Philosophy, and Film* (New York, 1991), pp. 60–70.

51. In addition to Fisher, see Klotz's analysis of Eugène Sue, Victor Hugo, Charles Dickens, and Emile Zola in *Die erzählte Stadt*, especially pp. 253, 381.

52. Pike, *The Image of the City*, pp. 58–59.

53. Ossip Mandelstam on Bely, cited in Berman, *All That Is Solid Melts into Air*, p. 267.

54. Klotz, *Die erzählte Stadt*, pp. 263–264, 312, 316.

55. Regarding this irritation, see Friedbert Stühler, *Totale Welten: der moderne deutsche Grossstadtroman* (Regensburg, 1989).

56. Harald Jähner, *Erzählter, montierter, soufflierter Text: Zur Konstruktion des Romans "Berlin Alexanderplatz" von Alfred Döblin* (Frankfurt, 1984), p. 116. See also Döblin, "Bemerkungen zum Roman" (1917), in *Aufsätze zur Literatur* (Olten, 1963), pp. 19–23.

57. Jähner, *Erzählter, montierter, soufflierter Text*, pp. 75, 22.

58. Fisher, "City Matters: City Minds," in Buckley, ed., *The Worlds of Victorian Fiction*, p. 88.

59. Letter of 18 Jan. 1907, cited in Eckhardt Köhn, *Strassenrausch: Flanerie und kleine Form. Versuch zur Literaturgeschichte des Flaneurs bis 1933* (Berlin, 1989), p. 135.

60. *Der Sturm*, no. 170/71 (July 1913), p. 71, cited in Harald Jähner and Krista Tebbe, eds., *Alfred Döblin zum Beispiel—Stadt und Literatur* (Berlin, 1987), p. 23.

61. Frisby, *Fragments of Modernity*, p. 47.

62. I am indebted here to the excellent analysis of Jeffrey S. Weiss, "Picasso, Collage, and the Music Hall," in Kirk Varnedoe and Adam Gopnik, eds., *Modern Art and Popular Culture: Readings in High and Low* (New York, 1990), pp. 83–115. See also Brunhilde Wehinger, "Bilderflut am Boulevard: Bühnenrevue und Boulevardpresse im Second Empire," in Helmut Pfeiffer et al, eds., *Art social und Art industriel. Funktionen der Kunst im Zeitalter des Indus-*

trialismus (Munich, 1987), pp. 411–413. The best analysis of popular entertainment in Berlin is Peter Jelavich, *Berlin Cabaret* (Cambridge, Mass., 1993).

63. Weiss, "Picasso, Collage, and the Music Hall," in Varnedoe and Gopnik, eds., *Modern Art and Popular Culture*, p. 94.

64. See Köhn, *Strassenrausch*; and Eva Becker, "'Zeitungen sind doch das Beste.' Bürgerliche Realisten und das Vorabdruck ihrer Werke in der periodischen Presse," in Helmut Kreuzer and Käte Hamburger, eds., *Gestaltungsgeschichte und Gesellschaftsgeschichte* (Stuttgart, 1969).

65. Cited in Frisby, *Fragments of Modernity*, p. 14. See also Eberhard Roters, "Weltstadt und Kiefernheide," in *Berlin um 1900* (Berlin, 1987), p. 21; Friedell, *Ecce poeta*; and Peter Fritzsche, "Vagabond in the Fugitive City: Hans Ostwald, Imperial Berlin and the *Grossstadt-Dokumente*," *Journal of Contemporary History* 29 (1994).

66. Bienert, *Die eingebildete Metropole*, p. 16.

67. Russell Berman, *The Rise of the Modern German Novel: Crisis and Charisma* (Cambridge, Mass., 1986), p. 135. The original is in Fontane, *Politik und Gesellschaft* (Munich, 1969).

68. The best analysis of the feuilleton is really Roland Barthes's essay on the related genre of *faits divers*. See his 1962 essay, "The Structure of the *Fait-Divers*," in Roland Barthes, *Critical Essays*, Richard Howard, trans. (Evanston, 1972), pp. 185–195, as well as Karl Prümm, "Die Stadt der Reporter und Kinogänger bei Roth, Brentano, und Kracauer: Das Berlin der zwanziger Jahre im Feuilleton der 'Frankfurter Zeitung,'" in Scherpe, *Die Unwirklichkeit der Städte*, pp. 86, 100–101.

69. Clark, *Painting of Modern Life*; and Christopher Prendergast, *Paris and the Nineteenth Century* (Oxford, 1992), pp. 1–45.

70. A. H. Kober, *Einst in Berlin*, Richard Kirn, ed. (Hamburg, 1956), pp. 7–16.

71. Kracauer, "Zeitungsausrufer" in "Berliner Figuren," (*Frankfurter Zeitung*, 10 July 1931), reprinted in *Strassen in Berlin und anderswo* (Frankfurt, 1964), pp. 151–153.

72. Cited in Roger Chartier, "Texts, Printing, Readings," in Lynn

Hunt, ed., *The New Cultural History* (Berkeley, 1989), p. 156. See also Wolfgang Iser, *The Act of Reading: A Theory of Aesthetic Response* (Baltimore, 1978).

2. Readers and Metropolitans

1. On the revolution in reading, see Rolf Engelsing, "Die Perioden der Lesergeschichte in der Neuzeit," *Archiv für Geschichte des Buchwesens* 10:2–3 (1969), pp. 945–1002. His classic argument about the transformation of intensive reading has been misread by other important historians of the subject: Cathy N. Davidson, *Revolution and the Word: The Rise of the Novel in America* (New York, 1986); and James Smith Allen, *In the Public Eye: A History of Reading in Modern France, 1800–1940* (Princeton, 1991).

2. Engelsing, "Die Perioden der Lesergeschichte," p. 984; B. R. Mitchell, *European Historical Statistics 1750–1975* (New York, 1980), p. 30.

3. Reinhard Wittmann, "Das literarische Leben 1848 bis 1880," in Max Bucher et al, eds., *Realismus und Gründerzeit: Manifeste und Dokumente zur deutschen Literatur, 1848–1880* (Stuttgart, 1976), vol. 1, pp. 228–237; idem, *Buchmarkt und Lektüre im 18. und 19. Jahrhundert: Beiträge zum literarischen Leben, 1750–1880* (Tübingen, 1982), pp. 199–204.

4. For this and other examples, see Engelsing's wonderfully rich article, "Perioden der Lesergeschichte," pp. 961–962, 971–972.

5. Arthur Eloesser, *Die Strasse meiner Jugend* (Berlin, 1919), pp. 13–14. See also Thomas C. Leonard, "News at the Hearth: A Drama of Reading in Nineteenth-Century America," *Proceedings of the American Antiquarian Society* 102/2 (1993), pp. 379–396.

6. Cited in Rudolf Schenda, *Volk ohne Buch: Studien zur Sozialgeschichte der populären Lesestoffe 1770–1910* (Frankfurt, 1970), p. 451. The twentieth-century figure of two metropolitans to every newspaper is confirmed in Vienna by Stephan Schreder, *Der Zeitungsleser* (Vienna, 1936), p. 29.

7. Alfred Döblin, *Alexanderplatz, Berlin: The Story of Franz Biberkopf*, Eugene Jolas, trans. (New York, 1931), pp. 5, 73–75, 274–275, 342.

8. Albert Südekum, *Grossstädtisches Wohnungselend* (Berlin, 1908), p. 16, describes a proletarian apartment as follows: "the sole table was covered with a couple of plates and glasses, newspaper pages, a comb and brush, soap, a box of ointment, leftover food, and other articles. . . . The few clothes hung on the wall; a couple of faded photographs and unframed lithographs from the illustrateds provided the only decoration." See also the photographs collected in Gesine Asmus, ed., *Hinterhof, Keller und Mansarde: Einblicke in Berliner Wohnungselend 1901–1920* (Reinbek, 1982).

9. Schenda, *Volk ohne Buch*, p. 451.

10. Schreder, *Der Zeitungsleser*, p. 29.

11. Karl Bücher, "Der Zeitungsvertrieb" (1923), in *Gesammelte Aufsätze zur Zeitungskunde* (Tübingen, 1926), p. 224. Karl Hauer, "Das Gehirn des Journalisten," *Die Schaubühne* 7 (12 Dec. 1911), also refers to a "mania" of newspaper reading.

12. Tucholsky, "Gebet des Zeitungslesers" (1927), *Gesammelte Werke*, Mary Gerold-Tucholsky and Fritz J. Raddatz, eds. (Reinbek, 1960), vol. 5, p. 301.

13. Engelsing, "Perioden der Lesergeschichte in der Neuzeit," p. 976; and Hans A. Münster, *Jugend und Zeitung* (Berlin, 1932), p. 6.

14. Eckhardt Köhn, *Strassenrausch: Flanerie und 'Kleine Form.' Versuch zur Literaturgeschichte des Flaneurs von 1830 bis 1933* (Berlin, 1989), p. 88. See also Peter de Mendelssohn, *Zeitungsstadt Berlin: Menschen und Mächte in der Geschichte der deutschen Presse* (Berlin, 1959), p. 50.

15. Gottfried Korff, "'Die Stadt aber ist der Mensch . . .'" in Reinhard Rürup and Korff, eds., *Berlin, Berlin. Die Ausstellung zur Geschichte der Stadt* (Berlin, 1987), p. 658.

16. Allen, *In the Public Eye*, p. 66.

17. Richard D. Altick, "English Publishing in 1852," in *Writers, Readers and Occasions: Selected Essays on Victorian Literature and Life* (Columbus, Ohio, 1989), p. 150.

18. Allen, *In the Public Eye*, p. 44; and Rudolf Schenda, *Die Lesestoffe der kleinen Leute: Studien zur populären Literatur im 19. und 20. Jahrhundert* (Munich, 1976), p. 28.

19. On the success of popular fiction see the excellent conclusion of Schenda, *Volk ohne Buch*, pp. 473–494. Magazines are discussed in Dieter Barth, "Das Familienblatt—ein Phänomen der Unterhaltungspresse des 19. Jahrhunderts," *Archiv für Geschichte des Buchwesens* 15 (1975).

20. Otto Groth, *Die Zeitung: Ein System der Zeitungskunde*, 4 vols. (Mannheim, 1928–1930), vol. 1, p. 42.

21. Jürgen Wilke, *Nachrichtenauswahl und Medienrealität in vier Jahrhunderten* (Berlin, 1984), pp. 146, 149. See also Erich Conrad, "Die Entwicklung des kommunalen Teils der grösseren Leipziger Tageszeitungen in der 2. Hälfte des 19. Jahrhunderts," Ph.D diss. (Leipzig, 1935). Michael Shudson, *Discovering the News: A Social History of American Newspapers* (New York, 1978), pp. 22–23, makes the same argument for the United States.

22. Groth, *Die Zeitung*, vol. 1, p. 940.

23. "Die Welt der Lucie Berlin," BT, no. 644, 19 Dec. 1904; BT, no. 448, 3 Sept. 1904.

24. See Fred Hildenbrandt, *Ich soll dich grüssen von Berlin* (Munich, 1966), p. 277.

25. Werner Theuer, "Zeitungsstadt," in Ulrich Baehr et al, eds., *Mythos Berlin. Zur Wahrnehumungsgeschichte einer industriellen Metropole* (Berlin, 1987), p. 167.

26. On this theme, see Richard Altick, *The Presence of the Present: Topics of the Day in the Victorian Novel* (Columbus, Ohio, 1991).

27. According to Hans O. Modrow, *Berlin 1900* (Berlin, 1936), p. 106. Paul Goldschmidt, *Berlin in Geschichte und Gegenwart* (Berlin, 1910), pp. 383–384, adds that 85% of all immigrants to Berlin in 1900 came from small towns. Altogether, 60% of Berlin's inhabitants in 1905 were born elsewhere. Of these, most came from districts east of the Elbe River: 18% were born in the province of Brandenburg, 6% in Pomerania, 7% in Silesia, and 19% in Germany's other eastern regions.

28. Gunther Barth, *City People: The Rise of Modern City Culture in Nineteenth-Century America* (New York, 1980), p. 59.

29. On "new journalism," see Joel H. Wiener, ed., *Papers for the Mil-*

lions: The New Journalism in Britain, 1850s to 1914 (Westport, Conn., 1988); George Juergens, *Joseph Pulitzer and the New York World* (Princeton, 1966); Judith R. Walkowitz, *City of Dreadful Delight: Narratives of Sexual Danger in Late-Victorian London* (Chicago, 1992), p. 84; and Edward Berenson, *The Trial of Madame Caillaux* (Berkeley, 1992), pp. 228–232.

30. Barth, *City People*, pp. 59, 76, 107.

31. Groth, *Die Zeitung*, vol. 1, p. 927.

32. "Berolina beim Einkauf. Aus dem Haushalt einer Millionstadt," in MP, no. 189, 13 Aug. 1905; no. 191, 16 Aug. 1905; no. 193, 18 Aug. 1905; no. 195, 20 Aug. 1905; no. 198, 24 Aug. 1905; and no. 202, 29 Aug. 1905; and "Der unpünktliche Geschäftsmann. Eine kleine Moralpredigt," BZ, no. 18, 11 Nov. 1904; "Die Psychologie des Detailverkaufs," no. 46, 23 Feb. 1905; and "Die Kunst des Einpackens," no. 57, 8 Mar. 1905.

33. See MP, no. 17, 21 Jan. 1906, for a front-page article on the problems provincial girls had working as maids in Berlin.

34. Emil Löbl, *Kultur und Presse* (Leipzig, 1903), p. 26. See also Robert Brunhuber, *Das moderne Zeitungswesen* (Leipzig, 1907), p. 45.

35. Erich Giese and H. Paetsch, *Polizei und Verkehr* (Berlin, 1926), p. 20; Erich Giese, *Das zukünftige Schnellbahnnetz für Gross-Berlin* (Berlin, 1919), p. 32.

36. BT, no. 77, 12 Feb. 1907, reported that the busiest single day for 1906 was Sunday, 17 June, with 1,188,773 riders; the least busy was Friday, 20 July, with 716,756. According to MP, no. 53, 3 Mar. 1904, 1.6 million commuters used all types of public transportation each day in 1903, a figure which certainly reached 2 million by 1914.

37. Grosse Berliner Strassenbahn to Polizei-Präsidenten, 31 Jan. 1911, Brandenburgisches Landeshauptarchiv, Potsdam, Rep. 30, C Tit. 1202/20559/89.

38. Walter Kiaulehn, *Berlin. Schicksal eine Weltstadt* (Munich, 1958), p. 23.

39. BLA, no. 350, 20 July 1905; Thomas Lindenberger, "Strassenpolitik: Zur Sozialgeschichte der öffentlichen Ordnung in Berlin, 1900–1914," Ph.D diss. (Berlin, 1992), p. 45.

40. *Statistik des Deutschen Reiches*, vol. 107 (Berlin, 1897); and vol. 207, 1 (Berlin, 1909).

41. "Die Frau im Kampf ums Dasein," serialized over 1898 and 1899 in the MP.

42. "Aus der Markthalle," MP, no. 67, 19 Mar. 1905.

43. Shudson, *Discovering the News*, pp. 104–105; Rachel Bowlby, *Just Looking: Consumer Culture in Dreiser, Gissing, and Zola* (London, 1985).

44. Robert Heymann, "Die Kultur in der Annonce," *Der Zeitungs-Verlag*, no. 24, 16 June 1911. In general, see Walkowitz, *City of Dreadful Delight*, pp. 46–49; Susan Porter Benson, *Counter Cultures: Saleswomen, Managers, and Customers in American Department Stores, 1890–1940* (Urbana, 1986), p. 18; and Miriam Hansen, *Babel and Babylon: Spectatorship in American Silent Film* (Cambridge, Mass., 1991), pp. 116–118.

45. With 1,029,461 visitors in 1906, Berlin was not far behind Paris with 1,193,619, although in Paris one in three of the tourists were foreigners, twice as many as in Berlin. See BLA, no. 537, 13 Aug. 1909; as well as Neil Harris, "Urban Tourism and the Commercial City," in William R. Taylor, ed., *Inventing Times Square: Commerce and Culture at the Crossroads of the World* (New York, 1991). pp. 66–82.

46. Otto von Leixner, *Soziale Briefe aus Berlin 1888 bis 1891* (Berlin, 1891), pp. 188, 200. See also Eric Hobsbawm, *Workers: Worlds of Labor* (New York, 1984), pp. 200–204.

47. BT, no. 77, 12 Feb. 1907. See also the statistics assembled by Eduard Buchmann, *Die Entwicklung der Grosse Berliner Strassenbahn und ihre Bedeutung für die Verkehrsentwicklung Berlins* (Berlin, 1910), p. 107; and *Die Grosse Berliner Strassenbahn und ihre Nebenbahnen 1902–1914* (Berlin, 1914), pp. 115–116.

48. BLA, no. 170, 5 Apr. 1907; no. 285, 7 June 1911.

49. Quoted in *Der Luna Park im Jubiläumsjahr 1929* (Berlin, 1929), p. 7.

50. MP, no. 133, 10 June 1906.

51. See letters to BLA, no. 430, 25 Aug. 1907; 443, 1 Sept. 1907.

52. (Berlin, 1913), p. 143.

53. Kurt E. Weckwarth, "Im Familienbad Wannsee," MP, no. 172, 26 June 1910. See also MP, no. 188, 13 Aug. 1907; BLA, no. 418, 19 Aug. 1907, which estimated the crowds at 200,000; and Heinrich Zille, *Rund ums Freibad* (Berlin, 1926).

54. H. Neumann, "Landpartie," MP, no. 110, 10 May 1908.

55. MP, no. 242, 15 Oct. 1907. See also BLA, no. 230, 11 May 1905.

56. "Blütezeit," BLA, no. 256, 28 May 1905.

57. The weekend outing is a recurring motif in Berlin novels. See Katherine Roper, *German Encounters with Modernity: Novels of Imperial Berlin* (Atlantic Highlands, N.J., 1991); and Marilyn Sibley Fries, *The Changing Consciousness of Reality: The Image of Berlin in Selected German Novels from Raabe to Döblin* (Bonn, 1980). See also Hans Ostwald, *Kultur- und Sittengeschichte Berlins* (Berlin, 1921), pp. 396–397.

58. Hans Ostwald, *Berliner Tanzlokale* (Berlin, n.d. [1905]), pp. 62–63.

59. Lindenberger, "Strassenpolitik," p. 76.

60. BLA, no. 512, 8 Oct. 1907.

61. Roger Jonathan Green, "'Haus Vaterland, Berlin:' Pleasure Architecture as a Mirror of Conflict in German History, 1912–1961," Ph.D diss. (University of Chicago, 1987). A major theme in Lindenberger's superb dissertation, "Strassenpolitik," is the creation of a shared metropolitan culture by 1914.

62. BLA, no. 557, 1 Oct. 1907; BT, no. 59, 2 Feb. 1906.

63. See the series "Aus dem Leben der Strassenbahner," MP, no. 249, 22 Oct. 1905; no. 255, 29 Oct. 1905; no. 260, 4 Nov. 1905; no. 270, 16 Nov. 1905; and "Auf der Elektrischen," BT, no. 199, 21 Apr. 1913.

64. Heinz Knobloch, ed., *Der Berliner zweifelt immer. Seine Stadt in Feuilletons von damals* (Berlin [East], 1977); Paul Schlesinger, *Das Sling-Buch* (Berlin, 1924), pp. 200–207; Johannes Trojan, *Berliner Bilder* (Berlin, 1903), p. 30; and "Gespräche im Stadtbahncoupé," BT, no. 285, 3 June 1907.

65. Richard Sennett, *The Fall of Public Man* (Cambridge, 1976), pp. 47, 39.

66. Walkowitz, *City of Dreadful Delight*, pp. 16–18.

67. Hermann Ullstein, *The Rise and Fall of the House of Ullstein* (New York, 1943), p. 69.

68. Hans A. Münster, *Geschichte der Deutschen Presse* (Leipzig, 1941), pp. 102–103; de Mendelssohn, *Zeitungsstadt Berlin*, pp.84–89; and Ullstein, *House of Ullstein*, pp. 69–71.

69. Barth, *City People*, p. 59; Shudson, *Discovering the News*.

70. de Mendelssohn, *Zeitungsstadt Berlin*, pp. 84–85. See also Hans Erman, *August Scherl*. *Dämonie und Erfolg in wilhelminischer Zeit* (Berlin, 1954), pp. 182–183.

71. Rainer Wagner, "*Berliner Morgenpost*," in W. Joachim Freyburgand Hans Wallenberg, eds., *Hundert Jahre Ullstein*, 4 vols. (Berlin, 1977), vol. 2, pp. 9–26.

72. Wilhelm Vogel, *Der Handelsteil der Tagespresse* (Berlin, 1914), pp. 185–186.

73. Arthur Brehmer, "Parteinehmer—nicht Parteigänger," MP, no. 1, 20 Sept. 1898, republished in Freyburg and Wallenberg, eds., *Hundert Jahre Ullstein*, vol. 3, pp. 519–520.

74. MP, no. 207, 3 Sept. 1904. The *Berliner Tageblatt* published the long lists of decorated Germans as well.

75. See, for example, the *Morgenpost*'s Easter issue, no. 88, 15 Apr. 1906.

76. "Zum Gaunerstreich in Köpenick," BLA, no. 530, 18 Oct. 1906; no. 546, 26 Oct. 1906.

77. See the statistics presented by Karl Bücher, "Die Anonymität in den Zeitungen" (1917), in his *Gesammelte Aufsätze*, pp. 162–63.

78. See MP, no. 295, 16 Dec. 1908; and also the 1898 series "Wie wird man eine gute Hausfrau?" nos. 77, 81, 82.

79. MP, no. 52, 22 Feb. 1910; BZ, no. 24, 29 Jan. 1910.

80. "Meine Hochzeitsreise im Automobil," MP, no. 135, 11 June 1899.

81. MP, no. 152, 1 July 1899.

82. MP, no. 219, 17 Sept. 1899. See also *Morgenpost* propaganda in Freyburg and Wallenberg, eds., *Hundert Jahre Ullstein*, vol. 4, pp. 66–67.

83. MP, no. 296, 17 Dec. 1899.

84. MP, no. 147, 1 June 1913. See also statistics in no. 222, 20 Sept. 1908.

85. Circulation figures for 1902–1912 can be found in BT, no. 565, 7 Nov. 1912.

86. End pages to Hans Hyan, *Aute mit'n Ast und andere Berliner Geschichten* (Berlin, 1904); BT, no. 313, 22 June 1912.

87. Egon Jameson, *Wenn ich mich recht erinnere: Das Leben eines Optimisten in der besten aller Welten* (Bern, 1963), p. 229.

88. Ernst Bayer, "Sport, Politik und Presse: Der Sport als Mittel des politischen Kampes und der parteipolitischen Propaganda in der Zeit des Weimarer Systems, 1919–1933" (Ph.D. diss., Heidelberg, 1936), p. 25. See also Vernon Lidtke, *The Alternative Culture: Socialist Labor in Imperial Germany* (New York, 1985); and Arno Arndt, *Berliner Sport* (Berlin, 1904).

89. "Ostermontag in Karlshorst," BZ, no. 96, 25 Apr. 1905.

90. Fritz Wirth, "Sport und Massenpresse," in Freyburg and Wallenberg, eds., *Hundert Jahre Ullstein*, vol. 2, p. 353.

91. Rupert Naumann in *Deutsche Presse*, no. 23 (1928).

92. On the growth of sports coverage, see Groth, *Die Zeitung*, vol. 1, pp. 935–937. See also Friedebert Becker, "Die Saga vom BZ-Sport," in Freyburg and Wallenberg, eds., *Hundert Jahre Ullstein*, vol. 1, pp. 265–293.

93. *Vorwärts*, 15 Nov. 1901, cited in Dieter and Ruth Glatzer, ed., *Berliner Leben 1900–1914* (Berlin, 1986), vol. 1, pp. 150–151. For more details on the distribution of job ads, see Thomas Lindenberger, "Strassenpolitik," pp. 113–123. See also Gustav Dahms, "Arbeitsmarkt auf Berliner Strassen," in Moritz Reymond and Ludwig Manzel, eds., *Berliner Pflaster* (Berlin, 1891), pp. 241–244; and Victor Noack, *Was ein Berliner Musikant erlebte* (Berlin, n.d. [1908]), pp. 29–30.

94. BT, no. 448, 3 Sept. 1904.

95. Döblin, *Alexanderplatz, Berlin*, pp. 274–275.

96. "Aufen auf!" MP, no. 314, 13 Nov. 1919.

97. Egon Jameson, "12 Stunden unerkannt durch Gross-Berlin," MP, no. 317, 16 Nov. 1919.

98. This is the conclusion of Helmut Lethen, "Chicago und Moskau: Berlins moderne Kultur der 20er Jahre zwischen Inflation und Weltwirtschaftskrise," in Jochen Boberg et al, eds., *Die Metropole:*

Industriekultur in Berlin im 20. Jahrhundert (Munich, 1986), pp. 193–194.

99. Egon Jameson, "Meine Erlebnisse auf der Flucht," MP, no. 324, 23 Nov. 1919.

100. Rudolf Lothar, "Das Auge der Grossstadt," BLA, no. 802, 13 Dec. 1909. See also, MP, no. 239, 11 Oct. 1899.

101. Günther Dahlke and Günter Karl, eds., *Deutsche Spielfilme von den Anfängen bis 1933* (Berlin, 1993), pp. 16–17; Ilona Brennicke and Joe Hembus, *Klassiker des deutschen Stummfilms 1910–1930* (Munich, 1983), p. 242. See also Sabine Hake, "Self-Referentiality in Early German Cinema," *Cinema Journal* 31 (1992), pp. 37–55, especially pp. 49–50.

102. Max Mack, *With a Sigh and a Smile: A Showman Looks Back* (London, 1943), pp. 90–91.

103. Michael Hanisch, *Auf den Spuren der Filmgeschichte: Berliner Schauplatz* (Berlin, 1991), p. 184.

3. Physiognomy of the City

1. Anna Behnisch-Kappstein, "Der Fensterplatz," BT, no. 200, 18 Apr. 1905.

2. Dana Brand, *The Spectator and the City in Nineteenth-Century American Literature* (Cambridge, 1991); Rüdiger Severin, *Spuren des Flaneurs in deutschsprachiger Prosa* (Frankfurt, 1988); and Eckhardt Köhn, *Strassenrausch: Flanerie und 'kleine Form.' Versuch zur Literaturgeschichte des Flaneurs von 1830 bis 1933* (Berlin, 1989).

3. Edgar Allan Poe, "The Man of the Crowd," in *Tales of Edgar Allan Poe* (New York, 1944), pp. 482–487. See also E. T. A. Hoffmann, *Des Vetters Eckfenster* (Stuttgart, 1980 [1822]).

4. Christopher Prendergast, *Paris and the Nineteenth Century* (Oxford, 1992), p. 2. See also Volker Klotz, *Die erzählte Stadt. Ein Sujet als Herausforderung des Romans von Lessing bis Döblin* (Munich, 1969).

5. See Rolf Lindner, *Die Entdeckung der Stadtkultur: Soziologie aus der Erfahrung der Reportage* (Frankfurt, 1990), pp. 46, 110; Walter Benjamin, "The Paris of the Second Empire in Baude-

laire," in *Charles Baudelaire: A Lyric Poet in the Era of High Capitalism*, Harry Zohn, trans. (London, 1973), p. 37.

6. Benjamin, "The Paris of the Second Empire in Baudelaire," in *Charles Baudelaire*, p. 36.

7. Christof Forderer, *Die Grossstadt im Roman: Berliner Grossstadtdarstellungen zwischen Naturalismus und Moderne* (Berlin, 1992), pp. 44–47; and Heinz Rölleke, *Die Stadt bei Stadler, Heym, and Trakl* (Berlin, 1966), pp. 105–108, 136. See also Oskar Hübner and Johannes Moegelin, eds., *Im steinernen Meer. Grossstadtgedichte* (Berlin, 1910).

8. Lindner, *Entdeckung der Stadtkultur*; Elisabeth Pfeil, *Grossstadtforschung: Entwicklung und Gegenwärtiger Stand* (Hanover, 1972), pp. 8–40, 158–191. See also John Czaplicka, "Pictures of a City at Work, Berlin, circa 1890–1930: Visual Reflections on Social Structures and Technology in the Modern Urban Construct," in Charles W. Haxthausen and Heidrun Suhr, eds., *Berlin: Culture and Metropolis* (Minneapolis, 1991), pp. 3–36.

9. Benjamin, "The Paris of the Second Empire in Baudelaire," in *Charles Baudelaire*, p. 37.

10. Gerd Mattenklott, *Der übersinnliche Leib: Beiträge zur Metaphysik des Körpers* (Reinbek, 1982), p. 38. See also Susanne Hauser, *Der Blick auf die Stadt: Semiotische Untersuchungen zur literarischen Wahrnehmung bis 1910* (Berlin, 1990).

11. Brand, *The Spectator and the City*, pp. 47–48.

12. Philip Fisher, "City Matters: City Minds," in Jerome Buckley, ed., *The Worlds of Victorian Fiction* (Cambridge, Mass., 1975), p. 386.

13. Lindner, *Entdeckung der Stadtkultur*, pp. 110–112.

14. Jürgen Wilke, *Nachrichtenauswahl und Medienrealität in vier Jahrhunderten* (Berlin, 1984), pp. 146, 149.

15. Richard Sieburth, "Same Difference: The French *Physiologies*, 1840–42," Norman Cantor, ed., *Notebooks in Cultural Analysis* (Durham, N.C., 1984), p. 174.

16. Thomas W. Laqueur, "Bodies, Details, and the Humanitarian Narrative," in Lynn Hunt, ed., *The New Cultural History* (Berkeley, 1989). See also Deborah Epstein Nord, "The City as Theater: From Georgian to Early Victorian London," *Victorian Studies* 31 (1988),

p. 188; and Judith R. Walkowitz, *City of Dreadful Delight: Narratives of Sexual Danger in Late-Victorian London* (Chicago, 1992).

17. Hans Ostwald, *Dunkle Winkeln in Berlin* (Berlin, 1905), p. ii.

18. Ostwald, *Dunkle Winkeln*, p. i. See also Peter Fritzsche, "Vagabond in the Fugitive City: Hans Ostwald, Imperial Berlin, and the *Grossstadt-Dokumente*," *Journal of Contemporary History* 29 (1994). The *Grossstadt-Dokumente* appeared as small pamphlets, but the authors contributed frequently to newspapers and individual chapters often appeared as feuilletons. For example, BT, no. 17, 11 Jan. 1904, published excerpts of Hans Ostwald, *Berliner Kaffeehäuser* (Berlin, n.d.); BZ, no. 80, 4 Apr. 1905, published selections from Eberhard Buchner, *Varieté und Tingeltangel in Berlin* (Berlin, 1905); MP, no. 189, 13 Aug. 1905, did the same for Franz Hoeniger, *Berliner Gerichte* (Berlin, n.d.); and BT, no. 279, 5 June 1906, published parts of Edmund Edel, *Neu-Berlin* (Berlin, 1908).

19. Robert Prutz cited in Hermann Haufler, *Kunstformen des feuilletonistischen Stils* (Stuttgart, 1928), p. 11.

20. Wilmont Haacke, *Handbuch des Feuilletons* (Emsdetten, 1951), vol. 1, p. 312. See also Severin, *Spuren des Flaneurs;* Köhn, *Strassenrausch;* Winfried Ranke, *Vom Milljöh ins Milieu: Heinrich Zilles Aufstieg in der berliner Gesellschaft* (Hanover, 1979); Ulrike Scholvin, *Döblins Metropolen: Ueber reale und imaginäre Städte und die Travestie der Wünsche* (Weinheim, 1985); and Heinz Brüggemann, "Stadt lesen—Stadt beschreiben. Ueber historische und ästhetische Bedingungen literarischer Stadterfahrung," *Literatur und Erfahrung* 14 (1984), pp. 32–35.

21. "Tiergartenbummel," BT, no. 307, 19 June 1904. For similar pieces, see "Morgens im 'Zoo.' Ein Stimmungsbild," BZ, no. 107, 8 May 1905; "Tiergartenbummel," no. 153, 5 July 1905; and "Berliner Bänke am Vormittag," no. 137, 14 June 1906; and Robert Walser, "Tiergarten" [1911] in Jürgen Schutte and Peter Sprengel, eds., *Die Berliner Moderne 1885–1914* (Stuttgart, 1987), pp. 321–323. See also Walter Benjamin, "A Berlin Chronicle," in *Reflections: Essays, Aphorisms, Autobiographical Writings*, Peter Demetz, ed. (New York, 1978), pp. 6–7.

22. "Der Tiergarten," MP, no. 164, 15 July 1905.

23. Buchner, *Variete und Tingeltangel*; and Hans Ostwald, *Berliner Tanzlokale* (Berlin, 1905).

24. Theodor Kappstein, "Droschke!" BT, no. 178, 6 Apr. 1905; "Typen aus dem Tippbureau," MP, no. 152, 20 July 1909.

25. Paul Schüler, "Auf der Elektrischen," BT, no. 199, 21 Apr. 1913. See also "Gespräche im Stadtbahncoupé," BT, no. 285, 3 June 1907.

26. "Strassenbahn-Ausblicke. Eine Rundreise mit Linie 74," MP, no. 172, 10 July 1909.

27. Louise Schulze-Brücke, "Ein Kinderparadies," BT, no. 365, 20 July 1905.

28. Walter Turszinsky, "Im Theater der kleinen Leute," BT, no. 84, 15 Feb. 1906; "Strassenhändlerin," MP, no. 175, 13 July 1909; Edmond Edel, "Unsere Strassen," BT, no. 279, 5 June 1906; and Victor Auburtin, "Berliner Nachtleben", BT, no. 245, 15 May 1911.

29. "Der 'lange Hermann,'" MP, no. 267, 12 Nov. 1905; "Die 'erste' Droschke," MP, no. 275, 22 Nov. 1905; "Bei der 'Grossen Berliner,'" MP, no. 285, 5 Dec. 1905; and "'In Treue fest,'" MP, no. 290, 10 Dec. 1905.

30. Erdmann Graeser, "Auf dem 'Rummel,'" MP, no. 125, 7 May 1911; Schulze-Brücke, "Ein Kinderparadies," BT, no. 365, 20 July 1905' "Der Haushalt in teurer Zeit," MP, no. 203, 30 Aug. 1905; and "Am Krögel," BZ, no. 88, 14 Apr. 1906.

31. Michael W. Jennings, *Dialectical Images: Walter Benjamin's Theory of Literary Criticism* (Ithaca, 1987), pp. 26–29.

32. Albert Borée, "Im Grünen," BZ, no. 143, 22 June 1909.

33. W. Fred, "Das sündige Berlin," BT, no. 229, 6 May 1912.

34. See Haufler, *Kunstformen des feuilletonistischen Stils*, for a masterly analysis of the rhetoric of the feuilleton.

35. R. O. Frankfurter, "Sechs Tage auf dem Rade," BZ, no. 68, 22 Mar. 1908. See also "Im Kinematographen-Theater," BZ, no. 262, 7 Nov. 1906.

36. Haufler, *Kunstformen des feuilletonistischen Stils*, pp. 36–40; Eberhard Roters, "Weltstadt und Kieferheide," in *Berlin um 1900* (Berlin, 1984), pp. 21–22; and Russell Berman, *The Rise of the*

Modern German Novel: Crisis and Charisma (Cambridge, Mass., 1986), pp. 143–146.

37. See A. J. C. Mayne, *The Imagined Slum: Newspaper Representations in Three Cities* (Leicester, 1993).

38. Walter Kiaulehn, *Berlin. Schicksal einer Weltstadt* (Munich, 1958), pp. 19–20. See also A. H. Kober, *Einst in Berlin*, Richard Kirn, ed. (Hamburg, 1956), pp. 7–11.

39. Charles W. Haxthausen, "'A New Beauty': Ernst Ludwig Kirchner's Images of Berlin," in Haxthausen and Suhr, eds., *Berlin*, pp. 58–94.

40. "Ueber den Potsdamer Platz," BZ, no. 240, 12 Oct. 1905.

41. "Geständnis," MP, no. 248, 23 Oct. 1906.

42. Edmund Edel, "Unsere Strassen," BT, no. 279, 5 June 1906. This piece was expanded and republished in Edel, *Neu-Berlin*.

43. See also "Um den Potsdamer Platz," MP, no. 243, 15 Oct. 1905; Georg Hermann in MP, no. 128, 3 June 1906; "Berliner Beobachter," BLA, no. 519, 11 Oct. 1908; and Michael Bienert, *Die eingebildete Metropole: Berlin im Feuilleton der Weimarer Republik* (Stuttgart, 1992).

44. Max Kretzer, *Die Verkommenen* (Berlin, 1882), p. 6.

45. "Ein Viertel nach acht," BT, no. 318, 26 June 1910.

46. "Berliner Nachtleben," BZ, no. 52, 2 Mar. 1907; Victor Auburtin, "Berliner Nachtleben," BT, no. 245, 15 May 1911; BIZ, no. 11, 15 Mar. 1903; and Edmond Edel, "Berlins leichte Kunst," reprinted in Dieter and Ruth Glatzer, eds., *Berliner Leben 1900–1914* (Berlin, 1986), vol. 2, pp. 356–359; and *Berlin für Kenner: Ein Bärenführer bei Tag und Nacht durch die deutsche Reichshauptstadt* (Berlin, 1913). Joachim Schlör, *Nachts in der grossen Stadt: Paris, Berlin, London 1840–1930* (Munich, 1992), provides an excellent study of night in the city.

47. "Die Früh-Bars," BZ, no. 22, 27 Jan. 1914. See also "Berliner Schlafenszeit," BLA, no. 567, 25 Aug. 1909; and Georg Hermann, "Hans Baluschek," *Nord und Süd* 33 (1909), p. 176.

48. Gottfried Korff, "Berliner Nächte: Zum Selbstbild urbaner Eigenschaften und Leidenschaften," in Gerhard Brunn and Jürgen Reulecke, eds., *Berlin . . . Blicke auf die deutsche Metropole*

(Essen, 1989), p. 83. See also Robert Walser, "Guten Tag, Riesin!" (1907), reprinted in Schutte and Sprengel, eds., *Berliner Moderne*, pp. 302–304.

49. Ostwald, *Berliner Tanzlokale*, pp. 6, 11–12.

50. "Berliner Passagen," BT, no. 471, 16 Sept. 1906; and Hans Ostwald, "In der Passage," in *Das neue Magazin* 73 (1904), pp. 438–442. See also Haxthausen, "'A New Beauty,'" in Haxthausen and Suhr, eds., *Berlin*, pp. 58–94.

51. Ostwald, "Prostitutionsmärkte," in *Das Berliner Dirnentum*, 2 vols. (Leipzig, 1905).

52. Edel, *Neu-Berlin*, pp. 14–15.

53. Lothar Brieger and Hanns Steiner, eds., *Zirkus Berlin: Bilder Berliner Lebens* (Berlin, 1919), p. 64.

54. Alfred Döblin, "Östlich um den Alexanderplatz," in *Zeitlupe*, pp. 60–63; and Ludovica Scarpa, "Abschreibungsmythos Alexanderplatz," in Jochen Boberg et al, eds., *Die Metropole: Industriekultur in Berlin im 20. Jahrhundert* (Munich, 1986), pp. 126–133.

55. "'Berlin im Omnibus,'" BZ, no. 156, 6 July 1906.

56. "Im Nordring," *Berlin für Kenner*, pp. 123–127. See also "Im Nordring," BT, no. 336, 5 July 1904.

57. Anselm Heine, "Berlins Physiognomie," in *Ich weiss Bescheid in Berlin* (Berlin, 1908), p. 4. See also Gottfried Korff, "Berlin— Berlin, Menschenstadt und Stadtmenschen," in Ulrich Eckhardt, ed., *750 Jahre Berlin. Stadt der Gegenwart* (Berlin, 1986), p. 151.

58. Hugo is cited and discussed in T. J. Clark, *The Painting of Modern Life: Paris in the Art of Manet and His Followers* (Princeton, 1986), pp. 25–30. See also Jacques Leenhardt, "Eine Aesthetik des Randgebietes," in Manfred Smuda, ed., *Die Grossstadt als 'Text'* (Munich, 1992), pp. 91–100; and Bernard Delvaille, "Vers les Banlieues," in Daniel Oster and Jean-Marie Goulemot, eds., *Ecrire Paris* (Paris, 1990), pp. 53–63.

59. Georg Hermann, *Kubinke* (Gütersloh, 1967 [1910]), pp. 6, 8–9, 314, which was also serialized in the *Berliner Tageblatt* in summer 1910. See also his "Hans Baluschek," *Nord und Süd* 33 (1909), pp. 171–177; and "Um Berlin," *Pan* 2 (1912), pp. 1101–1106.

Julius Bab and Willi Handl, *Wien und Berlin* (Berlin, 1918), prized both the novel and the novelist as most representative of the new Berlin. See, for example, Marilyn Sibley Fries, *The Changing Consciousness of Reality: The Image of Berlin in Selected German Novels from Raabe to Döblin* (Bonn, 1980), pp. 116–120.

60. Republished as Hans Fallada, *Ein Mann will nach oben* (Reinbek, 1970 [1943]), p. 120.

61. "Auf der Schillingsbrücke," BT, no. 181, 10 Apr. 1912.

62. "Die Armee der Arbeit," BIZ, no. 39 (29 Sept. 1912). The same emplotment informs "Nach Feierabend," BLA, no. 402, 10 Aug. 1907.

63. "Lohntag," MP, no. 66, 18 Mar. 1905.

64. "Im Kremser," BZ, no. 182, 5 Aug. 1905; "Im Grünen," no. 143, 22 June 1909; and "Berliner Sommernacht," no. 178, 31 July 1912.

65. "Am 25 Pfennigtag im 'Zoologischen,'" BIZ, no. 34 (24 Aug. 1902). See also "Im Zoologisch. Der billige Sonntag," MP, no. 154, 3 July 1904.

66. "Umzug," BT, no. 504, 3 Oct. 1908. See also "Die neue Wohnung," no. 503, 4 Oct. 1909; "Umzugsleiden," BLA, no. 653, 25 Sept. 1909; "In der neuen Wohnung," MP, no. 76, 31 Mar. 1906; no. 78, 3 Apr. 1906; "In der neuen Wohnung," no. 232, 4 Oct. 1906; no. 76, 31 Mar. 1907; "Wir ziehen um," no. 263, 23 Sept. 1910.

67. "Sonntagmorgen in der Schrippenkirche," BZ, no. 24, 19 Nov. 1904; "Bei den Gesundbetern," no. 6, 8 Jan. 1909; and "Am Wärmeofen der Stadt Berlin," no. 32, 29 Nov. 1904.

68. "Heimarbeiter," BZ, no. 134, 9 June 1905.

69. See, for example, Adolf Braun, *Berliner Wohnverhältnisse* (Berlin, 1893); Albert Südekum, *Grossstädtisches Wohnungselend* (Berlin, 1908); Alfred Lasson, *Gefährdete und verwahrloste Jugend* (Berlin, 1908); and Gesine Asmus, ed., *Hinterhof, Keller und Mansarde: Einblicke in Berliner Wohnungselend 1901–1920* (Reinbek, 1982).

70. Hermann, "Um Berlin," *Pan* 2 (1912), p. 1105.

71. BZ, no. 10, 2 Nov. 1904.

72. MP, no. 185, 9 Aug. 1905.

73. BZ, no. 65, 17 Mar. 1905. See also BLA, no. 130, 17 Mar. 1905.

74. Franz Hessel in *Die Literarische Welt*, 6 (1930), pp. 5–6, cited in

Severin, *Spuren des Flaneurs*, p. 219. See also Hessel's *Ein flâneur in Berlin* (Berlin, 1984 [1929]).

75. Cited in Severin, *Spuren des Flaneurs*, pp. 219–220.

76. See Fries, *Changing Consciousness of Reality*, pp. 97–99, 116–118.

4. The City as Spectacle

1. Ernst Blass, "An Gladys," in *Die Strassen komme ich entlang geweht*, Thomas B. Schumann, ed. (Munich, 1980 [1912]), p. 13.

2. Cited in Hannah Arendt's introduction to Walter Benjamin, *Illuminations*, Harry Zohn, trans. (New York, 1969), pp. 21–22.

3. Richard Sennett, *The Fall of Public Man* (Cambridge, 1977), p. 17.

4. Uwe Böker, "Von Wordsworths schlummerndem London bis zum Abgrund der Jahrhundertwende. Die Stadt in der englischen Literatur des 19. Jahrhunderts," in Cord Meckseper and Elisabeth Schraut, eds., *Die Stadt in der Literatur* (Göttingen, 1983), p. 36.

5. Ibid.

6. Bernhard von Brentano, "Berlin—von Süddeutschland aus gesehen," in *Wo in Europa ist Berlin? Bilder aus den zwanziger Jahren* (Frankfurt, 1981), p. 98.

7. "Die bunte Strasse," BT, no. 583, 16 Nov. 1910.

8. "Zeitungsständchem vom Zeitungsstand," *Der Zeitungshandel* 13 (9 Apr. 1923). See also Hans A. Münster, *Jugend und Zeitung* (Berlin, 1932), pp. 17–18, 56–57.

9. Sabine Hake, "Urban Spectacle in Walter Ruttmann's *Berlin: Symphony of the Big City*," in Thomas W. Kniesche and Stephen Brockmann, eds., *Dancing on the Volcano: Essays on the Culture of the Weimar Republic* (Columbia, S.C., 1994), pp. 127–137. Walter Benjamin, "Some Motifs in Baudelaire," in *Charles Baudelaire: A Lyric Poet in The Era of High Capitalism*, Harry Zohn, trans. (London, 1973), p. 120, also links mass literacy with mass consumption.

10. Dana Brand, *The Spectator and the City in Nineteenth-Century American Literature* (Cambridge, 1991), p. 4; and Susanne Hauser, *Der Blick auf die Stadt: Semiotische Untersuchungen zur literarischen Wahrnehmung bis 1910* (Berlin, 1990), pp. 17–18.

11. Lynn Abrams, *Workers' Culture in Imperial Germany: Leisure and Recreation in the Rhineland and Westphalia* (London, 1992),

pp. 169–195. See also the seminal analysis by Richard Hoggart, *The Uses of Literacy* (London, 1957).

12. Christopher Prendergast, *Paris and the Nineteenth Century* (London, 1992), p. 5; Benjamin, "Some Motifs in Baudelaire," in *Charles Baudelaire*, p. 117. See also Brand, *The Spectator and the City*, pp. 7–8.

13. Georg Simmel, "The Metropolis and Mental Life," in *The Sociology of Georg Simmel*, Kurt Wolff, ed. (New York, 1950). pp. 413–414. See also Siegfried Kracauer, *Die Angestellten* (Frankfurt, 1930).

14. Cited in Sennett, *Fall of Public Man*, p. 154.

15. Brand, *The Spectator and the City*, pp. 7–8, 195.

16. William R. Taylor, "The Evolution of Public Space in New York City: The Commercial Showcase of America," in Simon J. Bronner, ed., *Consuming Visions: Accumulation and Display of Goods in America, 1880–1920* (New York, 1989), pp. 288–291.

17. Erich Wagner, "BZ am Mittag und BZ," in W. Joachim Freyburg and Hans Wallenberg, eds., *Hundert Jahre Ullstein* (Berlin, 1977), vol. 2, p. 52.

18. D. H., "Betrachtungen aus dem Setzersaal," *Der Zeitungs-Verlag*, no. 37 (1903); Hermann Löns, "Noch etwas über Zeitungsausstattung," *Der Zeitungs-Verlag*, no. 30 (1904); and Erich Feldhaus, "Von Drahtberichten, Letzten Nachrichten und Extrablätter," *Der Zeitungs-Verlag*, no. 9 (1914); and "Vom Schaufenster der Zeitung," *Der Zeitungs-Verlag*, no. 53 (1926).

19. "Schweres Stadtbahnunglück bei Baumschulenweg," BZ, no. 31, 6 Feb. 1911.

20. "Bellestristik," in *Frankfurter Zeitung*, no. 667, 7 Sept. 1929, cited in Wilmont Haacke, *Handbuch des Feuilletons* (Emsdetten, 1951), vol. 1, pp. 251–252.

21. August Endell, *Die Schönheit der grossen Stadt* (Stuttgart, 1908), p. 68. See also Lothar Müller, "The Beauty of the Metropolis: Toward an Aesthetic Urbanism in Turn-of-the-Century Berlin," in Charles W. Haxthausen and Heidrun Suhr, eds., *Berlin: Culture and Metropolis* (Minneapolis, 1990), pp. 37–57.

22. "Der Schrecken von Berlin," BZ, no. 38, 15 Feb. 1909; BT, no. 75, 11 Feb. 1909; no. 76, 11 Feb. 1909. While the *Lokal-Anzeiger* fea-

tured the attacks on the front page of its morning edition, it generally eschewed a sensational tone and thus did not draw attention to
itself or the story. See BLA, nos. 75–88, 11 to 18 Feb. 1909.

23. In Matthais Flügge, *Heinrich Zille* (Berlin, 1979), p. 54.

24. W. T. Stead, *The Americanization of the World* (London, 1902),
p. 111; Erich Dombrowski, "Das Gesicht der Zeitung," *Deutsche
Presse*, no. 6 (1925); "Vom Schaufenster der Zeitung," *Der
Zeitungs-Verlag*, no. 53 (1926), pp. 2797–2798; and Otto Groth,
Die Zeitung: Ein System der Zeitungskunde (Mannheim,
1928–1930), vol. 1, p. 345.

25. BZ, no. 178, 2 Aug. 1909; and no. 66, 19 Mar. 1914.

26. The examples are all drawn from BZ, no. 2, 24 Oct. 1904. Inci-
dentally, the marvellous story of the Russian attack on English
fishermen was not featured in the *Berliner Tageblatt*, which maintained a very serious profile. See "Der russisch-englische
Konflikt," BT, no. 551, 28 Oct. 1904.

27. The examples are all drawn from BT, no. 495, 29 Sept. 1907.

28. A. H. Kober, *Einst in Berlin*, ed. Richard Kirn (Hamburg, 1956),
pp. 227–228, citing prewar advertisements.

29. Groth, *Die Zeitung*, vol. 3, pp. 227–229.

30. Larissa Reisner, *Im Lande Hindenburgs, eine Reise durch die
deutsche Republik* (Berlin, 1926), p. 217.

31. BLA, no. 130, 12 Mar. 1909.

32. Otto Nahnsen, *Der Strassenhandel mit Zeitungen und
Druckschriften in Berlin* (Berlin, 1920), pp. 37–38.

33. Werner Theuer, "Zeitungskioske," in Ulrich Baehr et al, eds.,
*Mythos Berlin. Zur Wahrnehmungsgeschichte einer industriellen
Metropole* (Berlin, 1987), pp. 158–159; Groth, *Die Zeitung*, vol. 3,
p. 141.

34. Münster, *Jugend und Zeitung*, pp. 17–18; Alfred Döblin, *Alexanderplatz, Berlin. The Story of Franz Biberkopf*, Eugene Jolas,
trans. (New York, 1931), pp. 73–75.

35. Nahnsen, *Strassenhandel*, pp. 39–40.

36. See Zille's drawings, for example, and MP, no. 294, 16 Dec. 1906.
Nahnsen discusses the sociology of street vendors in *Strassenhandel*, pp. 53–66.

37. Münster, *Jugend und Zeitung*, p. 57.

38. "40 Jahre Zeitungshändler," MP, no. 272, 3 Oct. 1911; Siegfried Kracauer, "Der Zeitungsverkäufer," FZ, 29 July 1930.

39. Walter Kiaulehn, *Berlin, Schicksal eine Weltstadt* (Berlin, 1958), p. 26.

40. As Franz Biberkopf's comings and goings around Alexanderplatz indicated, people used to browse among newspapers in cafés and restaurants as well. *BZ am Mittag*, no. 76, 30 Mar. 1905, for example, advertised its availability in a total of 154 cafés in downtown Berlin. Café Josty on Potsdamer Platz even engaged a *Zeitungskellner* to select the latest newspapers for customers, and Café Bauer, on the famous corner of Unter den Linden and Friedrichstrasse, offered patrons a selection of more than 600 newspapers and magazines, each attached to a wooden pole in the Viennese manner.

41. Nahnsen, *Strassenhandel*, pp. 51–52.

42. Marianne Thalmann, *Romantiker entdecken die Stadt* (Munich, 1965).

43. Hans Zapf, "Ecke Joachimsthaler," in Herbert Günther, ed., *Hier schreibt Berlin: Eine Anthologie von heute* (Berlin, 1929), p. 108.

44. Leo Colze, *Berliner Warenhäuser* (Berlin, 1905), pp. 11–12.

45. Edmund Edel, "Der Schrei der Litfasssäule," BT, no. 481, 21 Sept. 1908.

46. "Mehr Litfasssäulen," BT, no. 609, 29 Sept. 1912.

47. "Die Litfasssäule als Jubilarin," BLA, no. 315, 1 July 1905; "Mehr Litfasssäulen," BT, no. 609, 29 Sept. 1912.

48. Edmund Edel, "Der Schrei der Litfasssäule," BT, no. 481, 21 Sept. 1908.

49. Ibid.

50. *Litfasssäulen* are depicted on the cover of Jürgen Schutte and Peter Sprengel, eds., *Die Berliner Moderne 1885–1914* (Stuttgart, 1987) and Otto Friedrich, *Before the Deluge: A Portrait of Berlin in the 1920's* (New York, 1972). Consider also the contemporary literary journal *Litfass*.

51. "Litfasssäulen," BT, no. 90, 19 Feb. 1910.

52. "Die Tragödie an der Litfassäule," MP, no. 196, 22 Aug. 1905.

53. BLA, no. 377, 13 Aug. 1899; no. 510, 7 Oct. 1906. See also no. 315, 1 July 1905.

54. "Litfasssäulen," BT, no. 90, 19 Feb. 1910.

55. Oscar Justinus, "Zettel," in Moritz Reymond and Ludwig Manzel, eds., *Berliner Pflaster* (Berlin, 1891), pp. 66–68.

56. "Kartenlegerinnen," BLA, no. 340, 8 July 1910.

57. "Das Extrablatt," BZ, no. 19, 23 Jan. 1912; Karl Aram, "Unsere armen Augen," BT, no. 527, 17 Oct. 1910.

58. Max Brod, "Berlin für den Fremden," *Der Stürm*, no. 46 (14 Jan. 1911). See also "Die Plakatwand," MP, no. 201, 29 Aug. 1906; and Brunhilde Wehinger, "Bilderflut am Boulevard: Bühnenrevue und Boulevardpresse im Second Empire," in Helmut Pfeiffer et al, eds., *Art social und art industriel: Funktionen der Kunst im Zeitalter des Industrialismus* (Munich, 1987), pp. 422–423.

59. "Die bunte Strasse," BT, no. 583, 16 Nov. 1910.

60. Eckhardt Köhn, *Strassenrausch: Flanerie und 'Kleine Form.' Versuch zur Literaturgeschichte des Flaneurs von 1830 bis 1933* (Berlin, 1989), p. 128.

61. For reviews, see BZ, no. 29, 3 Feb. 1905; no. 61, 13 Mar. 1905; and BLA, no. 621, 6 Dec. 1908. On "Lappenparade," BT, no. 267, 30 May 1910. See also "Schaufenster und Sonntagsheilligung," BZ, no. 61, 13 Mar. 1905.

62. "Fensterpromenade," MP, no. 144, 29 May 1910.

63. "Eindrücke von der Schaufenster-Konkurrenz," BLA, no. 646, 23 Sept. 1909; "Der Wettbewerb der Schaufenster," MP, no. 260, 22 Sept. 1910; "An den Schaufenstern vorbei. Eindrücke eines Spaziergängers," no. 261, 23 Sept. 1910. See also "Vor dem Schaufenster," BT, no. 362, 20 July 1910.

64. See, for example, BLA, no. 658, 27 Sept. 1909; no. 488a, 26 Sept. 1910.

65. Hans Ostwald, *Dunkle Winkeln in Berlin* (Berlin, 1905), p. 21. See also "Strassenschönheiten," MP, no. 261, 5 Oct. 1905; Ernst Heilemann, *Die Berliner Pflanze* (Munich, 1908); and Hans Ostwald, *Berlin und die Berlinerin: Eine Kultur- und Sittengeschichte* (Berlin, 1911).

66. "Zwischen 5 und 7," BZ, no. 240, 12 Oct. 1906.

67. Gustav Eberlein, "Der Tauentzienstil," BZ, no. 270, 16 Nov. 1911.

68. "Strassenbekannschaften," MP, no. 257, 3 Oct. 1909.

69. Max Kretzer, *Die Verkommenen* (Berlin, 1882), p. 65.

70. Johannes Trojan, "Kalte Tage," in *Berliner Bilder* (Berlin, 1903), pp. 28–31; and Paul Schlesinger, "Isolde in der Strassenbahn," in *Das Sling-Buch* (Berlin, 1924), pp. 200–203.

71. Walter Benjamin, "The Paris of the Second Empire in Baudelaire," in *Charles Baudelaire*, p. 45.

72. Max Marcuse, *Uneheliche Mütter* (Berlin, 1906), pp. 47–48. See also Hans Ostwald, *Zuhältertum in Berlin* (Berlin, 1905); and Elizabeth Harvey, *Youth and The Welfare State in Weimar Germany* (Oxford, England, 1993), p. 33.

73. Paul Schüler, BT, no. 469, 14 Sept. 1908.

74. "Heiratsvermittlung und Wucher," BZ, no. 10, 2 Nov. 1904.

75. "Falschmünzer," BZ, no. 1, 22 Oct. 1904. See also "Skizzen zum Prozess Kluge," BZ, no. 82, 9 Apr. 1910.

76. On opera glasses, BLA, no. 243, 21 May 1905; and MP, no. 100, 1 May 1906.

77. MP, no. 35, 10 Feb. 1906; "Ein Gespräch mit Hennig," BZ, no. 34, 9 Feb. 1906.

78. "Die Jagd nach Hennig," BZ, no. 34, 10 Feb. 1906; "Die Hennig-Woche," no. 36, 12 Feb. 1906; "Trübe Folgen der Hennig-Hetze," no. 67, 20 Mar. 1906; "'Hennigs Vorführung' verboten," no. 95, 25 Apr. 1906. See also MP, no. 34, 10 Feb. 1906; and "Hennigs erstes Jubiläum," BT, no. 114, 3 Mar. 1906.

79. "Hennig vor den Geschworenen," BZ, no. 100, 30 Apr. 1906.

80. "Die Lebenskultur des Berliner Arbeiters," MP, no. 88, 12 Apr. 1908. See also "Der Kampf ums Brot. Ein Stimmungsbild aus dem Streikgebiet," BZ, no. 228, 28 Sept. 1905; and Hans Ostwald, *Kultur- und Sittengeschichte Berlins* (Berlin, 1921), p. 572.

81. See the testimony of impoverished homeworkers in "Heimarbeiter," BZ, no. 134, 9 June 1905.

82. "Sonntagspublikum," MP, no. 213, 28 Apr. 1907.

83. *Berlin für Kenner: Ein Bärenführer bei Tag und Nacht durch die deutsche Reichshauptstadt* (Berlin, 1913), pp. 10, 28–31.

84. "Zwischen 5 und 7," BZ, no. 240, 12 Oct. 1906.

85. "Vor dem Schaufenster," BT, no. 362, 20 July 1910. See also "Was zeigen wir den Fremden in Berlin?" BLA, no. 430, 1 Sept. 1905.

86. Hans Fallada, *Damals bei uns Daheim: Erlebtes, Erfahrenes, und Erfundenes* (Hamburg, 1955), pp. 33–38.

87. "Der silberne Sonntag," BLA, no. 629, 12 Dec. 1910; "Der goldene Sonntag," no. 642, 19 Dec. 1910. See also "Weihnachtspräludien," no. 593, 18 Dec. 1904; and "Der silberne Sonntag," no. 628, 18 Dec. 1905.

88. "Panik in der Passage," BLA, no. 590, 21 Nov. 1910.

89. BZ, no. 260, 5 Nov. 1906; no. 266, 12 Nov. 1906; no. 99, 29 Apr. 1907; and BLA, no. 304, 18 June 1906.

90. Robert Walser, "Friedrichstrasse" (1909), in *Das Gesamtwerk*, Jochen Greuen, ed. (Geneva, 1982), vol. 1, pp. 298–301.

91. Kurt Aram, "Unsere armen Augen," BT, no. 527, 17 Oct. 1910. See also Ruth Kraft, "Die Shimmytreppe" (1925?), cited in Klaus Strohmeyer, ed., *Berlin in Bewegung* (Berlin, 1987) vol. 1, p. 30.

92. "In ein Lichtmeer getaucht," BT, no. 107, 28 Feb. 1906. See also "Die Illumination in Berlin," no. 49, 28 Jan. 1904.

93. Felix Escher, *Berlin und sein Umland. Zur Genese der Berliner Stadtlandschaft bis zum Beginn des 20. Jahrhunderts* (Berlin, 1985), p. 310.

94. Jules Huret, *Berlin* (Munich, 1909), p. 11.

95. "Abgesperrt!" BZ, no. 262, 7 Nov. 1905. See also MP, no. 207, 3 Sept. 1904; and no. 272, 20 Nov. 1906.

96. "Parade," BT, no. 276, 1 June 1908. See also BIZ, no. 10 (6 Mar. 1910). The *Lokal-Anzeiger* made no critical comments and even referred to the "Ovationen des Volkes" on Belle-Alliance-Platz. See nos. 275–276, 1 June 1908. To cope with the complete disruption of traffic, the paper suggested building a parallel bridge across the Landwehrkanal. See no. 291, 10 June 1908.

97. See incidents recounted in "Polizei und Schiller-Feier," BT, no. 239, 11 May 1905; "Die Klinge des Leutnants," no. 243, 14 May 1906.

98. BZ, no. 104, 4 May 1905.

99. "Parade," BT, no. 276, 1 June 1908.

100. "Das lautlose Berlin," BT, no. 588, 17 Nov. 1912. See also Arthur

Eloesser, "Die Blumen des Herrn von Jagow" (1913), in *Die Strasse meiner Jugend. Berliner Skizzen* (Berlin, 1987 [1919]), pp. 57–61.

101. "Demonstrationen," BZ, no. 11, 14 Jan. 1908; "Wahlrechts-Demonstrationen," no. 18, 22 Jan. 1908; "Berlin auf die Strasse," no. 37, 14 Feb. 1910; "Strassendemonstrationen," BT, no. 57, 1 Feb. 1909; "Die Wahlrechtskundgebung im Zirkus Busch," no. 106, 28 Feb. 1910; MP, no. 43, 13 Feb. 1910; no. 243, 4 Sept. 1911. For the much less sympathetic attitude of the BLA, see "Warnung des Polizeipräsidenten vor Strassendemonstrationen," no. 79, 13 Feb. 1910; "Wovon man spricht," no. 81, 15 Feb. 1910; and "Berliner Beobachter," no. 131, 13 Mar. 1910.

102. "Das Recht auf die Strasse," BIZ, no. 10 (6 Mar. 1910). The proclamation read:

Bekanntmachung
Es wird das Recht auf die Strasse verkündet.
Die Strasse dient lediglich dem Verkehr.
Bei Widerstand gegen die Staatsgewalt erfolgt Waffengebrauch.
Ich warne Neugierige.
Berlin, den 13. Februar 1910

Der Polizei-Präsident
von Jagow

103. "Die Massenkundgebungen," BT, no. 81, 14 Feb. 1910. See also the front-page editorial in MP, no. 43, 13 Feb. 1910; and "Berlin auf die Strasse," BZ, no. 37, 14 Feb. 1910.

5. Illegible Texts

1. Franz Hessel, *Ein flâneur in Berlin* (Berlin, 1984 [1929]), p. 145.

2. Kurt Aram, "Unsere armen Augen," BT, no. 527, 17 Oct. 1910. Some years later, Walter Benjamin referred to "Heuschrecken-schwärme von Schrift." See the discussion in Erhard Schütz, "'Kurfürstendamm' oder Berlin als geistiger Kriegsschauplatz: Das Textmuster 'Berlin' in der Weimarer Republik," in Klaus Sieben-haar, ed., *Das poetische Berlin: Metropolenkultur zwischen Gründerzeit und Nationalsozialismus* (Berlin, 1992), pp. 169–170.

3. Roth in April 1921, cited in Karl Prümm, "Die Stadt der Reporter

und Kinogänger bei Roth, Brentano, und Kracauer: Das Berlin der zwanziger Jahre im Feuilleton der *Frankfurter Zeitung,*" in Klaus R. Scherpe, ed., *Die Unwirklichkeit der Städte: Grossstadtdarstellungen zwischen Moderne und Postmoderne* (Reinbek, 1988), pp. 84–85. See also Gottfried Benn, "Das Plakat," in *Gedichte. Gesammelte Werke,* Dieter Wellershoff, ed. (Wiesbaden, 1963), vol. 3, p. 39.

4. "Grossstadt Reklame," *Zeitungs-Verlag,* no. 18 (1910).

5. Georg Simmel, *The Philosophy of Money,* trans. Tom Bottomore and David Frisby (Boston, 1978). For a similar description of turn-of-the-century advertisements in Washington D.C., see William Leach, *Land of Desire: Merchants, Power, and the Rise of a New American Culture* (New York, 1993), p. 47.

6. Theodor Lessing, *Kampfschrift gegen die Geräusche unseres Lebens* (Wiesbaden, 1908), p. 15, cited in Ulrike Scholvin, *Döblins Metropolen: Ueber reale und imaginäre Städte und die Travestie der Wünsche* (Weinheim, 1985), p. 60. See also "Das Recht auf Stille," BLA, no. 208, 24 Apr. 1908.

7. Dana Brand, *The Spectator and the City in Nineteenth-Century American Literature* (Cambridge, 1991), p. 2. See also Susanne Hauser, *Der Blick auf die Stadt: Semiotische Untersuchungen zur literarischen Wahrnehmung bis 1910* (Berlin, 1990).

8. Christoph Asendorf, *Batterien der Lebenskraft: Zur Geschichte der Dinge und ihrer Wahrnehmung im 19. Jahrhundert* (Giessen, 1984), p. 51; and Hermann Kähler, *Berlin—Asphalt und Licht. Die Grosse Stadt in der Literatur der Weimarer Republik* (Berlin [East], 1986), pp. 119–132.

9. Harald Jähner, *Erzählter, montierter, soufflierter Text: Zur Konstruktion des Romans "Berlin Alexanderplatz" von Alfred Döblin* (Frankfurt, 1984), p. 116.

10. Russell Berman, *The Rise of the Modern German Novel: Crisis and Charisma* (Cambridge, Mass., 1986), p. 257. See also Klaus R. Scherpe, "The City as Narrator: The Modern Text in Alfred Döblin's *Berlin Alexanderplatz,*" in Andreas Huyssen and David Bathrick, eds., *Modernity and the Text: Revisions of German Modernism* (New York, 1989).

11. Guy Debord, *Society of the Spectacle* (Detroit, 1977); and Thomas Richards, *The Commodity Culture of Victorian England: Advertising and Spectacle, 1851–1914* (Stanford, 1990).

12. Patrick Brantlinger, *Bread and Circuses: Theories of Mass Culture as Social Decay* (Ithaca, 1983); idem, *Crusoe's Footprints: Cultural Studies in Britain and America* (New York, 1990); and Marshall Berman, *All That Is Solid Melts into Air: The Experience of Modernity* (New York, 1982).

13. Roland Barthes, "Structure of the *Fait-Divers*," in *Critical Essays*, Richard Howard, trans. (Evanston, Ill., 1972), pp. 185–195. Weimar feuilletonist Fred Hildenbrandt makes a similar point in "Tragödien," in *Grosses schönes Berlin* (Berlin, 1928), p. 94.

14. Otto Groth, *Die Zeitung: Ein System der Zeitungskunde* (Mannheim, 1928–1930), vol. 1, pp. 42–43. See also David Paul Nord, "Teleology and News: The Religious Roots of American Journalism, 1630–1730," *Journal of American History* 76 (1990), pp. 9–38.

15. On this theme, Gary D. Stark, "Cinema, Society, and the State: Policing the Film Industry in Imperial Germany," in Stark and Bede Karl Lackner, eds., *Essays on Culture and Society in Modern Germany* (Arlington, Texas, 1982), pp. 122–166; and James Retallack, "From Pariah to Professional? The Journalist in German Society and Politics, from the Late Enlightenment to the Rise of Hitler," *German Studies Review* 16 (1993). See also the texts collected in Anton Kaes, ed., *Kino-Debatte: Literatur und Film 1908–1929* (Tübingen, 1978).

16. "Sensation," *Der Zeitungs-Verlag*, no. 6 (1906).

17. Erich Feldhaus, "Von Drahtberichten, Letzten Nachrichten und Extrablättern," *Der Zeitungs-Verlag*, no. 9 (1914).

18. "Die moderne Zeitung," *Der Zeitungs-Verlag*, no. 7 (1914).

19. Hans Traub, *Zeitungswesen und Zeitungslesen* (Berlin, 1928), p. 132. See also Karl Bücher, "Der Zeitungsvertrieb" (1923), in *Gesammelte Aufsätze zur Zeitungskunde* (Tübingen, 1926), p. 199; and Brunhilde Wehinger, "Bilderflut am Boulevard: Bühnenrevue und Boulevardpresse im Second Empire," in Helmut Pfeiffer et al, eds., *Art social und Art industriel: Funktionen der Kunst im Zeitalter des Industrialismus* (Munich, 1987), pp. 420–421.

20. Wilhelm Foerster, "Die Tagesberichte über sensationelle Vorgänge," *Der Zeitungs-Verlag*, no. 5 (1910). See also Foerster in "Was lehrt der Mordprozess Berger?" BLA, no. 606, 27 Dec. 1904.

21. Jakob Julius David, *Die Zeitung* (Frankfurt, 1906), pp. 74–75.

22. Donald M. Lowe, *History of Bourgeois Perception* (Chicago, 1982), p. 38; Jürgen Wilke, *Nachrichtenauswahl und Medienrealität in vier Jahrhunderten* (Berlin, 1984), pp. 170–171.

23. Wilke, *Nachrichtenauswahl*, pp. 119–122.

24. Rudolf Wendorff, *Zeit und Kultur. Geschichte des Zeitbewusstseins in Europa* (Opladen, 1980), p. 419.

25. Paul Knoll, "Das Anzeigewesen des Ullsteinhauses," in *50 Jahre Ullstein 1877–1927* (Berlin, 1927), p. 308.

26. Walter Kiaulehn, *Berlin, Schicksal eine Weltstadt* (Berlin, 1958), p. 26; BZ, no. 250, 25 Oct. 1920.

27. Ernst Wallenberg, "Wie meistern wir das Tempo?" *Deutsche Presse*, no. 23 (1928).

28. Bücher, "Der Zeitungsvertrieb" in *Gesammelte Aufsätze*, p. 202; Groth, *Die Zeitung*, vol. 3, p. 147.

29. On "the glare of the present," see Richard Altick, *The Presence of the Present: Topics of the Day in the Victorian Novel* (Columbus, Ohio, 1991), p. 21.

30. Emil Löbl, *Kultur und Presse* (Leipzig, 1903), p. 62; and David, *Die Zeitung*, p. 16.

31. Gustav Stresemann, "Die Entwicklung des Berliner Flaschenbiergeschäfts," Ph.D diss. (Leipzig, 1900), pp. 22–23, cited in Gottfried Korff, "Mentalität und Kommunikation in der Grossstadt: Berliner Notizen zur 'inneren' Urbanisation," in Theodor Kohlmann and Hermann Bausinger, eds., *Grossstadt: Aspekte empirischer Kulturforschung* (Berlin, 1985), p. 352.

32. Karl Bücher, "Das Zeitungswesen," in Paul Hinneberg, *Die Kultur der Gegenwart: Ihre Entwicklung und ihre Ziele* (Leipzig, 1906), p. 510; Groth, *Die Zeitung*, vol. 1, pp. 131–132; Jöhlinger, *Zeitungswesen und Hochschulstudium*, p. 158; Löbl, *Kultur und Presse*, p. 218; and "Die Elektrizität tötet das Buch," BT, no. 348, 12 July 1910.

33. Bernhard von Brentano, "Berlin—von Suddeutschland aus

gesehen," in *Wo in Europa ist Berlin? Bilder aus den zwanziger Jahren* (Frankfurt, 1981), p. 99.

34. Groth, *Die Zeitung*, vol. 3, p. 73.

35. In general, see Berman, *Rise of the Modern German Novel*.

36. Robert Brunhuber, *Das moderne Zeitungswesen* (Leipzig, 1907), pp. 73–74. See also Fritz Mauthner in H. Bulthaupt, ed., *Ueber den Einfluss des Zeitungswesens auf Literatur und Leben* (Kiel, 1891), p. 13.

37. Karl Hauer, "Das Gehirn des Journalisten," *Die Schaubühne*, no. 51 (1911), pp. 596–597.

38. Groth, *Die Zeitung*, vol. 4, pp. 211–214; Karl Dovifat, "Die Zeitung," in Kurt Weidenfeld, ed., *Die deutsche Wirtschaft und ihre Führer* (Gotha, 1925), vol. 3, 104–106; Richard Jacobi, *Der Journalist* (Hanover, 1902), pp. 165–66; Jöhlinger, *Zeitungswesen und Hochschulstudium*; and Rüdiger von Bruch, "Zeitungswissenschaft zwischen Historie und Nationalökonomie: Ein Beitrag zur Vorgeschichte der Publizistik als Wissenschaft im späten deutschen Kaiserreich," *Publizistik* 25 (1980), pp. 590–592.

39. Jutta Birmele, "The Mass-Circulation Press and the Crisis of Legitimization in Wilhelmine Germany, 1900–1918," Ph.D diss. (Claremont, Calif., 1991), p. 60; and "Auswüchse im modernen Zeitungswesen," *Der Zeitungs-Verlag*, no. 50 (1901).

40. Groth, *Die Zeitung*, vol. 1, pp. 117, 950.

41. Wilhelm Fischer, "Die Frau in der Zeitungsliteratur," *Der Zeitungs-Verlag*, no. 17 (1902); Otto Hellmut Hopfen, *Verdorben zu Berlin* (Breslau, 1914), pp. 276, 287; Paul Dobert, "Wie ich mir eine Tageszeitung denke," *Deutsche Presse*, 17 Mar. 1922 and 24 Mar. 1922; as well as Retallack, "From Pariah to Professional?" pp. 207–209.

42. Groth, *Die Zeitung*, vol. 1, pp. 738–739; Jöhlinger, *Zeitungswesen und Hochschulstudium*, p. 55; and Hopfen, *Verdorben zu Berlin*, pp. 242–243.

43. Hopfen, *Verdorben zu Berlin*, pp. 392–393, 404–405, 422–423, 453–456. See also Alan J. Lee, *The Origins of the Popular Press in England* (London, 1976), pp. 231–33.

44. Siegfried Kracauer, "Wiederholung," *Frankfurter Zeitung*, 29

May 1932, cited, translated, and discussed in David Frisby, *Fragments of Modernity: Theories of Modernity in the Work of Simmel, Kracauer, and Benjamin* (Cambridge, Mass., 1986), p. 141.

45. On this theme, see Donald Fanger, *Dostoevsky and Romantic Realism: A Study of Dostoevsky in relation to Balzac, Dickens, and Gogol* (Cambridge, Mass., 1965), p. 27.

46. Karl Scheffler, *Berlin. Ein Stadtschicksal* (Berlin, 1910), p. 267.

47. "Ueber den Potsdamer Platz," BZ, no. 240, 12 Oct. 1905.

48. Paul Gurk, *Berlin* (Berlin, 1934), pp. 16, 101, 255.

49. Winfried Ranke, *Vom Milljöh ins Milieu. Heinrich Zilles Aufstieg in der berliner Gesellschaft* (Hanover, 1979), pp. 30–31, 174–175; Hans O. Modrow, *Berlin 1900* (Berlin, 1936), pp. 131–132; and Dieter Kramer, "Das Neue in der Geschichte der Arbeiterkultur. Berliner Beispiele und ihre überregionalen Wirkungen," in Theodor Kohlmann and Hermann Bausinger, eds., *Grossstadt: Aspekte empirischer Kulturforschung* (Berlin, 1985), p. 331.

50. Albert Südekum, *Grossstädtisches Wohnungselend* (Berlin, 1908), p. 17.

51. "Grossstadtkinder," BLA, no. 325, 4 July 1905.

52. Oscar Stillich, *Die Lage der weiblichen Dienstboten in Berlin* (Berlin, 1902), p. 267.

53. Carl Schneidt, *Das Kellnerinnen-Elend in Berlin* (Berlin, 1893), p. 30.

54. Ibid, pp. 36–53; Abraham Flexner, *Prostitution in Europe* (New York, 1914), p. 10.

55. "Tippe," BT, no. 54, 30 Jan. 1911. Similar alarms were rung by the BLA, no. 323, 27 June 1908; and no. 643, 22 Sept. 1909. The bourgeois fears projected onto maids are discussed in Karin Walser, *Dienstmädchen: Frauenarbeit und Weiblichkeitsbilder um 1900* (Frankfurt am Main, 1986), pp. 59–73. See also the cautionary guide to strangers and swindlers, J. Werthauer, *Berliner Schwindel* (Berlin, 1905).

56. "Berliner Schlafburschen," MP, no. 242, 14 Oct. 1899.

57. Thomas Schäfer, "Die Welt der Lucie Berlin," BT, no. 644, 19 Dec. 1904; "Grossstadtjammer," BT, no. 655, 24 Dec. 1904; "Ackerstrasse 130," MP, no. 302, 24 Dec. 1905.

58. On 102-year-old Auguste Heinrichs, BT, no. 350, 18 July 1914.

59. Richard Dietrich, "Berlins Weg zur Industrie- und Handelsstadt," in Dietrich, ed., *Berlin: Neun Kapitel seiner Geschichte* (Berlin, 1960), pp. 171–172.

60. "Die Sandsteinstadt," BT, no. 270, 30 May 1906. See also "Der Zaun," MP, no. 229, 30 Sept. 1906; and "Im Zeichen des Bauzauns," BLA, no. 268, 27 May 1908.

61. "Die Fangarme der Grossstadt," BT, no. 252, 19 May 1906. My guess is that this unsigned article was written by Georg Hermann.

62. Max Osborn, "Die Schönheit des neuen Berlin. Spaziergänge eines Lithographen," BZ, no. 233, 3 Oct. 1912.

63. Anselm Heine, "Berlins Physiognomie," in *Ich weiss Bescheid in Berlin* (Berlin, 1908), p. 24. See also Hans Hyan, "Auf den Bau," BT, no. 431, 25 Aug. 1911; Alexander Baron von Roberts, "Geschichte einer Berliner Strasse im W," in Moritz Reymond and Ludwig Manzel, eds., *Berliner Pflaster* (Berlin, 1891), pp. 49–58; and Georg Hermann, *Kubinke* (Gütersloh, 1967 [1910]), pp. 6–9.

64. Jules Huret, *Berlin* (Munich, 1909), pp. 26–27.

65. Gurk, *Berlin*, pp. 164–165.

66. "Krieg im Frieden," BT, no. 255, 20 May 1905.

67. Hermann Konsbrück, "Neu-Berlin," *März* (7 Jan. 1908), pp. 7–15.

68. See, for example, "Endlose Buddelei," MP, no. 249, 24 Oct. 1906; "Berlin auf Abbruch," MP, no. 256, 1 Nov. 1906; "Die Saison der grossen Strassenbuddeleien," BLA, no. 202, 22 Apr. 1910; "Das bauende Berlin," BT, no. 377, 27 July 1905; "Unterirdischer Spaziergang," no. 54, 30 Jan. 1908; "Die Untergrundbahn," no. 293, 12 June 1909; and "Die neue Brückenstrasse," no. 488, 25 Sept. 1913.

69. Fedor von Zobeltitz quoted in Dieter and Ruth Glatzer, eds., *Berliner Leben 1900–1914* (Berlin, 1986), vol. 1, pp. 115–116.

70. Arthur Eloesser, "Die Strasse meiner Jugend" (1907) in *Die Strasse meiner Jugend* (Berlin, 1919), p. 12.

71. Heine, "Berlins Physiognomie," in *Ich weiss Bescheid in Berlin*, pp. 1–2.

72. On the *Kremser*, "Im Kremser," BZ, no. 182, 5 Aug. 1905; and "Sonntagsfahrt im Autobus," BT, no. 419, 19 Aug. 1907; on the

Droschke, "Das letzte Droschkenpferd," BT, no. 215, 29 Apr. 1906; "Einzug des 'Eisernen Gustav' in Paris," MP, no. 133, 5 June 1928; no. 135, 7 June 1928; no. 219, 13 Sept. 1928; Fritz Wirth, "Sport und Massenpresse," in W. Joachim Freyburg and Hans Wallenberg, eds., *Hundert Jahre Ullstein* (Berlin, 1977), vol. 3, pp. 343–344; and Hans Fallada, *Iron Gustav,* Philip Owens, trans. (London, 1940); on the Pferdeomnibus, Egon Jameson, "Der letzte Pferdeomnibus," MP, 23 June 1920, reprinted in *Augen auf! Streifzüge durch das Berlin der zwanziger Jahre* (Frankfurt, 1982), pp. 88–89; and on the Krögel, "'Am Krögel,'" BZ, no. 88, 14 Apr. 1906; Eloesser, "Die Strasse meiner Jugend," in *Die Strasse meiner Jugend,* p. 13. See also Ernst Friedel, "Der Kampf um die alten Bauwerke Berlins," BLA, no. 1, 1 Jan. 1910; Albert Dresdner, "Stadtzerstörung und kein Ende!" BLA, no. 435, 28 Aug. 1910; and "Ein Stück des alten Berlin geht wieder dahin," BLA, no. 451, 7 Sept. 1910. Gottfried Korff, "Mentalität und Kommunikation," in Kohlmann and Bausinger, eds., *Grossstadt,* p. 353, draws attention to the folkloric appreciations of old Berlin, a genre elaborated by Heinrich Zille and Hans Ostwald.

73. "Unter den Linden 13. Ein Abschiedswort," BZ, no. 171, 24 July 1906. See also "Das alte Schöneberg verschwindet," BZ, no. 232, 3 Oct. 1906.

74. "Nun auch die Wilhelmstrasse . . . ," BZ, no. 245, 18 Oct. 1911.

75. "Das Verschwinden von Alt-Berlin," BZ, no. 137, 13 June 1912. See also Max Osborn, "Die Zerstörung Berlins," *Die Nation,* no. 31 (1906), pp. 488–492; "Ein Rest des alten Berlin," BIZ, no. 6, 9 Feb. 1896; Wolf Jobst Siedler in Manfred Schlenke, ed., *Preussen: Beiträge zu einer politischen Kultur* (Reinbek, 1981), p. 314; and Siedler, *Die gemordete Stadt: Abgesang auf Putte und Strasse, Platz und Raum* (Munich, 1961).

76. Walther Rathenau, "Die schönste Stadt der Welt" (1899), in *Impressionen* (Leipzig, 1902), p. 144.

77. Observers frequently noted the absence of *Pietät* in the redesigned city, which corresponds to Simmel's notion of the disappearance of *Vornehmheit.* See Eloesser, "Die Strasse meiner Jugend," in *Die Strasse meiner Jugend,* pp. 12–13; Heine, "Berlins Physiog-

nomie," in *Ich weiss Bescheid in Berlin*, p. 24; and "Die Sandsteinstadt," BT, no. 270, 30 May 1906.

78. "Die Sandsteinstadt," BT, no. 270, 30 May 1906.
79. Konsbrück, "Neu-Berlin," *März*, p. 8.
80. Scheffler, *Berlin*, pp. 52, 59.
81. Max Osborn, "Die Zerstörung Berlins," *Nation*, p. 488.
82. Scheffler, *Berlin: Ein Stadtschicksal* (Berlin, 1910), p. 181.
83. Osborn, "Die Zerstörung Berlins," *Nation*, p. 488.
84. "Die Sandsteinstadt," BT, no. 270, 30 May 1906.
85. Robert Walser, "Guten Tag, Riesin!" (1907), reprinted in Schutte and Sprengel, *Die Berliner Moderne*, p. 303.
86. Ibid.
87. Siegfried Kracauer, "Strasse ohne Erinnerung," *Frankfurter Zeitung*, 16 Dec. 1932, reprinted in *Strassen in Berlin und anderswo* (Frankfurt, 1964), pp. 19–24. Bernhard von Brentano, Kracauer's predecessor at the *Frankfurter Zeitung*, made the same observation earlier. See his "Berlin—von Süddeutschland aus gesehen," in *Wo in Europa ist Berlin?* pp. 96–97.
88. Modrow, *Berlin*, pp. 38–39.
89. "Die Friedrichstrasse von heute," BIZ, no. 36, 7 Sept. 1919.
90. Kiaulehn, *Berlin*, p. 56.
91. Siegfried Kracauer, "Wiederholung," *Frankfurter Zeitung*, 29 May 1932, cited, translated, and discussed in Frisby, *Fragments of Modernity*, p. 141.

6. Plot Lines

1. Burton Pike, *The Image of the City in Modern Literature* (Princeton, 1981), p. 100; Christof Forderer, *Die Grossstadt im Roman: Berliner Grossstadtdarstellungen zwischen Naturalismus und Moderne* (Berlin, 1992), p. 232; Dana Brand, *The Spectator and the City in Nineteenth-Century American Literature* (Cambridge, 1991), p. 88, pp. 102–103; and generally, Walter Benjamin, "The Paris of the Second Empire in Baudelaire," in *Charles Baudelaire: A Lyric Poet in the Era of High Capitalism*, Harry Zohn, trans. (London, 1973).
2. Pike, *Image of the City*, p. 100.

3. Döblin, "Modern. Ein Bild der Gegenwart," ms. dated 6 Oct. 1896, quoted in Krista Tebbe and Harald Jähner, eds., *Alfred Döblin zum Beispiel: Stadt und Literatur* (Berlin, 1987), p. 12.

4. Alfred Döblin, *Alexanderplatz, Berlin: The Story of Franz Biberkopf*, Eugene Jonas, trans. (New York, 1931), pp. 220–221.

5. Alfred Döblin, "Der Geist des naturalistischen Zeitalters," *Neue Rundschau* 35 (1924), p. 1293.

6. Walter Benjamin, "Some Motifs in Baudelaire," in *Charles Baudelaire*, p. 132.

7. This excellent point is fully developed in Thomas Lindenberger, "Strassenpolitik: Zur Sozialgeschichte der öffentlichen Ordnung in Berlin, 1900–1914," Ph.D diss. (Berlin, 1992), pp. 103–113.

8. Stephen Schreder, *Der Zeitungsleser* (Vienna, 1936), p. 29.

9. A. H. Kober, *Einst in Berlin*, ed. Richard Kirn (Hamburg, 1956), pp. 36–37. A useful map of the newspaper quarter can be found in Friedrich Leyden, *Gross-Berlin—Geographie der Weltstadt* (Berlin, 1933), p. 153.

10. Hermann Kesser, *Die Stunde des Martin Jochner* (Berlin, 1921 [1915]), p. 50. See also Kober, *Einst in Berlin*, p. 29.

11. Hans Fuchs, "Technik im modernen Zeitungsbetrieb," Ph.D diss. (Heidelberg, 1916), pp. 78–79.

12. Quoted in Helmut Lethen, "Chicago und Moskau: Berlins moderne Kultur der 20er Jahre zwischen Inflation und Weltwirtschaftskrise," in Jochen Boberg et al, eds., *Die Metropole: Industriekultur in Berlin im 20. Jahrhundert* (Munich, 1986), p. 212.

13. Gustav Kauder, "Bezett—Bezett am Mittag! Die Geschichte eines neuen Zeitungstyps. Zeitgeist und Sportgeist," in *50 Jahre Ullstein 1877–1927* (Berlin, 1927), pp. 198–199.

14. Kauder, "Bezett—Bezett am Mittag!" in *50 Jahre Ullstein*, pp. 201–202.

15. "Der schnellste Weg zum Leser," *Der Zeitungshandel* 16 (1 May 1926), p. 3.

16. Otto Groth, *Die Zeitung: Ein System der Zeitungskunde* (Mannheim, 1928–1930), vol. 3, p. 33.

17. BZ, no. 257, 31 Oct. 1912.

18. Cited in Modris Eksteins, *The Limits of Reason: The German De-*

mocratic Press and the Collapse of Weimar Democracy (Oxford, 1975), p. 113.

19. Hermann Diez, *Das Zeitungswesen* (Leipzig, 1910), p. 1.

20. Groth, *Die Zeitung*, vol. 1, p. 557. See also Menahem Blondheim, *News over the Wires: The Telegraph and the Flow of Public Information in America, 1844–1897* (Cambridge, Mass., 1994).

21. Groth, *Die Zeitung*, vol. 3, p. 70.

22. Gottfried Korff, "Mentalität und Kommunikation in der Grossstadt: Berliner Notizen zur 'inneren' Urbanisation," in Theodor Kohlmann and Hermann Bausinger, eds., *Grossstadt: Aspekte empirischer Kulturforschung* (Berlin, 1985).

23. "Berliner Beobachter," BLA, no. 5, 7 Jan. 1889. This feisty tone is remarkable in view of the *Berliner Lokal-Anzeiger*'s later development.

24. "Berliner Sommernacht," BZ, no. 178, 31 July 1912. See also Max Osborn, "Gedränge. Die Pein und Wonne des Grossstädters," no. 32, 7 Feb. 1911; and Lothar Müller, "Modernität, Nervosität und Sachlichkeit. Das Berlin der Jahrhundertwende als Hauptstadt der 'neuen Zeit,'" in Ulrich Baehr et al, eds., *Mythos Berlin—Zur Wahrnehmungsgeschichte einer industriellen Metropole* (Berlin, 1984), pp. 86–87.

25. BT, no. 60, 2 Feb. 1906; no. 77, 12 Feb. 1907; no. 290, 11 June 1913.

26. BZ, no. 240, 12 Oct. 1905; BT, no. 248, 19 May 1910; BZ, no. 57, 27 Feb. 1927.

27. Alfred Döblin, "Grossstadt und Grossstädter," in *Die Zeitlupe. Kleine Prosa* (Olten, 1962), p. 229, originally the introduction to Mario von Bucovich, *Berlin* (Berlin, 1928). See also Fred Hildenbrandt, "Die Stadt von aussen," in *Grosses schönes Berlin* (Berlin, 1928), p. 10; "Das Tempo," ibid., pp. 115–122; and Erich Kästner, "Berlin in Figures," in *Let's Face It*, Patrick Bridgwater, ed. (London, 1963).

28. Müller, "Modernität, Nervosität und Sachlichkeit," in *Mythos Berlin*, p. 84.

29. Eloesser, "An der Stadtbahn" (1918), in *Die Strasse meiner Jugend* (Berlin, 1987 [1919]), p. 98.

30. Paul Gurk, *Berlin* (Berlin, 1934), p. 100. See also David Harvey, *The Urban Experience* (Baltimore, 1989), p. 173.

31. Erwin Alexander-Katz, "Berliner Sommernacht," BZ, no. 178, 31 July 1912.

32. Georg Simmel, "The Metropolis and Mental Life," in *The Sociology of Georg Simmel*, Kurt Wolff, ed. (New York, 1950), p. 410.

33. Richard Hamann, *Der Impressionismus in Leben und Kunst* (Cologne, 1907), p. 204.

34. Baroness von Spitzemberg, diary entry for 20 Dec. 1898, quoted and analyzed in Müller, "Modernität, Nervosität und Sachlichkeit," in *Mythos Berlin*, p. 88. The idea of apprenticeship is borrowed from Müller as well. See also "Um den Potsdamer Platz," MP, no. 243, 15 Oct. 1905; "Grossstadtschmerzen einer Kleinstädterin," BLA, no. 525, 22 Oct. 1905.

35. Eduard Höber, "Die Erziehung zum Potsdamer Platz," BT, no. 335, 4 Feb. 1905. See also VZ, no 625, 8.12.12, discussed in Lindenberger, "Strassenpolitik," p. 54.

36. "Pflichten des Fussgängers," BT, no. 378, 27 July 1911. See also "Die Disziplin der Strasse," no. 581, 14 Nov. 1911; and "Berliner Beobachter," BLA, no. 243, 25 Apr. 1909.

37. "Die Hupe," BT, no. 617, 5 Dec. 1907.

38. See, for example, Osborn, "Gedränge. Die Pein und Wonne des Grossstädters"; "Verlängerte Französische Strasse," BZ, no. 61, 13 Mar. 1911; and "Der alte Westen," BT, no. 99, 24 Feb. 1908.

39. See Ludovica Scarpa, "Abschreibungsmythos Alexanderplatz," in Boberg et al, eds., *Die Metropole*, pp. 126–133; and W. Graemkow, "Zur Berliner Verkehrsregelung," *Der Motorwagen* 33 (30 Nov. 1924), pp. 631–637.

40. Osborn, "Gedränge. Die Pein und Wonne des Grossstädters."

41. "Paul Singers letzte Fahrt," MP, no. 37, 6 Feb. 1911.

42. Osborn, "Gedränge. Die Pein und Wonne des Grossstädters."

43. On this theme, Peter Fritzsche, "Breakdown or Breakthrough? Conservatives and the November Revolution," in Larry Eugene Jones and James Retallack, eds., *Between Reform, Reaction and Resistance: Studies in the History of German Conservatism from*

1789 to 1945 (New York, 1993). For a more general discussion of Singer's funeral, see Lindenberger, "Strassenpolitik," pp. 417–420.

44. "New York-Paris im Automobil," BZ, no. 15, 18 Jan. 1908; "New York-Paris im Auto," no. 22, 27 Jan. 1908.

45. *Der Strassenhändler*, 5 Aug. 1908, cited in Hildegard Kriegk, "Die politische Führung der Berliner Boulevardpresse," Ph.D diss. (Berlin, 1941), pp. 72–73.

46. "Der deutsche Wagen auf dem Wege nach Berlin," BZ, no. 171, 23 July 1908; "Die Weltumfahrer in Berlin," no. 172, 24 July 1908; MP, no. 172, 24 July 1908; no. 173, 25 July 1908; Fritz Wirth, "Sport und Massenpresse," in W. Joachim Freyburg and Hans Wallenberg, eds., *Hundert Jahre Ullstein* (Berlin, 1977), vol. 2, p. 343.

47. "Der deutsche Wagen auf dem Wege nach Berlin," BZ, no. 171, 23 July 1908.

48. "Automobil und Kultur," BZ, no. 173, 25 July 1908.

49. See Peter Fritzsche, *A Nation of Fliers: German Aviation and the Popular Imagination* (Cambridge, Mass., 1992), chapter 1.

50. "Berlin in Erwartung Zeppelins," MP, no. 220, 27 Aug. 1909.

51. "Berlins Zeppelin-Tag," MP, no. 221, 28 Aug. 1909. It should be noted that the *Lokal-Anzeiger* also published extra editions, erected a 24-meter wind gauge, and purchased a section of bleachers at Tempelhof. See no. 580, 30 Aug. 1909.

52. "Unser Zeppelin-Sonntag," MP, no. 223, 30 Aug. 1909.

53. Adolf Petrenz in *Tägliche Rundschau*, 8 July 1913, quoted in Adolf Saager, *Zeppelin: Der Mensch, Der Kämpfer, Der Sieger* (Stuttgart, 1916), pp. 173–174.

54. BT, no. 438, 30 Aug. 1909.

55. Eduard Buchmann, *Die Entwicklung der Grosse Berliner Strassenbahn und ihre Bedeutung für die Verkehrsentwicklung Berlins* (Berlin, 1910), p. 107.

56. BT, no. 438, 30 Aug. 1909.

57. "Das Volk von Berlin," BZ, no. 203, 31 Aug. 1909.

58. See the comments in BT, no. 438, 30 Aug. 1909, and more generally, Fritzsche, *Nation of Fliers*, pp. 27–35.

59. BZ, no. 134, 10 June 1911; MP, no. 157, 10 June 1911.
60. "Um den BZ Preis der Lüfte," BIZ, no. 25, 18 June 1911. See the *Vossische Zeitung*, 12 June 1911, quoted in Dieter and Ruth Glatzer, eds., *Berliner Leben 1900–1914* (Berlin, 1986), vol. 2, p. 230.
61. Lindenberger, "Strassenpolitik," p. 65.
62. Conrad Alberti, "Masse und Maschine. Der Flug-Sonntag in Berlin," BZ, no. 135, 12 June 1911. The *Morgenpost*, no. 189, 12 July 1911, made the same point.
63. The *Lokal-Anzeiger* endeavored to organize its own "Scherl-Sensation" when it sponsored Orville Wright's exhibition flights at Tempelhof. Publisher August Scherl paid millions of marks to Wright and attracted hundreds of thousands of Berliners to the two-week-long rally in September 1909. But Scherl never matched the showmanship of Ullstein. See Hans Erman, *August Scherl: Dämonie und Erfolg in wilhelminischer Zeit* (Berlin, 1954), p. 243; and BLA, no. 2 Sept. 1909; no. 608, 9 Sept. 1909; and no. 636, 19 Sept. 1909.
64. Jutta Birmele, "The Mass-Circulation Press and the Crisis of Legitimation in Wilhelmine Germany, 1908–1918," Ph.D diss. (Claremont, Calif., 1991).
65. Max Osborn, "Berlin bei der Arbeit," BZ, no. 289, 24 Nov. 1914.
66. Fritz Koch, "Berlin im vierten Kriegsjahr. Kleine Bilder aus der Weltstadt im Herbst, festgehalten für unsere Enkel," BIZ, no. 44, 4 Nov. 1917.

7. Other Texts of Exploration

1. Lewis Mumford, *The City in History* (New York, 1961), pp. 97–98.
2. David Frisby, *Fragments of Modernity: Theories of Modernity in the Work of Simmel, Kracauer and Benjamin* (Cambridge, 1985).
3. Jürgen Schutte and Peter Sprengel, eds., *Die Berliner Moderne 1885–1914* (Stuttgart, 1987), p. 49.
4. Georg Simmel, *The Philosophy of Money*, trans. Tom Bottomore and David Frisby (Boston, 1978), p. 484.
5. Lothar Müller, "Die Grossstadt als Ort der Moderne: Ueber Georg Simmel," in Klaus R. Scherpe, ed., *Die Unwirklichkeit der Städte: Grossstadtdarstellungen zwischen Moderne und Postmoderne*

(Reinbek, 1988), pp. 21–23, 26–31. On Simmel as *Wanderprediger* and Simmel's reflections, Hans Simmel, "Auszüge aus den Lebenserinnerungen," in Hannes Böhringer and Karlfried Gründer, eds., *Aesthetik und Soziologie um die Jahrhundertwende: Georg Simmel* (Frankfurt, 1976), pp. 258, 265. See also Kurt Gassen and Michael Landmann, eds., *Buch des Dankes an Georg Simmel: Briefe, Erinnerungen, Bibliographie* (Berlin, 1958); Gianfranco Poggi, *Money and Modern Mind: Georg Simmel's Philosophy of Money* (Berkeley, 1993); Patrick Watier, ed., *Georg Simmel: La sociologie et l'expérience du monde moderne* (Paris, 1986); and David Frisby, *Sociological Impressionism: A Reassessment of Georg Simmel's Social Theory* (London, 1981).

6. Hans Ostwald, *Dunkle Winkeln in Berlin* (Berlin, 1905), p. i.

7. Hans Ostwald, *Vagabunden*, ed. Klaus Bergmann (Frankfurt, 1980).

8. For more details, see Peter Fritzsche, "Vagabond in the Fugitive City: Hans Ostwald, Industrial Berlin, and the *Grossstadt-Dokumente*," *Journal of Contemporary History* 29 (1994), pp. 385–402.

9. Eckhardt Köhn, *Strassenrauch: Flanerie und "Kleine Form." Versuch zur Literaturgeschichte des Flaneurs von 1830 bis 1933* (Berlin, 1989), esp. p. 137. *Kleine Prosa* has its counterpart in *Kleinkunst*, the art of cabaret for instance, which thrived as a form of "metropolitan collage." See Peter Jelavich, *Berlin Cabaret* (Cambridge, Mass., 1993).

10. Charles Baudelaire, "The Painter of Modern Life," in his *The Painter of Modern Life and Other Essays*, J. Mayne, ed. and trans. (London, 1964).

11. Quoted and translated by Eberhard Roters, "The Painter's Nights," in Carol S. Eliel, *The Apocalyptic Landscapes of Ludwig Meidner* (Los Angeles, 1989), pp. 75–77. See also Charles W. Haxthausen, "Images of Berlin in the Art of the Secession and Expressionism," in *Art in Berlin 1815–1989* (Seattle, 1989), pp. 68–73.

12. Haxthausen, "Images of Berlin," in *Art in Berlin*, p. 70; Ludwig Meidner, "An Introduction to Painting Big Cities," in Victor H. Meisel, ed., *Voices of German Expressionism* (Englewood Cliffs, N.J., 1970), pp. 111–115.

13. Both self-assessments are cited, translated, and ably discussed by Charles Haxthausen, "'A New Beauty': Ernst Ludwig Kirchner's Images of Berlin," in Haxthausen and Heidrum Suhr, eds., *Berlin: Culture and Metropolis* (Minneapolis, 1990), pp. 66–67.

14. Nowhere is this argument made better than in Haxthausen, ibid.

15. Georg Hermann, "Um Berlin," *Pan* 2 (August 1912), p. 1104.

16. Zille is still awaiting scholarly treatment. The best to date is Winfried Ranke, *Vom Milljöh ins Milieu. Heinrich Zilles Aufstieg in der berliner Gesellschaft* (Hanover, 1979). For Baluschek, see Margrit Bröhan, *Hans Baluschek* (Berlin, 1985).

17. Silvio Vietta, "Grossstadtwahrnehmung und ihre literarische Darstellung. Expressionistischer Reihungsstil und Collage," *Deutsche Vierteljahrsschrift für Literaturwissenschaft und Geistesgeschichte* 48 (1974), pp. 354–373. See also Heinz Rölleke, *Die Stadt bei Stadler, Heym, und Trakl* (Berlin, 1966).

18. See also Christof Forderer, *Die Grossstadt im Roman: Berliner Grossstadtdarstellungen zwischen Naturalismus und Moderne* (Berlin, 1992).

19. *Dunkle Winkeln*, 21. The same point is made for Booth by Judith R. Walkowitz, *City of Dreadful Delight: Narratives of Sexual Danger in Late-Victorian London* (Chicago, 1992), p. 34; and for the Chicago School of Sociology by Rolf Lindner, *Die Entdeckung der Stadtkultur: Soziologie aus der Erfarhung der Reportage* (Frankfurt, 1990), pp. 110–112.

20. On the bowler, Fred Miller Robinson, *The Man in the Bowler Hat: His History and Iconography* (Chapel Hill, 1993).

21. On neighborhood subcultures, see Eve Rosenhaft, *Beating the Fascists?: The German Communists and Political Violence, 1929–1933* (Cambridge, 1983).

22. Erhard Schütz, "'Kurfürstendamm' oder Berlin als geistiger Kriegsschauplatz: Das Textmuster 'Berlin' in der Weimarer Republik," in Klaus Siebenhaar, ed., *Das poetische Berlin: Metropolenkultur zwischen Gründerzeit und Nationalsozialismus* (Berlin, 1992); "Kleinstadt Berlin," *Reclams Universum* 48, no. 50 (8 Sept. 1932), pp. 1840–1841.

23. Hans Ostwald, *Sittengeschichte der Inflation: Ein Kulturdokument aus den Jahren des Marksturzes* (Berlin, 1931).

24. Michael Geyer, "The Stigma of Violence, Nationalism, and War in Twentieth-Century Germany," *German Studies Review* (Winter 1992), pp. 75–110.

INDEX